# LATIN AMERICAN
# BUSINESS CULTURES

# LATIN AMERICAN BUSINESS CULTURES

**Robert Crane**

**Carlos Rizowy**

PEARSON

Prentice
Hall

Upper Saddle River, New Jersey 07458

*Dedicated with love to:*
*Brian, Yael, and Michal*
*–Carlos Rizowy*

**Library of Congress Cataloging-in-Publication Data**

Latin American business cultures / Robert Crane, Carlos G. Rizowy.
   p. cm.
   Includes bibliographical references and index.
   ISBN 0-13-067048-0 (alk. paper)
   1. Business anthropology–Latin America. 2. Corporate culture–Latin America. 3. Cross-cultural orientation–Latin America. 4. Business communication–Latin America. 5. Intercultural communication–Latin America. I. Crane, Robert. II. Rizowy, Carlos G.

GN564.L29L37 2005
302.3'5'094–dc22

2004052285

**Project Manager:** Ashley Keim
**Senior Acquisitions Editor:** Jennifer Simon
**Editor-in-Chief:** Jeff Shelstad
**Executive Marketing Manager:** Shannon Moore
**Marketing Assistant:** Patrick Dansuzo
**Managing Editor:** John Roberts

**Permissions Supervisor:** Charles Morris
**Manufacturing Buyer:** Michelle Klein
**Production Manager:** Arnold Vila
**Cover Design:** Kiwi Design
**Composition:** Laserwords
**Full-Service Project Management:** BookMasters, Inc.

Credits and acknowledgments borrowed from other sources and reproduced, with permission, in this textbook appear on appropriate page within text.

Pearson Education LTD.
Pearson Education Singapore, Pte. Ltd
Pearson Education, Canada, Ltd
Pearson Education–Japan

Pearson Education Australia PTY, Limited
Pearson Education North Asia Ltd
Pearson Educación de Mexico, S.A. de C.V.
Pearson Education Malaysia, Pte. Ltd

10 9 8 7 6 5 4 3 2
ISBN 0-13-067048-0

# CONTENTS

# ACKNOWLEDGMENTS

We would like to thank all those who contributed to this book, particularly the chapter authors: Roque B. Fernandez Avenida, Katherina Fernandez, Luis Alberto Machado, Jose Maria Rodriguez Ramos, Otto Nagami, Hernán Felipe Errázuriz, Jose Manuel Cardenas, Ricardo Monge-Gonzalez Roberto Saladin, Luis Valencia Rodriguez, Bobby James Calder, Nicholas Ardito Barleta, Father Juan Julio Wicht, Ignacio de Posadas, and Carlos Steneri.

We would also like to thank two wonderful women who generously gave of their time to format the book, Ana Maria and Esther—Ana Maria for meticulously reviewing every chapter for consistency and accuracy and for organizing the final manuscript, and Esther for the diligent follow-up with all the authors throughout the project.

We also thank all of those unnamed individuals who contributed to give us inspiration, courage and energy to start and conclude the book.

Finally, we wish to thank those who gave selflessly of the time we might have devoted to them rather than the book—that is, our families.

Robert Crane and Carlos Rizowy

# CONTRIBUTORS

## ARGENTINA

Roque B. Fernandez Avenida, a former Minister of Finance, is a member of the National Academy of Economics in Argentina.

Co-author Katherina Fernandez is an economic law analysis consultant for the House of Representatives in Argentina.

## BRAZIL

Luis Alberto Machado is Dean of the Graduate School of Economics at FAAP Fundação Armando Alvares Penteado, Brazil.

Co-author Jose Maria Rodriguez Ramos is Coordinator of the Graduate School of Economics at FAAP Fundação Armando Alvares Penteado, Brazil.

Co-author Otto Nagami is also a member of the Graduate School of Economics at FAAP Fundação and has background experience as CFO and CEO of many companies.

## CHILE

Hernán Felipe Errázuriz, former Ambassador to the United States of America in Chile and former Minister of Foreign Affairs, is presently Senior Partner of the law firm Guerrero, Olivos, Novoa y Errázuriz.

## COLOMBIA

Jose Manuel Cardenas, a former Vice-Minister of Economic Development and former Vice-Minister of Foreign Relations, is a Doctor in law and political science of the law faculty of the Universidad Nacional de Colombia with a specialization in international law, diplomacy and European integration of the Université Libre de Bruxelles.

## COSTA RICA

Ricardo Monge-Gonzalez is Executive Director of the Costa Rican High Technology Advisory Committee Foundation (CAATEC), Vice President of Banco Internacional de Costa Rica (BICSA) and Board Member of Banco Nacional de Costa Rica (BNCR).

## DOMINICAN REPUBLIC

Roberto Saladin, former CEO of the Banco de Reservas, the largest commercial bank in the Dominican Republic, and former Governor of the Central Bank and President of the Monetary Board, is the Ambassador of the Dominican Republic to the United States of America.

## ECUADOR

Luis Valencia Rodriguez, a former Minister for Foreign Affairs, is a Professor of Private International Law at the International University of Ecuador.

## MEXICO

Bobby James Calder is the Distinguished Professor of Marketing and Professor of Psychology at The Charles H. Kellstadt, Kellogg Graduate School of Management, Northwestern University, Chicago.

## PANAMA

Nicholas Ardito Barleta, former Vice President of The World Bank (IBRD), Washington, D.C., is Chairman for Asesores Estrategicos, S.A., a consulting firm in Panama and Chairman for Panam Development Corporation, an investment firm in Panama.

## PERU

Father Juan Julio Wicht, former Economic Advisor at the Head of the Instituto Nacional de Planificación (Peruvian Government), is presently Dean of Economics at the Universidad del Pacífico in Lima, Peru and a Jesuit Priest at the Church of Fatima in Miraflores, Lima, Peru.

## URUGUAY

Ignacio de Posadas, former Minister of Finance, is a Partner at the law firm of Posadas, Posadas & Vecino in Uruguay and director at Merrill Lynch, P.F. & S. in Uruguay.

Co-author Carlos Steneri is the Financial Representative of the Ministry of Finance and Central Bank of Uruguay in the United States of America.

# ABOUT THE EDITORS

## DR. ROBERT CRANE

Having worked in the field of management education for over twenty years, Dr. Robert Crane has built a solid reputation for competence in the areas of international development, cross-cultural business applications and institutional entrepreneurship in eastern and western Europe and North America. Throughout his career he has been involved with such management institutions as the J. L. Kellogg School of Management at Northwestern University near Chicago, EM-Lyon in France and the International Management Center (now the Business School of the Central European University) in Budapest. He has developed and/or run customized programs for executives for such firms as Baker & McKensie (one of the world's largest law firms), McKinsey and Company, Societe Generale (now SoGen) and others.

Thanks to his wide travels and long-term residence in both Europe and North America, Dr. Crane possesses a privileged viewpoint on cultural issues. This perspective has allowed him to create customized cross-cultural business programs for multinational firms such as Royal Ten Cate (NL) and publish a series of books on cross-cultural business with publishing houses in the United Kingdom and the United States.

His breadth of vision has also led him to create consortia both of universities offering joint degrees he helped design and of researchers working on collective publications. His long experience in advising companies has allowed him to facilitate idea sharing among firms as well as internal brainstorming for single companies. Finally, he has had the entrepreneurial vision and audacity to develop or enhance the global dimension of institutions (IMC, IGS) and companies (Baker & McKensie, Royal Ten Cate).

As an entrepreneur, he created the first global executive education program in 1992; the first globally televised MBA program (through the National Technological University); and The Peace School, the first primary school to teach peace making to small children through a knowledge of cultures and religions.

Dr. Crane holds degrees in French literature (B.A., M.A., Ph.D. from the University of North Carolina at Chapel Hill) and translation (maitrise or M.A. from the University of Lyon, France). He also studied management (Young Managers' Programme or Executive MBA at Cranfield University in the U.K.).

## DR. CARLOS G. RIZOWY

Dr. Carlos G. Rizowy holds degrees in international relations (B.A. from The Hebrew University of Jerusalem, M.A. and Ph.D. from the University of Chicago), political science (Ph.D. from the University of Chicago) and law (J.D. Illinois Institute of Technology, Chicago Kent College of Law).

Dr. Rizowy was born in Uruguay, South America. In demand as a public speaker and media commentator, Dr. Rizowy routinely addresses over seventy audiences each year. Groups addressed include the Council on Foreign Relations, Rotary International, Latin American Chamber of Commerce and many major universities. In addition, he has spoken with and/or given interviews to a large number of trade, business and civic organizations, including The Executive Committee ("TEC," a national organization of chief executives of significant, privately held companies), NPR, BBC, ABC, CBS and NBC. Topics include foreign policy, security, political violence, terrorism, doing business in Latin America, foreign trade and international issues.

Dr. Rizowy's law practice has focused on corporations, government relations and international transactions. He is of counsel to the firm of Sonnenschein, Nath and Rosenthal, LLP with offices in Chicago, St. Louis, Kansas City, San Francisco, Los Angeles, New York and Washington, D.C. His international business consulting focuses on government relations. He has counseled governmental as well as non-governmental organizations. He has authored articles in professional and popular journals on topics in law, business and international relations.

As former chairman of the political science department at Roosevelt University in Chicago, he inspired a generation of students and faculty.

Dr. Rizowy is listed in the 11th Edition of *Who's Who in America* and the 54th Edition of *Who's Who in American Law*. He is also listed in the *Who's Who in the Midwest* and *Who's Who of the Emerging Leaders of America*.

# CHAPTER 1
# INTRODUCTION

Dr. Robert Crane
Dr. Carlos G. Rizowy

To deal with what is an inherently vague and as yet ill-defined subject, the cross-cultural relations of Latin America, we use a series of filters to detect the elusive cultural factors in Latin American life. All of the following approaches are used in the chapters, with individual authors varying the dosing and order.

First, the historical background of each nation is examined. What are the tribal origins of the people and their influence today on economic culture? What were the governments over time? Is there a democratic, monarchical, or autocratic tradition? What is the faith of the people? What are its strengths? Are there several faiths juxtaposed? Do they coexist peacefully? Is there a tradition of free trade and individual initiative or is central control of economic affairs the historical bias? What are the values of the country? In Hofstede's terms, are they more masculine and aggressive or more feminine and nurturing? What are the nation's dreams?

Second, what are the national attitudes toward the regional economic organizations [Mercosur, Andean Community, Caribbean Community (CARICOM), Central American Common Market (CACM) and NAFTA] while the United States remains as the sole superpower and the European Union struggles to reassert Europe's political and economic might?

While the United States as the sole remaining superpower in the world today is involved in globalization, the rest of the world is involved in regionalism. Regionalism seems to be one of the mechanisms evolving in the relationship between the other countries and the United States as a means of protecting themselves from being overwhelmed militarily, economically, socially, politically and culturally by the sole remaining superpower. The same nations that are pursuing regionalism also advocate the development of strong international organizations as a means of complementing regionalism.

Third, a look is taken at the national stake in the regional trade groups (Mercosur, Andean Community, CARICOM, CACM and NAFTA). Naturally, this stake is perceived in large part through the national attitude previously discussed. However, in this section a closer look is taken at the economic implications of trade group membership in both financial and emotional terms. This section deals with both the economic reality of group membership and the present national perception of the benefits of that membership.

Fourth, as we mentioned earlier, Latin America is a continent of regions not always corresponding to national borders. The ethnic strife in Mexico and Bolivia and the ongoing border war between Peru and Ecuador are proof of this fact. A possible part of the role of Mercosur and the Andean Community is to gather these regions, often drawn from the tribes and their customs of pre-Colombian times, into their

**FIGURE 1-1** Map of South America

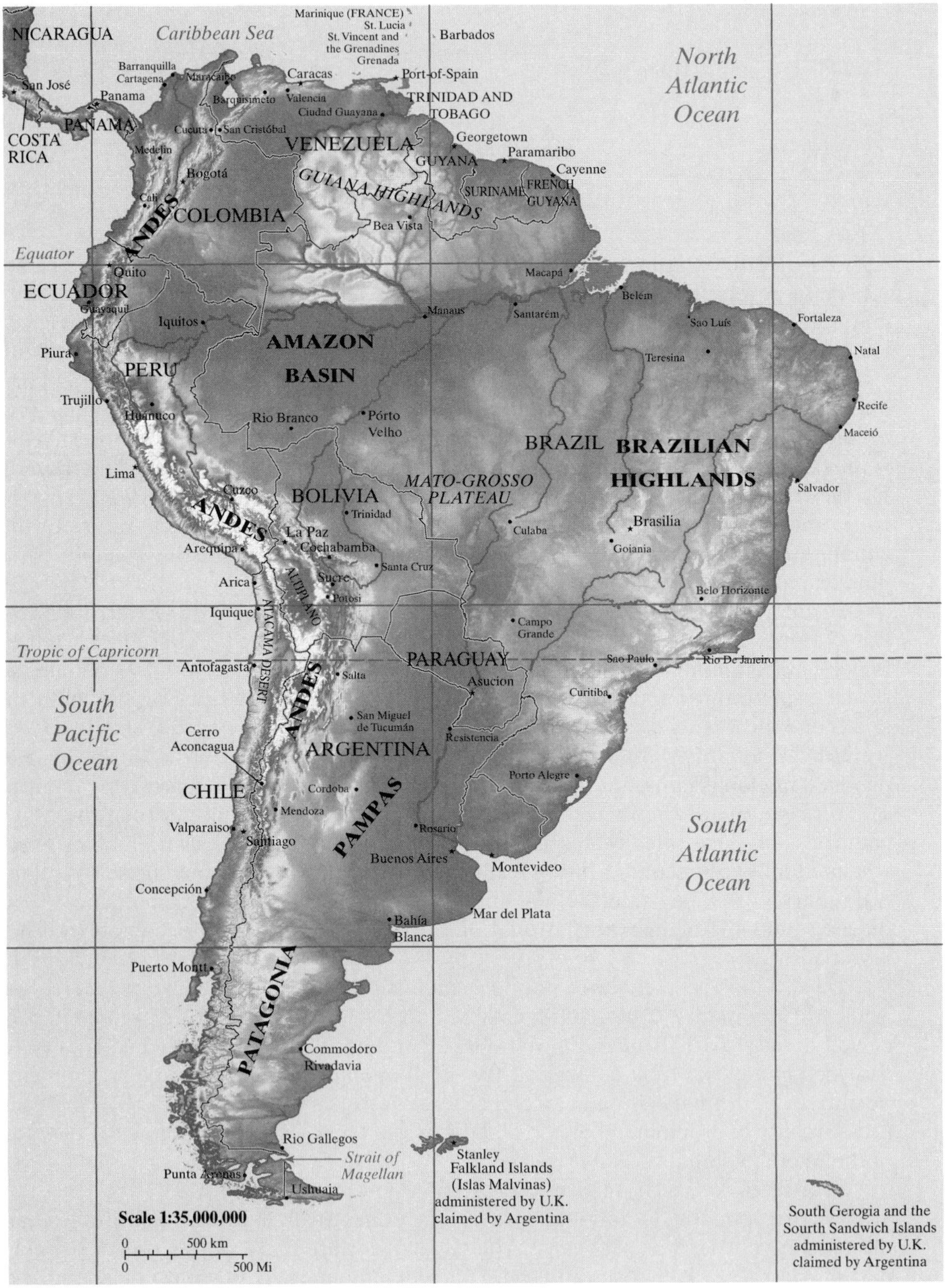

supranational structures. How do these regions fit into their national contexts, or do they not fit? What is the benefit of trade agreements to these regions? How are the three groups perceived by the regions' leaders?

Fifth, the latest trend of several Latin American countries toward populism (e.g., Venezuela, Brazil and Uruguay) and reservations toward market economies strengthen the cultural ties of the southern countries versus the northern countries. Cultural affinity acts as a complement to regionalism. In other countries of Latin America poor indigenous people are radicalizing politics while challenging democracy. Will the Latin American countries affected by this trend allow the democratic process to incorporate them into the political system or will they threaten democracy? In Ecuador, indigenous people formed an alliance with other opposition groups and some military officers succeeded in deposing a democratically elected president. In Mexico, the Zapatista movement is comprised mostly of peasants, indigenous Mayan people. Brazil has a long history of indigenous peoples rebelling against legal and illegal land seizures by industrialists. In Colombia and Peru civil strife affects the indigenous people's land in their quest for civil rights. This struggle is tied to the drug trade. The indigenous people support the Latin American populist movements in Venezuela and Brazil. The clash of cultures poses a challenge to the democratic institution in Brazil, Mexico, Ecuador, Colombia, Peru and Venezuela.

Sixth, a look is taken at the business impact of Mercosur, the Andean Community and NAFTA, present and future, on the nation. How do businesspeople see the present climate inside and outside these trading blocs? What are their predictions for the future in both cases? What is the present reality of these common markets? What are the cultural implications of Free Trade Area of the Americas?

Latin America is an important world region with societies that are extremely different, facing major challenges in democracy, poverty and inequity. Disparities in the distribution of wealth have created deep social problems. Politically, there are no boundaries between the public and private sectors. Political parties are generally clientelistic, with low ideological content, and opportunistic in their positions, with little discipline.

Nonetheless, most Latin American countries have the characteristics of democracy such as institutionalized elections and the exercise of such political freedoms as expression, opinion, association and movement and access to the media. There are variations in the degree of state participation and control of these elements. As a consequence, the governments lack legitimacy, which translates as discontent among the population.

In addition, recessions and crises are fertile ground for populist movements, such as those in Peru after the 2000 crisis, Argentina after the 2001 crisis, Uruguay following the Argentine crisis, Brazil with the 2002 presidential victory of a left-wing party with Lula Da Silva, and Venezuela in 1998 with the election of a leader of the 1992 military coup (Hugo Chavez). The majority of these populist groups attributed their economic misery to the pro-market policies promoted by the United States.

As an outcome, Brazil's leftist President Luis Inacio Lula Da Silva hoped to lead a South American diplomatic bloc with the support of Argentina. However, countries such as Mexico, Chile and Colombia wanted to maintain the Rio Group.

Another ongoing problem of the state in Latin America is that there are some areas into which its legality does not extend. Instead, authoritarian subnational regimes coexist with democratic national regimes. Thus, in Colombia, revolutionary groups control large areas of the territory.

## MULTIETHNICITY OF THE POPULATIONS

It is important to point out that, in most cases, the construction of the Latin American state was characterized by violence and cruelty. One might say that in Latin America there were states looking for a nation rather than nations looking for a state. The establishment of political regimes was aristocratic or oligarchic from the beginning. The emergent states were the result of domination arrangements, with a legacy of colonialism that excluded a large part of the population (indigenous peoples, women). Later, these sectors of the population were included through indigenous policies. Today many of the populist movements are motivated by the indigenous population's desire to participate in and get a share of the national wealth.

The indigenous population in Latin America is estimated at between 34 and 40 million persons, or about 8 to 10 percent of the total population. The majority of this population is found in Bolivia, Guatemala and Peru. Some 30 to 40 percent of the total population in Ecuador is indigenous. In the other countries of Latin America, the indigenous population constitutes less than 6 percent, so the process of inclusion did not reach an emergency state.

We should clearly identify the problems that arise from the identification of this kind of population; in certain countries, we can observe that the indigenous population is increasing, which may be a consequence of a new-found identity and policies recognizing that identity.

The emergence of new movements and constitutional changes in Latin American countries recognizing the multiethnicity of the populations[1] present new challenges for the governments and societies. There is a tendency toward a Latin American regional model of multicultural constitutionalism, and toward a democratizing process of emancipation. This trend is not yet consistent with globalization but with cultural regionalism.

## CURRENT INDIGENOUS MOVEMENTS

The demands of indigenous people are included in the "second generation" reforms. Indigenous movements can be observed in two different ways. There are direct or indirect associations, which differ in their degree of government recognition of the indigenous right to self government. There are also specific lands recognized as belonging to the indigenous peoples and loyal to their own political and legal cultures and traditions (e.g., the Kuna in Panama, the Resguardos in Colombia and the Oaxaca in Mexico).

## ECONOMIC CULTURE

The different chapters deal with each country's economic culture. However, the trend at the beginning of the 1990s was that most of the countries in Latin America had as their primary goal economic growth through reform and anti-inflationary policies.

---

[1]Guatemala (1985), Brazil (1988), Nicaragua (1986), Colombia (1991), Mexico (1992–2001), Paraguay (1992), Argentina (1994), Bolivia (1994), Ecuador (1998), Venezuela (1999) and Chile (1993).

Measures were taken to open the economy to market forces and to reduce the size of the public sector through structural reforms. As a consequence, there was an inclination toward privatization and the diminution of the role of governments.

The globalization process involved all countries in specific challenges to become a part of the global economy. Most of the Latin American countries assumed that regional economic integration was a necessity in order to promote internal development and regional integration. This process of regionalism was paving the way for global integration. As an outcome of this objective, free trade agreements such as the Southern Common Market (Mercosur), the Andean and Caribbean Community (CARICOM) and the Free Trade Area of the Americas (FTAA) were created.

Trade liberalization in agriculture and manufactured products, the liberalization of certain services and a reduction in barriers to trade in agricultural products and manufactured goods between developing countries are among the key subjects discussed in world trade negotiations like those in Cancun, Mexico (September 2003). However, this kind of negotiation implies gains for the Latin American and Caribbean countries only if at the same time the rich countries open their markets.

Hopeful favorable results of such negotiations include the improvement of investment in the region, and the creation of a stable basis to open the markets and of an appropriate climate to attract foreign investment. An example is Mexico. The NAFTA agreement established a good atmosphere for both foreign direct investment and national investments in all the industries involved in exports to the United States.

One illustration of the advantages is the Mercosur free trade agreement (1991) among Uruguay, Argentina, Paraguay and Brazil, which was made to formalize and strengthen regional trade flows. Argentina and Brazil are the pact's two major markets. Imports tariffs are reduced; duties on imports of most products from outside Mercosur are set under a common external tariff (0–20 percent). Within this frame, the countries can acquire considerable advantages, enlarging their markets. Moreover, some goods defined traditionally as non-tradable become tradable thanks to this regional trade.

However, despite the commitments made by the countries, there are many problems of regional obstacles that must successfully be dealt with for the achievement of full integration, for example:

- Exchange policy coordination is a paramount challenge.
- Lack of a common goal linking Mercosur to other regional agreements.
- Is a limitation to bilateral trade agreements with other countries, especially the United States, a platform for their? reinforcement of macroeconomic coordination?
- Degree of flexibility for member countries to negotiate bilateral agreements with other regional blocs and/or individual countries to facilitate the transition toward a fully integrated regional trade area, etc.

The extreme economic hardship suffered by most of the member countries of these groups has occasionally led them to suspend, postpone or even default on some of their commitments to strengthening free trade within their respective subregions. Despite the serious effects of international crises, countries have persevered in order to uphold and, wherever possible, expand regional cooperation substantially. Thus, Mercosur is improving regulations for settling trade disputes and strengthening joint negotiations with third parties. The Andean Community is facilitating the fuller reintegration of Peru and has finally adopted a common external tariff, initially covering some 62 percent of all tariff items.

There are also Western Hemisphere trade negotiations, looking toward a free trade zone, which should be completed by 2005. Negotiations with third world countries and groups of countries and multilateral forums are very important to strengthening regional integration and leveling the playing field of globalization. Governments are realizing that through deepened and more efficient subregional cooperation, they gain stronger individual ability to negotiate with more powerful trading partners. This phenomenon has enhanced the importance of the current talks between the Andean Community and Mercosur with a view to the formation of a South American free trade area, before the creation of the Free Trade of the Americas that includes the NAFTA partners.

In the Latin American region, Brazil has emerged as the political and economic leader, pushing Mexico aside. As a member of Mercosur, Brazil has great impact on key hemispheric issues such as the creation of the Free Trade Area of the Americas.

The political and economic ambivalence and the pressing economic situation of several of the Latin American countries pushes toward parallel, bilateral trade negotiations with the United States, the most important market for Latin America. These dual bilateral and regional negotiations could mutually reinforce one another and have positive results. However, some countries have difficulty obtaining political consensus on unilateral trade liberalization because of the internal perceived and real disparities in the groups that benefit from those policies.

In the Latin American region the pursuit by the United States of policies such as the promotion of economic and political liberalization, support for free markets and trade liberalization did not achieve a perceived long-term benefit to the countries of the region. Economic improvement was followed by recessions, economic crises and political instability that fed a certain anti-Americanism which translated into the failure of pro-market policies. In spite of this, the U.S.–Chile Free Trade Agreement (FTA) is an important first step toward building bilateral partnerships with Latin American countries.

In sum, free trade agreements are an excellent framework both for negotiating lower trade barriers and for setting the rules for reform, transparency and respect for the rule of law. In addition, expanding free trade with the United States would enhance economic opportunity for the region.

What then is our goal in describing cross-cultural Latin America? We want to sound the depths of feeling of Latin Americans for each other and for the region. We want to reveal the half-submerged basis of the ways people think and feel in the region. We want to lay the groundwork for others to define and predict which way Latin America will develop in the future. We want to define how those outside the region perceive Latin America and speculate on how these perceptions impinge on the evolution of Latin America's relations with the world. It is an ambitious task, but one whose time has come. We hope we have advanced it.

# CHAPTER 2
# ARGENTINA

Dr. Roque B. Fernandez Avenida
Katherina Fernandez

## THE LAND AND ITS PEOPLE

Argentina is located on the South American continent. With a total population of 36,027,041, a surface area of 2,780,400 square kilometers and a density of 13 inhabitants per square kilometer, it is surrounded by Chile in the west; the Atlantic Ocean in the east; and Peru, Bolivia, Uruguay and Brazil in the north. Argentine's ancestors mostly came from Europe, mainly Spaniards and Italians. There were also, in smaller numbers, German, French and English immigrants. The Mestizos (a mixture of whites and Indians) account for approximately 4.5 percent of the population, whereas pure Aboriginals account for only 0.5 percent of the total population.

There is freedom of religion in Argentina, but Argentines are for the most part Roman Catholic. However, Jews, Protestants, Muslims and many other religions live together peacefully. The type of government since the 1853 National Constitution is representative, republican and federal. The country is divided into 23 provinces, the federal capital and Buenos Aires, an autonomous city. This autonomy was granted by a modification of the Constitution in 1994.

The government is divided into three branches: the Executive, formed by the President and Ministers; the Legislative, with two houses—the Senate and the House of Representatives; and the Judicial, with a Supreme Court of Justice and different jurisdictions.

The main economic activity in Argentina is agriculture, taking advantage of the good conditions of the temperate pampas. Other important activities are livestock raising and fishing. As in many developing countries, the industrial sector of moderate size has been influenced by periods of protective measures and periods of free trade policies.

## A BRIEF REVIEW OF ARGENTINA'S CULTURAL AND ECONOMIC HISTORY

### THE BEGINNINGS

The survival of many heterogeneous aboriginal groups has shaped the culture in Latin America. Argentina has incorporated many characteristics of the European cultures, introduced mainly by conquerors and afterward by immigrant streams mainly from European countries at the end of nineteenth and beginning of the twentieth century.

**FIGURE 2-1** Map of Argentina

Many indigenous groups from different cultures occupied the Argentine territory before its colonization. The Diaguitas from the middle-west territory domesticated animals, wove and hunted. The Querandies, Comechingones, Patagones and Onas inhabited Patagonia, the Litoral and Pampa regions. These people were nomads and lived by hunting and fishing. The Calchaquies and Matacos inhabited the north region and cultivated the land and domesticated animals.

Juan Díaz de Solís, a Spanish colonist, discovered the River Plate in 1516. Cabot first penetrated the territory in 1526 and established the first Spanish colony in the region. In 1536, Pedro de Mendoza founded Santa María del Buen Ayre, but the rebellious natives who refused to provide food to the Spaniards burnt down the city. However, Domingo Martinez de Irala is considered the first colonist since he was able to approach the indigenous groups peacefully, achieving the unification between Spaniards and natives. Colonizing streams from Peru, Chile and Spain started penetrating Argentine territory in 1560, populating the region and giving birth to new cities. Jesuit missionaries also began to make their way into the area during this time.

In 1776, the River Plate viceroyalty was created, integrating Argentina, Bolivia, Uruguay, Paraguay and southern Brazil. Buenos Aires was its capital. In 1777, the Port of Buenos Aires began free trade with other ports in Spain.

## THE ROAD TO INDEPENDENCE

In 1810, the viceroy was replaced by an Open Municipal County (Cabildo Abierto), moved by popular beliefs influenced by emancipating ideas from the French Revolution and North American independence. Liberating armies propagated the revolutionary doctrine to neighboring countries, trying to evict the Spaniards from their territories. General José de San Martín, one of the nation's most important characters in history, freed Chile and Peru, assuring the independence of the south of the continent. In 1816, independence from Spain was declared. In 1853, the National Constitution was created, establishing a republican, representative and federal form of government.

The economic culture in Argentina was greatly influenced by characters like the Frenchman Quesnay who favored wealth creation through work on the land, that is, developing agriculture. Influence also came from the English, through the ideas of Locke and Adam Smith, favoring freedom and private property as basic human rights, and free trade.

One major exponent of these economic principles during the viceroyalty period was Mariano Moreno, who defended farmers' interests. He strongly defended free trade and counseled the viceroy against monopolies that tended to generate contraband. He confronted Spanish public officials who denied the colonies the right to trade directly with London merchants. However, Spain's dominant colonial attitude became more flexible due to its economic decadence (due to debilitating wars with European countries) at the beginning of the 1800s.

Releasing the constraint on foreign trade established the basis for free trade with England, after the country's independence in 1816, and shaped Argentina's attitude until World War I. Consequently, the trade derived from cattle—such as leather, wool and chilled beef—began shaping external trade. Of course, the other side of the coin was the import of manufactured goods, mainly from England. These imports enhanced competition and produced discomfort for the Argentines involved in businesses competing with them. Although some protectionist policies were set in motion to protect certain industries, free trade was the general policy thanks to the revenues stemming from customs. This policy favored internationally competitive sectors such as agricultural production.

At the beginning of the 1800s, agriculture played a subordinate role to cattle. Much of the country's interior, where agricultural conditions were optimal, had not been extensively populated. However, this tendency started to reverse in the 1820s with the stimulation of fruit and other agricultural export policies.

The country tried to develop mining activity with no success. The goal was to supplement the wealth generated by stock exports and to attend to the great financial needs of supporting a revolution for independence. People's lack of knowledge on how to exploit mines dissipated this dream and made the economy dependent first on cattle, second on agriculture and lastly on manufactured goods.

The direct consequence of the lack of mineral wealth was a shortage of coins to back up commercial transactions. Thus, paper money was printed to substitute for the lack of coins.

After achieving independence from Spain with much effort, the young Argentine republic enjoyed a unique place in the world. It had vast natural resources, a huge internal market, and free direct access to the sea. Again, derivatives from cattle easily found eager importers such as Brazil, North America, Europe and Cuba. The following decades, however, were tainted by the imbalances between Buenos Aires, the center of commercial activity due to its proximity to a port, as well as of financial, political and economical activity, and the other provinces. Nevertheless Argentina was headed to positioning itself as one of the most powerful countries in Latin America.

### THE SEE-SAW CENTURY: DEALING WITH POPULISM AND COUPS D'ETAT

In 1904, the working class party gained representation. H. de Yrigoyen assumed the presidency in 1916, maintaining the country's neutrality during World War I. A succession of military coups took place from 1930 until 1946, replacing democratic governments. In 1944, diplomatic relations were broken with Germany and its allies and war was declared on them.

In 1946, General Juan Domingo Perón was elected president with the massive support of the working class. His government characterized itself by adopting populist measures. Perón and his wife, Eva Perón (who died in 1952), favored policies to enhance social welfare. However, these policies produced unsustainable macroeconomic pressure and social unrest that ended with Perón's exile in 1955. A new succession of democratic governments and coups d'état characterized the period from 1955 to 1973.

In 1972, Perón was reelected with substantial popular support, but he died the following year. His widow, María Estela de Perón, the vice president, succeeded him. But the period was characterized by waves of violence due to the lack of economic policies to support the nation's development and control the fiscal deficit and inflation. A new military coup again ended the democratic government.

The years that followed were cruel and brutal, and will always be remembered as a tragic piece of Argentina's history. The period called *Proceso Nacional de Reorganización* (National Reorganization Process) was characterized by a sort of civil war with massive violation of human rights. The results of this era were thousands of missing people, a great increase in the external deficit, a deep recession and the closure of many private firms, as well as the military occupation of the Malvinas Islands in 1982, which had been seized in 1833 by the United Kingdom.

## THE LEADER CHALLENGED: GAINING STABILITY

This last phase of Argentine history culminated in a lost war. Democratic elections were reestablished in 1983. New president Raúl Alfonsín, from the Radical Union Party, was elected for a six-year period. He worked hard on establishing and protecting the basic pillars of democracy and institutional stability. However, he was not successful in controlling the constant increases in prices that finally led to hyperinflation. As a result, he surrendered the presidency in 1989 to Carlos S. Menem, from the Justice Party, a few months before the end of his mandate.

Menem was reelected for the period 1995–1999. During his decade of administration he achieved price stability by creating the convertibility plan, based on a fixed exchange rate. He also privileged a free trade and capital mobility. The outcome of these policies was an increase in gross national product (GNP) that made Argentina the second largest economy in Latin America after Brazil. However, in the second half of 1998, after the Russian debt default, Argentina began a period of recession, which was worsened by the Brazilian devaluation at the beginning of 1999. The economy started to recover in the second half of 1999.

In the year 2000, the Alliance Party (named after the alliance of the Radical Union and Frepaso parties) won the presidential elections under Fernando de la Rúa. A high tax increase aborted the recovery and a new period of recession began. The return to populist policies and uncontrolled fiscal deficit together with the lack of attention to badly needed structural changes produced social turmoil that ended with de la Rúa's resignation in December 2001. A new provisional government, under the Justice Party, assigned the presidency to Eduardo Duhalde to finish de la Rua's mandate. The new administration is facing a debt default, high country risk and vast social discomfort due to devaluation, political uncertainty and the deterioration of institutions. The years to come will surely be difficult. The leadership will certainly be challenged.

## ARGENTINA AND WORLD ECONOMIC ORGANIZATIONS

### TRADE AND GROWTH IN THE COUNTRY

As we have seen before, Argentina enjoyed a comfortable position in world trade at the end of the 1800s. However, the country became progressively poorer compared to the development of other nations from the beginning of the last century. For example, Argentina's output grew 157 percent from 1900 to 1997, whereas Canada's output grew 603 percent over the same period. The explanation for this very low growth seems to be an inward orientation and macroeconomic instability. President Juan Peron's administration particularly favored import substitution policies over export policies in order to encourage domestic industrial development. He also favored an expansionary fiscal policy. However, empirical evidence[1] shows that output grew 5.6 percent annually between 1900 and 1930, whereas from 1930 to 1965, output grew only by 3.7 percent, thus putting into question the success of import substitution measures.

At present, due to the difficulty of dismantling trade barriers, controlling public spending and reducing government intervention in the industrial sector, Argentina is experiencing instability and low growth rates. However, when barriers to growth were eliminated under Menem's administration, output experienced a higher annual growth rate of 6 percent. This tendency decreased as other developing countries' crises spread around the globe. These results suggest that when Argentina follows relatively free trade policies, it tends to grow more rapidly than over periods of protectionism.

## TRADE LIBERALIZATION: THE BIRTH OF MERCOSUR

The recent attempts by Argentina to liberalize trade started at the end of the 1980s. The first attempt at free trade started in 1988, unilaterally, by abandoning the previous protectionist policies that tended to autarky, import substitution and exchange and price controls.

There were also efforts to open trade multilaterally by deepening the country's compromises with GATT (General Agreement on Tariffs and Trade) and the WTO (World Trade Organization) and by lowering tariffs and quota restrictions.

Regional openness started with Brazil in 1986 under the signing by both countries of the Acta de Cooperación e Integración Argentino-Brasileño. In November 1988, a new treaty—Tratado de Integración, Cooperación y Desarrollo—was signed, whereby both countries agreed not only to a free trade union but to recognize the importance of coordinating monetary, fiscal and exchange policies.

Later, in 1991, the Tratado de Asunción was signed, which gave birth to Mercosur (Mercado Común del Sur). A 40 percent tariff decrease was agreed upon among the participating countries—Argentina, Brazil, Uruguay and Paraguay—starting June 1991. The remaining tariff would gradually decrease to a zero tariff in 1995, thus establishing a free trade area and a new external common tariff for other nonmember countries. However, the members of Mercosur agreed to keep certain products under a specific tariff. Such was the case for Argentine products related to the steel, textile, paper and shoe industries.

Moreover, the sugar and automobile industries were given special treatment ad hoc due to divergences in policy among the countries regarding the protection of these vulnerable industries. Still, the main objective was to move to a Customs Union by 2001 by gradually eliminating these restrictions on trade.

In 1996, Chile and Bolivia were included in the Mercosur treaty as "associate economies," which meant that they could negotiate bilaterally with Mercosur. Nevertheless there were still negotiations going on to fully incorporate Chile as a new member and, later, Bolivia as well.

Mercosur also served as an enforcing technology. Due to the international commitment among countries, the job of local lobbyists to press the government for protection for certain industries was made more difficult. This task is particularly valuable for a country like Argentina, accustomed as it is to protectionist policies. In this area in particular, regionalism is preferable to unilateralism.

---

[1]Refer to Díaz (1970).

Mercosur has remained stable in spite of changes of government and economic crises. This stability is noteworthy considering that many projects involving Latin American countries have failed over time.

## WHAT'S BEHIND THE TRADE AGREEMENT?

Many authors have analyzed the determining factors of regional trade.[2] Unilateral liberalization together with geographic features seems to be an important factor in determining intra-regional trade among countries. There appears to be a concept of the Natural Bloc, drawn from common frontiers, similar cultural inheritance and similar languages, that reduces the costs of transactions between these related countries compared to others. There is empirical evidence suggesting that Mercosur is such a "Natural Bloc."

Although the four member countries are neighbors with markets close enough to lower transaction costs, there are different national interests. Argentina, Paraguay and Uruguay are economies that view integration as a way to increase trade. These nations look at Mercosur as a stage in opening commerce to other countries outside their current trading bloc. However, Brazil's economy is the largest of the bloc partners. As a result, membership in Mercosur seems to have an additional geopolitical interest: to generate a very large economic area so as to increase negotiation power relative to other trade areas in Europe, Asia and the United States.

Thus, Mercosur's pitfall is differing interests. In Argentina's case, the country would obtain more benefits by opening up to the rest of the world than by belonging to a bloc in which Brazil's economic leadership leads to higher tariffs for countries outside the bloc. Chile's reluctance to adhere to Mercosur might be taken as proof of the advantage for this country to play the role of a small world economy rather than that of a member of a group of countries not offering all the advantages of trade creation and suffering from trade diversion within the region, as well. In spite of the different interests among countries, Mercosur is a useful tool for all its members since it can be used as a transitional stage to greater global integration and can be used for leverage during negotiations. As a result, the member nations are more powerful as a bloc than individually.

## TRADE DEVELOPMENT

Table 2-1 gives some insight into the trade statistics of the Mercosur bloc.

As can be seen from the information in the table, trade within Mercosur has grown much more quickly than trade outside the bloc. However, the balance of trade accounts moved from an initial surplus to a deficit starting in 1995. This can be explained by the underlying macroeconomic movements that members of the bloc have experienced in opening their economies and abolishing external capital rationing. These movements also explain why the balance of trade deficit has produced discomfort for those who favor protectionist policies. Nonetheless, Argentina and the bloc still have a low degree of openness relative to other economies of similar size. Exports relative to gross domestic product (GDP) in Argentina are on average 7.75 percent, and for Mercosur they are 13 percent. This observation implies there is much to be done in order to improve economic efficiency by opening trade.

---

[2]Refer to Sanguinetti and Garriga (1997).

**TABLE 2-1:** Trade statistics in millions of US$

| | 1991 | 1992 | 1993 | 1994 | 1995 | 1996 | 1997 | 1998 | 1999 | 2000 | Var. 91-100 % |
|---|---|---|---|---|---|---|---|---|---|---|---|
| Exports within bloc | 5,104 | 7,215 | 10,065 | 12,049 | 14,444 | 17,037 | 20,542 | 20,356 | 15,158 | 17,671 | 246,2 |
| Exports outside bloc | 40,807 | 43,273 | 43,981 | 50,079 | 56,051 | 57,909 | 62,742 | 61,008 | 59,164 | 66,813 | 63,7 |
| Total exports | 45,911 | 50,488 | 54,046 | 62,128 | 70,495 | 74,946 | 83,284 | 81,364 | 74,322 | 84,484 | 84 |
| Imports within bloc | 5,097 | 7,282 | 9,059 | 11,708 | 13,972 | 17,151 | 20,699 | 20,905 | 16,015 | 17,637 | 246 |
| Imports outside bloc | 27,231 | 31,574 | 37,205 | 48,092 | 61,735 | 66,329 | 78,325 | 75,371 | 64,559 | 69,061 | 153,6 |
| Total imports | 32,328 | 38,856 | 46,264 | 59,800 | 75,707 | 83,480 | 99,024 | 96,276 | 80,574 | 86,698 | 168,2 |
| Balance with rest of the world | 13,576 | 11,699 | 6,776 | 1,987 | –5,684 | –8,420 | –15,583 | –14,363 | –5,395 | –2,248 | |

*Source:* CEI(2000).

Nonetheless, the trade balance reversed to a surplus in 2001. This seemingly happy turn of events was due not to an increase in competitiveness but to an ongoing recession. Clearly then, Argentina is not a net exporter but merely exports whatever is left after satisfying domestic demand.

## THE PRESENT AND FUTURE OF TRADE IN ARGENTINA

### MERCOSUR AT PRESENT

There is an ongoing debate as to whether Mercosur has been trade creating or trade diverting. There is empirical evidence that supports both positions. An economist at the World Bank released the first publicly available document that suggested that Mercosur was trade diverting.[3] This document produced justified discomfort for all bloc members and prompted many responses to suggest that overall Mercosur had been trade creating.[4]

Before Mercosur began, many of its members—especially Argentina—had relatively closed economies. So, it is not wide of the mark to consider that any degree of opening to commerce is trade creating, at least at the beginning of the agreement.

Indeed, Mercosur produced a strong initial expansion and encouraged trade and investment. However, this tendency has decreased in the last few years and trade in Mercosur has become stable. This trend is not surprising considering that Mercosur is small compared to total world production.

Nevertheless, policies that protect vulnerable industries still remain. There are tariffs, nontariff restrictions, export subsidies and production subsidies, which distort trade. This state of affairs has also produced decreased exports to both NAFTA and the European Union.

These protectionist policies have prevailed due to lobbying by different sectors of the economy. The power of these lobbyists has had considerable influence and has coddled the so-called "infant industries" in Argentina to the ripe old age of 50 years! These small business groups, which hold a more protectionist view, are suspicious of economic integration programs. They try to maintain a system of protection of the products they represent. Such is the case, for example, of industrial products represented by the Industrial Union. Nevertheless, these goods do not represent a high proportion of the GNP.

On the whole, the business community has accepted Mercosur and supranational organizations as a good plan for growing international trade. In short, the business communities envision the opening of the economy as growth enhancing.

Recently, Argentina has experienced successive trade balance surpluses due to the deep recession that began around 1998. This recession has reduced local consumption, thus increasing sales to the rest of the world and reducing imports. However, it is not possible to constantly increase exports without considerable cost reduction to increase

---

[3]Refer to Yeats (1997).
[4]Refer to Bohara, Kishore and Sanguinetti (2001).

competitiveness. Therefore, it is important to deregulate the economy even further. Yet these measures do not enjoy public support; most of the Argentine people are strong supporters of nationalism and are accustomed to populist measures to protect them.

There has also been some discomfort about the opening of the economy due to such external shocks as Brazil's devaluation in 1999. However, in January 2002, Argentina abandoned the convertibility plan by devaluating its currency and moved to a floating exchange rate. The country expects its terms of trade to improve. Exporters received the reaction to Argentina's devaluation of the peso with great relief. They felt that the rule 1 peso = 1 dollar had made tradable products less competitive, due to the appreciated value of the local currency that was pegged to the dollar.

The lack of an institution to resolve these types of macroeconomic conflicts within Mercosur has caused intraregional relations to deteriorate and has produced a negative impact on direct investments from countries that could have taken advantage of the enlarged trade area. There is an urgent need to establish international policy coordination in order to avoid these hurtful consequences.

### MERCOSUR'S FUTURE: FAILURE OR SUCCESS?

As regards trade in Argentina in the future, the government is working on several issues in order to sell local goods in other countries' markets.

Many simulations have been run to determine the impact of eliminating barriers to agricultural goods—a field in which Argentina has a comparative advantage.[5]

In particular, this exercise has been run for the United States and the European Union. The results for the latter are very favorable, suggesting that if barriers are eliminated for this type of produce, meat exports will increase 350 percent and sugar exports will increase 143 percent, for example. This result is a direct consequence of the European Union's distorting measures toward agricultural goods. Argentina already exports this type of goods despite the European Union's policies.

If the United States eliminates agricultural trade barriers, the results are more moderate as compared to those of the European Union. For example, sugar exports would increase 60 percent and dairy products 20 percent. The explanation for these modest increases in exports is that there are fewer barriers and distortions to these goods and that the United States is more efficient in producing them.

Although negotiations regarding tariff reductions and/or elimination have started among these countries, Argentina, like many other developing countries, faces additional costs when settling multilateral agreements. Due to poor management infrastructure, to comply with standards and technical norms many countries require expensive tests and certificates of exporters. One recent example of this kind of cost was the outbreak of Aftosa (hoof-and-mouth disease) in the country. Argentina's ineffectiveness in controlling this type of virus resulted in the closure of the meat market to almost all importers for a very long time.

In spite of this incident, the country's agricultural and cattle industry is considered competitive relative to the United States. So, it might be better to improve trade with those countries that do not have a comparative advantage in this particular market segment.

---

[5]Refer to Fundación Mediterránea, 2000.

There is a new debate on whether the country should try to separate itself from its present bloc and search for other markets unilaterally. Currently, given market conditions, there might be more trade creation if the country entered NAFTA directly, even if it meant abandoning Mercosur. One of the advantages of entering NAFTA is the possibility of using the fast track policy of the United States in order to negotiate tariffs more easily. The reduction of transaction costs is a valuable tool in trying to reach an agreement with NAFTA. At present, Brazil's reluctance to lower the Mercosur external tariff is unfavorable to the other members who wish to have greater trade gains.

## CULTURE VS. GLOBALIZATION

There is an ongoing debate as to whether the growth in globalization has been detrimental to culture and tradition within a country.

The different ethnic groups in Argentina have integrated perfectly well into the democratic system. As was previously mentioned, there is a very small ethnic population in the country. These peoples' claims concerning their territory and culture are always heard, and they have been protected by specific legislation. International agreements such as Mercosur, NAFTA and the Andean Pact are recognized by the ethnic groups and are considered to be a normal process of integration among nations. The indigenous tribes do not believe that their cultural features are threatened since they are well protected by specific laws. Moreover, they have greatly benefited from the sale of their handcrafts to tourists, especially in the north of the country where these groups are mostly found.

Trade is definitely a factor of cultural integration in many other ways. Argentina has incorporated many modern practices, such as marketing structures and the development of economies of scale for mass production. All these practices are sooner or later translated into educational or business culture.

Buying bread at the bakery, meat at the butcher's shop and then vegetables at the grocery is, for many Argentineans, the culture of the small merchant. So when large companies enter the country with big, efficient supermarkets, with better price and quality and mass production, people argue that such behavior destroys culture.

The argument is accurate from that point of view. That is, in a competitive system, the more efficient baker will compete successfully in the market, and the inefficient baker might find himself arranging bread on the supermarket's aisles. Thus small merchants might argue that life was better before globalization. However, as consumers wish to optimize price and quality, this argument is not true for them.

Should consumers sacrifice themselves for culture's sake? In Argentina, although the small merchant culture still exists in some places, especially in the most rural regions, the more traditional political parties, such as the Radical and the Justice Parties, do not reject globalization. Moreover, they tend to promote economic integration with other countries.

Free markets and democracy are relatively new in Argentina. They started in 1983, and freedom of the press started in the 1990s. Political competition is relatively new. There has not been enough time to allow the system to fully work in favor of efficient allocation of resources and strong monetary, fiscal and political institutions.

## CONCLUSION

Argentina has been able to improve its terms of trade by becoming an important participant in the Mercosur trade agreement. Yet there is an urgent need to coordinate macroeconomic policies in order to minimize negative external shocks to the bloc.

Until the strong peso depreciation at the beginning of 2002, the debate in Argentina was whether the country should separate from the other bloc members (that had previously depreciated their own currencies) to be able to negotiate unilaterally with the United States, the Economic Union or enter NAFTA, from which Argentina could benefit by penetrating these markets. On the one hand, it could be stated that real exchange rate volatility affected and will affect regional economic integration in the future. On the other hand, culture and tradition have integrated nicely with globalization. The country's ancient and rich culture is maintained by the prevailing ethnic groups, which have accepted the challenge of an integrating world.

## BIBLIOGRAPHY

Bohara, A., Kishore, G., Sanguinetti, P. (2001) *Trade Diversion and Declining Tariffs: Evidence from Mercosur.* Working Paper, January 2001, Universidad Torcuato Di Tella.

CEI (2000) *Mercosur 2000, Crecimiento económico y nuevas oportunidades de inversión.*

Díaz, A. (1970) *Essays on the Economic History of the Argentine Republic.* New Haven: Yale University Press.

Fernández, R. (1991) *What Have Populists Learned from Hyperinflation? The Macroeconomics of Populism in Latin America,* ed. R. Dornbusch and S. Edwards. The University of Chicago Press.

Fernández, R., Mantel, R. (1988) *Fiscal Lags and the Problem of Stabilization: Argentina's Austral Plan. Latin American Debt and Adjustment,* ed. P. Brock, M. Connolly and C. Gonzalez. New York: Praeger Publishers.

Fundación Mediterránea (2000) *Las distorsiones de los mercados mundiales de alimentos y su impacto en la Argentina.* Mimeo.

Kendel, P. *Claves(1983) de la Economía Argentina 1810–1983,* ed. Sudamericana.

Krugman, P., Obstfeld, M. (2001) *International Economics, Policy and Theory,* Fifth Edition. Addison-Wesley Publishing.

Nogués, J., Sanguinetti, P., Sturzenegger, F. (2001) *Argentina y la Agenda de negociaciones comerciales internacionales: El Mercosur, el NAFTA, y la Unión Europea.* ABA, Buenos Aires, Junio 2001.

Sanguinetti, P., Garriga, M. (1995) *The Determinants of Regional Trade in Mercosur: Geography and Commercial Liberation.* Working Paper 016, Universidad Torcuato Di Tella.

Yeats, A. (1997) *Does Mercosur Trade Performance Raise Concerns about the Effect of Regional Trade Agreements?* World Bank Policy Research Working Paper.

# CHAPTER 3
# BRAZIL

PROF. LUIS ALBERTO MACHADO

## BACKGROUND

Brazil was "discovered" by the Portuguese on April 22, 1500. Following three centuries under the rule of Portugal, Brazil became an independent nation in 1822. For the last 14 years under Portuguese rule, Brazil was the seat of the Portuguese throne, due to the invasion of the Iberian Peninsula by Napoleon. By far the largest and most populous nation in South America, Brazil has overcome more than twenty years of military intervention in the governance of the country and has pursued industrial and agricultural growth and development of the country's interior. Exploiting vast natural resources and a large labor pool, Brazil became Latin America's leading economic power by the 1970s. However, highly unequal income distribution remains a pressing problem.

## A COUNTRY WITH CONTINENTAL DIMENSIONS

Situated in eastern South America, bordering on the Atlantic Ocean, Brazil is the fifth largest country in the world. It has a total area of 8,511,965 square kilometers (3,286,000 square miles); 8,456,510 square kilometers are land and 55,455 square kilometers are water. This figure includes Arquipelago de Fernando de Noronha, Atol das Rocas, Ilha da Trindade, Ilhas Martin Vaz and Penedos de São Pedro e Sao Paulo.

The countries bordering Brazil (and the length of each border) are, from south to north, Uruguay (985 km), Argentina (1,224 km), Paraguay (1,290 km), Bolivia (3,400 km), Peru (1,560 km), Colombia (1,643 km), Venezuela (2,200 km), Guyana (1,119 km), French Guiana (673 km) and Suriname (597 km). The coastline runs for more than 9,170 kilometers, almost of all of it along the South Atlantic Ocean.

The country comprises 27 states and the Federal District of Brasília, the capital. The states are divided into municipalities, which are further divided into districts.

Geographically, Brazil consists of five basic regions:

1. North (mainly the Amazon basin and the state of Tocantins).
2. Northeast (roughly, east from 46° west longitude and north from 16° south latitude).
3. Southeast (the coastal states south of the Northeast region as far as São Paulo, plus the state of Minas Gerais).
4. South (from Parana south).
5. Central-West (Mato Grosso, Mato Grosso do Sul, Goiás and the Federal District).

More than half of Brazil lies at about 200 meters (650 feet) above sea level, and only a small part rises above 915 meters (3,000 feet). The highest peaks have an altitude of

**FIGURE 3-1** Map of Brazil

about 3,000 meters (10,000 feet); only twelve of them exceed 2,130 meters (7,000 feet), four in the far North and eight in the Southeast. The Great Escarpment runs the length of the coast from Bahia south and falls away inland at varying distances, most of the terrain being broken by fertile valleys.

Arable land is found mainly in the South, but this is changing with the need to develop land for agriculture throughout the rest of the country, particularly in the Central-West and the North. Forest still covers substantial areas. The river system is extensive; the Amazon and its tributaries, which are great rivers themselves, drain over half of Brazil's area. Other large rivers include the Sao Francisco in the Northeast and the Parana and the Paraguay in the Southwest, both of which are tributaries of the River Plate.

The equator runs north of the Amazon River, and the Tropic of Capricorn crosses the metropolitan area of the city of São Paulo. Most of Brazil is therefore in the tropical zone; only the southern part is in the temperate zone. The North is hot, humid and rainy. Along the coast the tropical heat is tempered by sea breezes, whereas inland, especially along the Central Plateau, the altitude keeps the temperature lower. Humidity is high all along the coast, and rainfall is heavy. There is a drought area inland in the Northeast region.

Nearly every type of climate can be found in Brazil except the very cold. The country is free from earthquakes, hurricanes and cyclones, but rainstorms, drought and frost occasionally cause considerable damage.

There are areas of great scenic beauty, particularly along the coastline.

## THE POPULATION AND ITS PARTICULAR CHARACTERISTICS

The population is estimated at 169,799,170 and is growing at just under 2 percent per year. About 55 percent of population is under 20 years of age, and less than 10 percent is over 60. The average life expectancy is 63 years. The major social problem of recent years has been the continuous influx of people to the urban centers.

The comparative distribution of population, area and personal income by region is summarized in Table 3-1.

Approximately 25 percent of the population are rural dwellers and 75 percent urban. About 30 percent live in the ten principal metropolitan areas.

The metropolitan areas of São Paulo and Rio de Janeiro have populations of around 15 million and 10 million, respectively. São Paulo is one of the fastest-growing cities in the world. Its population is second only to Mexico City and is ahead of Tokyo, New York and Shanghai. Some 20 other metropolitan areas in Brazil have populations of more than one million, the principal cities being Belo Horizonte, Brasília, Curitiba, Fortaleza, Porto Alegre, Recife and Salvador. Population growth is fairly evenly spread over all regions, but the North and Central-West are projected to grow at faster rates in the future.

A majority of Brazilians is of European or African descent. Apart from the original Portuguese settlers, others who have settled in Brazil and significantly influenced its culture include Germans (mainly in the southern states), Italians and Japanese (in the state of São Paulo). In the larger cities there are many smaller ethnic communities representing most nationalities. There are also some sparse indigenous tribes in the jungle regions.

**TABLE 3-1:** Population distribution by area and income

| Region | Population | | Land mass | Personal |
| | In millions | % | (%) | income (%) |
| --- | --- | --- | --- | --- |
| North | 10 | 6 | 42 | 3 |
| Northeast | 45 | 30 | 18 | 15 |
| Southeast | 63 | 42 | 11 | 59 |
| South | 23 | 15 | 7 | 15 |
| Central-West | 11 | 7 | 22 | 8 |

All these people, during the past three decades, mixed among themselves, beginning a new culture to become typical Brazilian citizens.

## LANGUAGE

The language of Brazil is Portuguese. There are no significant local dialects or other deviations from the official language, but a number of words and phrases are at variance with those used in Portugal. English is the foreign language most used by the business community.

## RELIGION

The predominant religion is Roman Catholicism. Many other religions are also practiced, since immigrants of different creeds have settled in Brazil. There is religious freedom, and religion is not a source of unrest.

## EDUCATION

Government-subsidized (free) and private educational facilities from primary school through university offer full- and part-time curricula. The government also subsidizes national apprenticeship training programs to develop the labor force for various industrial and commercial sectors and an educational program to reduce illiteracy. About 75 percent of the population above ten years of age is considered to be literate. The general level of education requires much improvement. Approximately 5 percent of all students go on to higher education.

## LIVING STANDARDS

The standard of living of a large proportion of the population is very low, while that of the top stratum is extremely high. This gap between rich and poor has been a constant preoccupation of government administration after government administration.

The gross domestic product (GDP) per capita in 2000 was the equivalent of about US$3,570 per annum.

The percentage of home ownership is low. There is a chronic shortage of housing, especially for the working classes.

## CULTURAL AND SOCIAL LIFE

With its mixed background of Portuguese, Italian, German, Japanese, East European and African immigrants, Brazil offers a wide diversity of cultural and social activities, depending on the region of the country concerned. Most major cities support cultural institutions. Leisure and recreational activities are mainly outdoors, taking advantage of the favorable climate. Many clubs in Brazil offer extensive sports and social facilities.

## BRAZILIAN CULTURE

How to explain the joy of this people? Why don't we see the sadness that completes this same spirit of the "Brazilian way"? Brazilian people spring from a mix of the original natives and a large list of nationalities and different races that came over its 500 years of history. This original blend has produced a juxtaposition that includes the largest Japanese city outside Japan and the largest Italian city outside of Italy—all in São Paulo, one of the largest and most populous cities in the world.

We also have to see the big picture of all the influences of outsiders who have come to Brazil in all of its regions. These influences have produced different ways of expression in the arts, music, social rules and behavior that are included in the concept of culture. It's important to know that in this large country there are no dialects, but just small accent differences or different meanings for the same word.

The particular way of occupying the land by foreign people from very different parts of the world produces this special thing called Brazilian culture. This culture is highly visible and can be found in music, from erudite composers like Heitor Villa Lobos, to the original and most popular rhythm called *samba*, with Noel Rosa and others, the *chorinho*, with Pixinguinha, and more recently (about 40 years), the *bossa nova* rhythm, which has its roots in American jazz, and through the work of composers that have classical and erudite studies like João Gilberto, Antonio Carlos Jobim, Chico Buarque de Hollanda, Caetano Veloso, Gilberto Gil and many others.

In architecture Brazil's biggest name is Oscar Niemeyer, who planned and designed Brasília, and other significant buildings. There are also Lucio Costa and Lina Bo Bardi, who came from Italy and carried out important work such as the MASP (São Paulo Museum of Art). Jaime Lerner, another name in contemporary engineering and architecture, did important work in the urban (re)planning of Curitiba, one of the best cities in which to live today.

Brazil is a tropical country with a friendly environment that offers an enormous variety of fruits and vegetables. From the arrival of the first adventurous Portuguese and the African slaves to the generally pacific arrival of other nationalities, the people developed one of the most spectacular varieties of culinary styles, which include dishes such as *feijoada* (black beans), *vatapá* (dendê oil, coconut milk, fish and shrimp*), pato no tucupi* (duck cooked with a special vegetable), or the small "cheese bread." Most of the time, the world knows Brazil by the wonderful beaches, soccer and friendliness of the people, and especially the beauty of Brazilian woman. But the country has more to offer than that.

For interest, one thinks of visiting canyons in Chapada Diamantina; or an original rain forest in Amazônia, where different nations of natives found only in the last few years still live; or the biggest river in the world, the Amazon, that features the phenomenon called *pororoca*, which happens when the river meets the Atlantic Ocean; or even the amazing waterfalls in Iguaçu. The national sport, soccer, has its popularity because it is a simple game that boys, especially, play from their early years. It does not require any special equipment other than a ball, which can be made of lots of different materials, like a simple sock.

To understand Brazilian culture, we have to take a look at the history, geography and circumstances of colonization in the past, as well as at the consequences of world wars and crises in other countries that facilitated the existence of all this variety we call Brazil. Also, we have to take a look at the Brazilian position in the modern world and the success of people in different fields such as business, fashion and international politics.

Brazil has many important cultural institutions and cultural events in both big and small cities that take place the whole year round. There are special folk exhibitions, civic and religious celebrations at which all the multicultural influences from over 500 years coexist peacefully.

Some scholars propose that the Brazilian misunderstanding *jeitinho*, which is translated as "to always take advantage," is actually a lovely way of life that means having a good relationship with others (people, culture, business), and it is the best way to look at this country named Brazil.

This friendly attitude, this open mindedness toward other viewpoints, this permanent willingness to help everyone is the best way to explain the people and the Brazilian culture.

## POLITICAL SYSTEM

The federal government consists of three branches: the executive, the legislative, and the judiciary.

The president heads the executive branch. Under the president are a number of executive departments, the heads of which are appointed and known collectively as the Cabinet. The Cabinet is responsible to the president. Unlike those in many parliamentary democracies, Cabinet members are not also members of the legislature. Besides the executive departments there are a number of independent agencies, many of which are regulatory. Note—the president is both the chief of state and head of government.

The legislative branch, the bicameral National Congress, or *Congresso Nacional*, is made up of two chambers: the Federal Senate, or *Senado Federal*, and the Chamber of Deputies, or *Câmara dos Deputados*. There are 81 senators, three from each state or federal district elected by a majority vote to serve eight-year terms; one-third elected after a four-year period and two-thirds elected after the next four-year period. The total membership of the Chamber of Deputies is 513, the number of representatives from each state depending on its population, and the members are elected to serve four-year terms. Voting is compulsory from the age of 18 to 70, and people of 16 and 17 can opt to vote.

The judicial branch consists of a system of federal, state and local courts throughout the country, headed by the Supreme Federal Tribunal. The federal courts rule on the constitutionality of laws and decisions appealed from the lower courts in which the Federal Union is a party. There is no appeal to the Supreme Court's decisions. The state (Higher Tribunal of Justice) and municipal (Regional Federal Tribunals) courts operate independently of the federal courts within the bounds of the Constitution. The judges are appointed for life.

State governments follow a pattern similar to that of the federal government. Each state has a governor as chief executive, and power is divided among the state executive, legislative and judicial branches.

There are many political parties. However, ideologies are not highly developed, as the democratic system of government in Brazil returned only in 1985. Parties normally represent specific economic groups and interests within the country.

## LEGAL SYSTEM

The Brazilian legal system is based on Roman codes, not on common law. The administration of justice is slow and cumbersome.

## HISTORY

Brazil was discovered in 1500 by the Portuguese navigator Pedro Alvares Cabral. Although invaded by the French and later by the Dutch, who occupied the coast of Pernambuco in the Northwest for some years, Brazil remained a Portuguese colony for more than 300 years. In 1822, Brazil declared its independence. A constitutional government has been maintained for most of the time since then. The country continued to be ruled by members of the Portuguese royal family until 1889, when the Republic was proclaimed.

In 1964, after considerable political, economic and social unrest, a new government structure was installed by the armed forces. Considerable economic growth and development was achieved during the following 20 years, although not without political and social repercussions. In 1985, the country returned to a democratic regime.

The present Constitution was promulgated in October 1988. It is lengthy, comprising 83 articles.

## ECONOMY

The economy is basically one of free enterprise, although there is still considerable state and semi-state participation in various strategic sectors, such as transport and utilities. The petroleum industry is a government monopoly, except for distribution. Special legislation was enacted to privatize many companies for which the presence of the state is not considered essential.

Natural resources and agriculture have been the traditional mainstay of the economy, backed by abundant human resources. Since the 1960s, however, emphasis has been placed on industrial development financed largely by international loans. As a result, exports today reflect a more balanced mix of commodities and manufactured items. Also, the profile of imports became more restricted during the 1970s and 1980s due to a policy of import substitution and the scarcity of foreign exchange. With the lowering of trade barriers, this profile is changing.

Following the oil crises of the 1970s and 1980s, Brazil developed its sugarcane-alcohol industry, which for many years fueled a large part of the private-car fleet.

The official GNP in 2000 was US$587.5 billion. However, the underground economy is not included. It is said to vary between 30 and 40 percent of GNP depending on the sector.

**TABLE 3-2:** Major trends

|  | 1990 | 1995 | 2000 |
|---|---|---|---|
| Gross domestic product (US$ billions) | 469,318 | 705,449 | 595,393 |
| Per capita (US$) | 3,221 | 4,542 | 3,584 |
| Real annual growth (%) | –5.05 | 4.22 | 4.36 |
| Agriculture | –2.76 | 4.08 | 3.03 |
| Industry | –8.73 | 1.91 | 4.87 |
| Services | –1.15 | 1.30 | 3.71 |
| Consumer price index–INPC (%) | 2,863.90 | 65.96 | 5.27 |
| General price index–IGP-DI (%) | 2,740.23 | 67.46 | 9.81 |
| Exchange devaluation (%) | 1,569.58 | 13.75 | 6.54 |
| Trade balance–FOB (US$ billions) | 10,753 | –3,158 | –636 |
| Exports | 31,414 | 46,506 | 55,086 |
| Imports | 20,661 | 49,664 | 55,722 |
| Foreign currency reserves (US$ billions) | 9,973 | 51,840 | 33,011 |
| Total foreign debt (US$ billions) | 96,546 | 129,313 | 189,501 |

*Source:* Fundacao Getulio Vargas. *Cojuntura Economica.* Vol. 56, No. 8, Agosto 2002.

## MINERAL AND ENERGY RESOURCES

Brazil is rich in natural resources. It has some of the largest iron ore deposits in the world and is now one of the biggest gold producers. Many other metals, minerals and precious stones are also mined on an increasing scale. There is significant hydroelectric potential, which is slowly being harnessed as a source of energy. The Itaipu dam in the extreme southwest is the largest hydroelectric power producer in the world. Self-sufficiency in petroleum consumption in 1993 was about 54 percent. Participation by foreign investors in the mineral and energy sectors has not been encouraged.

## AGRICULTURE, FISHERIES AND FORESTRY

Vast areas of land are suitable or adaptable to agriculture. The advance in land clearing is mainly in the Central-West and North regions. Brazil is a major exporter of soybeans and orange juice in addition to the traditional coffee and cocoa. Ownership of rural land by foreigners is restricted.

The fishing potential along the 5,700 miles (9,170 km) of coastline is significant but has not been fully exploited.

Forest areas still abound, particularly in the Amazon basin, and international protests have been raised against forest clearance and its potential damage to the world environment.

The principal agricultural products are summarized in Table 3-3.

## MANUFACTURING

Major manufacturing industries include petrochemicals, steel, automobiles, mining, cement, paper and allied products, agro-industry and food processing. None of these

TABLE 3-3: Principal agricultural products

|  | 1990 | 1995 | 2000 |
|---|---|---|---|
|  | (In thousands) | | |
| Banana (bunches) | 554,052 | 561,598 | 559,288 |
| Oranges | 94,682 | 98,286 | 89,889 |
|  | (In metric tons '000s) | | |
| Staples crops: | | | |
| Beans | 2,744 | 2,800 | 2,464 |
| Cocoa | 320 | 328 | 346 |
| Coffee | 3,041 | 2,587 | 2,551 |
| Cotton | 2,079 | 1,885 | 1,139 |
| Maize | 23,624 | 30,557 | 29,967 |
| Rice | 9,488 | 9,962 | 10,193 |
| Soybeans | 14,938 | 1,915 | 22,710 |
| Sugarcane | 260,888 | 271,432 | 251,408 |
| Tobacco | 413 | 578 | 663 |
| Wheat | 2,917 | 2,796 | 2,201 |
| Other crops: | | | |
| Manioc | 24,538 | 21,917 | 21,719 |
| Onions | 888 | 886 | 910 |
| Peanuts | 141 | 171 | 151 |
| Potatoes | 2,567 | 2,421 | 2,365 |
| Tomatoes | 2,343 | 2,132 | 2,315 |
| Meat and poultry: | | | |
| Beef | 2,885 | 3,036 | 3,100 |
| Pork | 802 | 882 | 900 |
| Poultry | 1,794 | 1,992 | 2,100 |

industries is in decline. There is great potential for expansion in all areas, assuming the current economic difficulties can be overcome. There are still restrictions on foreign investments in some sectors.

Industrial output is summarized in Table 3-4.

## HIGH-TECH INDUSTRIES

The high-tech sector comprises mainly the assembly of imported components and parts. Multinationals dominate, but there are several large Brazilian groups.

## SERVICE INDUSTRIES

Service-providing industries are now a significant and growing part of the economy. There is good growth potential for the tourist and information services areas. Business services are considered to be fairly sophisticated. In advertising, computer services and management consultancy, multinationals are well represented. The wholesale, distribution and retail trade is populated by some very large national companies, a few

**TABLE 3-4:** Industrial output

|  | 1991 | 1992 | 1993* |
|---|---|---|---|
|  | (In thousands) | | |
| Crude oil (barrels daily) | 623 | 627 | 638 |
| Alcohol (barrels daily) | 207 | 202 | 210 |
| Iron ore (MT) | 109,415 | 107,029 | 110,000 |
| Steel ingots (MT) | 22,617 | 23,897 | 25,169 |
| Aluminum ingots (MT) | 1,140 | 1,193 | 1,440 |
| Cement (MT) | 27,257 | 23,889 | 24,835 |
| Vehicles | 964 | 1,074 | 1,391 |
| Tractors | 19 | 19 | 28 |
| Airplanes | 92 | 55 | 66 |
| Tires | 28,926 | 30,306 | 31,796 |
| Electric power (GWh) | 209 | 213 | 221 |
| Chemicals (MT) | 22,914 | 22,060 | 24,126 |
| Paper and paperboard (MT) | 4,914 | 4,921 | 5,100 |
| Orange-juice concentrate (MT) | 887 | 1,059 | 1,030 |

*Some 1993 figures are estimates.

multinationals, some large regional companies and a large number of small family-owned businesses. Many large industrial groups have their own distribution networks. Apart from restrictions in the banking, financial services and telecommunications areas, foreign investors may participate in the service industries.

## TRANSPORT AND COMMUNICATIONS

There has been no significant development or modernization of the government-controlled railroad network over the past years, although there are plans for some major extensions, particularly in the North and Central-West regions. Therefore, road transport dominates, both for long-distance and intercity traffic. Nevertheless, construction of new highways has been slow in recent years. Also, most of the major federal and state highways have not been well maintained. Nearly all road transport and haulage companies are privately owned.

## HISTORY

Brazilian economic and political development reveal two clearly different phases. The first is from the discovery to the beginning (around 1930) of the twentieth century. In this period the characteristic is a growth model based on exports. In the second phase, the growth model is turned inward. Each of the phases presents its own characteristics, such as can be observed in Figure 3-2.

During the phase of the growth model based on exports, the economic cycles of sugar, coffee and rubber (as described later in this chapter) occurred. In this period Brazil became independent from Portugal however the Brazilian economy was not affected.

In relation to inward-turned development, a clear evolution can be observed with emphasis on different types of production over time. The strategy was based on import

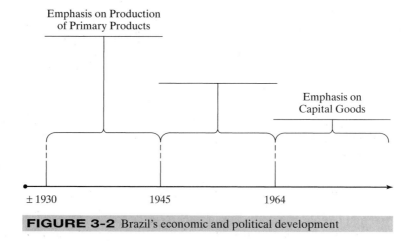

**FIGURE 3-2** Brazil's economic and political development

substitution and was related to the development of know-how and technology, as can be observed in Figure 3-3.

## PORTUGUESE AMERICA

The period between the discovery of Brazil on April 22, 1500, until the foundation of the first village (São Vicente) in 1530 is known as the Pre-Colonial period. From this time until King D. Pedro's declaration of Brazil's national independence, Portugal occupied the colony, promoting colonization and creating domestic economic and financial mechanisms. In terms of cultural life the system was designed to keep Brazil isolated and dependent and thus incapable of establishing any kind of independence from Portugal.

The colonial period was, therefore, marked by the conquest and control of the territory, as well as by exploration of agricultural and natural resources. In the beginning,

**FIGURE 3-3** Brazil's evolution of production

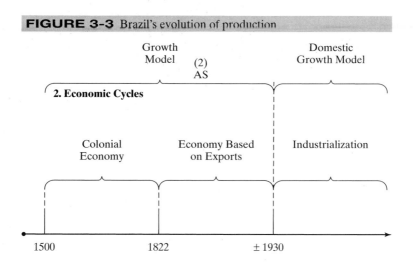

thanks to its immediate appearance, its abundance and its easy exploration with a minimum of necessary investment, Pau-Brasil (Brazil-Wood) gave origin to the first economic cycle called the Cycle of Brazil-Wood. The most intense period of its exploration goes from Brazil-Wood's discovery until the middle of the sixteenth century. The industry was developed along the coast, from the Rio Grande do Norte to the region of Rio de Janeiro, through a lease system between the State and particular companies, that paid one-fifth of the production to the Portuguese government. During this period the cutting and local hauling were done by the Indians, under the control of administrators, traders and colonists. Later, Black slaves were used.

In the period between 1570 and 1650 another important cycle in the colonial period known as the Cycle of Sugar took place. The success of this crop was favored by the experience acquired by the Portuguese in the islands of the Atlantic Ocean, by the favorable climate and soil in the Northeast region, by the abundance of enslaved manpower and by the expansion of the consumer market in Europe. Together with this activity, subsistence agriculture cattle grazing developed. Sugar production favored the occupation and colonization of the territory. These developments assured considerable profits to the aristocracy and to the Portuguese Crown. However, the decline in consumption in Europe and the competition from the production of sugar in the Antilles by the Dutch led to the end of the monopoly in sugar production in the second half of the seventeenth century.

Coincidently, with the beginning of the decline of the Cycle of Sugar, the colony of Brazil started to experience a new period of wealth and prosperity, which was confirmed at the turn of the eighteenth century by the discovery of gold in the region of Minas Gerais (at the time equivalent to what is today the state of Minas Gerais, Goiás and Mato Grosso). This event sparked a shift in migratory streams coming from the Northeast region to the region of São Paulo, which led to the founding of new villages.

Estimates indicate that the population of Brazil in 1770 was around 2 million, with 20.5 percent in Minas Gerais, 18.5 percent in Bahia and 15.4 percent in Pernambuco. In the mining regions society was already urbanized, with core populations and the diversification of activities, functions and jobs. In other regions, the population was organized around farms for cotton, tobacco and cattle. Power was concentrated in the hands of the agricultural aristocracy who, in many cases, substituted for the public authorities, ordering the lives of the people around them. It was a patriarchal society.

## A PRIMARY EXPORTING ECONOMY

Imperial Brazil is the period extending from independence, on September 7, 1822, until the announcement of the Republic on November 15, 1889. This period is marked by a centralized monarchy in conflict with rebellious liberal ideals and by the emerging economic diversification of the coffee expansion.

The second half of the nineteenth century was marked by diverse economic transformations. The influx of European immigrants was absorbed as qualified, wage-earning manpower. The immigrants began to consume national products, thus contributing to industrial and economic expansion. They also increased the hold of internal capital over the economy after prohibition of the importing of slaves. Part of this capital found its way into the farming of coffee and commercial and industrial enterprises. Another part went into the constitution of companies, plants, railroads and banks.

The crisis in the French colony of Haiti provoked a rise in the price of coffee on international markets and stimulated an increase in production in Brazil, and coffee became the leading national export. The expansion started in the highlands near Rio de Janeiro. It took advantage of idle manpower from the mining areas. From there, the coffee culture spread to Minas Gerais and São Paulo, thus forming the main axes of production. With the prohibition of the Black slave trade in 1850, enslaved manpower was replaced by contracting for European immigrants, attracted by the incentives offered by the Brazilian government.

The social-economic transformations in this period led, in the middle of the nineteenth century, to conflicts of interests, which led in turn to the end of the monarchy. On November 15, 1889, the Republic was proclaimed, thus initiating a period of great social, economic and political change that has continued until the present.

During the last decades of the nineteenth century and the first decade of the twentieth century, the Amazon region was transformed into the scene of the fastest economic cycle of Brazil—the Cycle of Rubber. The cycle began with the invention of the tire in 1890, and the expansion of the automobile industry, mainly in the United States. These developments raised the demand for the product, increasing its price and bringing prosperity to the main cities in the Amazon region. Production reached its height in 1912 and began to decline with the arrival, in 1910, of the production of rubber in the British colonies in Southeast Asia.

This period of the primary exporting economy was marked by a great boom in the economy, based on coffee. At the end of nineteenth century, 70 percent of the worldwide production of coffee came from the coffee plantations of Brazil. The expansion of coffee farming created the conditions for the appearance of a consumer market and contributed to the accumulation of capital. This development was accompanied by further industrial development, particularly of the center-south region.

Until the time of the announcement of the Republic, there were barely six hundred industries in the country that produced food, textiles and clothes. World War I changed this picture. With the disorganization of the worldwide economy, the Brazilian economy benefited thanks to the difficulties in importing certain products, such as food. The government tried to advance the industrialization process, granting financing for the importing of machinery and stimulating immigration.

The result of these measures can be measured by the number of companies in 1920, more than 13,000 industrial establishments. During this period much the same happened to the banking sector. Despite this industrial expansion, the dominant sectors of the Brazilian economy continued to be trade (importing and exporting) and the great coffee plantations. This picture remained basically unchanged up to 1929, when worldwide economic depression began. The crisis was reflected in Brazil, leading coffee producers to bankruptcy due to the fall in prices in the international market.

## INDUSTRIAL ECONOMY

The depreciation of the main export, coffee, contributed to successive harvest records. This fact generated a major crisis, beginning in 1930 and extending to 1944. Looking for a solution, the Brazilian government acquired and destroyed about 80 million bags of coffee.

The crisis led to the exploration of new products such as fruits, cotton, oil and ore, and to the development of an economy based on the domestic market. The government granted funds to the credit system, set up safeguard tariffs, controlled prices and established a policy of wage control. In the sectors in which the private sector could not invest, the government built its own companies, such as the Companhia Siderurgica Nacional (National Steel Company), created in 1941. The Companhia Vale do Rio Doce was established in 1942 for ore mining.

Industrial growth suffered a decline during World War II because of the difficulty in importing machinery and industrial equipment. In 1944, the government devised a plan for infrastructure development and the creation of basic industries.

With the coffee crisis, the power of the coffee barons declined, and the social and political space for an industrial bourgeoisie and for the middle class increased, giving them more participation in political life. The laboring classes also grew considerably, but their expansion was controlled by government interventionist mechanisms.

From the middle of the 1950s, the country lived through a phase of real economic progress, under the stimulation of the Plano Nacional de Desenvolvimento (National Plan for Development). Industrial production grew by 80 percent. Basic industries expanded, and other projects such as the construction of hydroelectric plants and the construction of Brasília modernized the country. These events contributed to the increase in internal migration and an increase in the rural exodus.

The Brazilian economy opened to foreign capital, through the concession of special incentives to spur the equipment input indispensable for industry. To the national private sector, the government offered advantageous credit policies that assured the expansion of internal demand. These strategies received favorable reactions from both national and foreign entrepreneurs. At this time the country reached self-sufficiency in certain key sectors, such as the automobile industry. However, at the beginning of the 1960s, the investment tax started to decline and inflation went up uncontrollably.

On March 31, 1964, the military regime began. It continued until the re-democratization of the country. For the economy, a new model was adopted to support income concentration and sacrifice low-wage earners. At the same time, the Brazilian government reopened the country to foreign capital and took on more external indebtedness to make investments in major public works projects.

Based on key security development, a new model for growth was undertaken to promote the growth of industrialization with resources drawn from foreign capital, national entrepreneurs and the government as economic agent. The country's borders opened to multinational companies, which were attracted by the extremely favorable conditions to establish and expand their industries—especially the cheap price of manpower, because of government intervention limiting real increases in wages.

If these measures aggravated the income distribution imbalance, the results from the economic point of view were positive. From 1968 to 1973, GDP growth was around 10 percent annually. Added to the great public works projects, they characterized the "Brazilian Miracle."

However, from the second half of the 1970s, external indebtedness speeded up, inflation returned, the public sector went into crisis and the economy as a whole started to plunge. In 1981, the economy's contraction reached depression level, with a sharp fall in industrial production. In the following years, the crisis grew, the external debt reaching US$80 billion in 1982 and US$100 billion in 1983. Consequently, the

Brazilian government had to appeal to the International Monetary Fund. At this stage, the government could not even pay the interest on the debt.

From 1986, the government tried through successive economic plans (Cruzado, Bresser and Verão) to control the high inflation, without success. Collor Plan #1 (1990) once more adopted the freezing of prices and wages. It increased the taxes and tariffs. It announced the privatization of state-owned companies, with the objective of containing public debt. It suspended tax incentives not guaranteed by the Constitution and created mechanisms to prevent tax evasion. Soon after its implementation, there was a drastic reduction in the productivity of the economy. After one year, the plan's impotence in the struggle with inflation was evident.

After difficult periods of contraction in the economy and the persistent growth of inflation, in July 1994 a new plan is was unveiled—The Real Plan. The Real Plan solved the problem and led the Brazilian economy to a new phase, with low inflation and a steady currency. The role of the State was redefined. Protectionist laws were abandoned and market controls eliminated. Through this act, national industry became competitive with foreign industry on the domestic market. Moreover, national industry was forced to adapt to a global economy.

## BIBLIOGRAPHY

Caldeira, J. (1997) *Viagem pela História do Brasil.* São Paulo: Companhia das Letras.

Da Matta, R. *Carnavais, Malandros e Heróis.* Rio de Janeiro: Rocco.

Freire, G. (2000) *Casa Grande e Senzala.* Rio de Janeiro: Record.

Instituto Brasileiro de Geografia e Estatística (IBGE) (2001) Brazil in Figures.

Lucci, E. A. (2000) *Geografia. Homem e Espaço.* São Paulo: Editora Saraiva.

Maddison, A. (1989) "Desempenho da Economia Mundial desde 1870." In Gall, N., et al., *Nova Era da Economia Mundial.* São Paulo: Pioneira.

Nêumanne, J. (1992) *Reféns do Passado.* São Paulo: Siciliano.

Senna, J. J. (1995) *Os Parceiros do Rei.* Herança Cultural e Desenvolvimento Econômico no Brasil. Rio de Janeiro: Topbooks.

Skidmore, T. (1986) *Politics in Brazil, 1930–1964: An Experiment in Democracy.* Oxford: Oxford University Press.

Skidmore, T. (1990) *The Politics of Military Rule in Brazil, 1964–1985.* Oxford: Oxford University Press.

# CHAPTER 4
# URUGUAY

❧

DR. IGNACIO DE POSADAS
DR. CARLOS STENERI

## INTRODUCTION

One of the smallest countries in South America, wedged between the two largest, Argentina and Brazil, Uruguay has a population of slightly over 3 million, a temperate climate and a geography devoid of spectacular features. Low demography, calm geography and moderate climate quite possibly account for some of the country's traits. See Table 4-1.

## ORIGINS

Unglamorous to the conquistadores due to its lack of gold and silver, Uruguay was noticed late in the colonizing process and then only because of its military potential, as an outpost from which to keep an eye on the River Plate estuary and, even more importantly, on the Portuguese, ever eager to extend their domination all the way to the Atlantic Coast.

These port origins also help to explain part of the country's history. Even today, the city-port of Montevideo accounts for virtually half of the total population and most of the political power. From garrison to commercial center, the region, attached to the viceroyalty of the River Plate, slowly started to develop and to develop its rivalry with the capital city of Buenos Aires. The area, roughly bordered by the Uruguay and Plate rivers, the Atlantic and its diffuse and changing land border with Brazil, was sparsely populated by a few Indian tribes. These tribes were very primitive, mostly nomadic and in some cases (the Charrúas) quite indomitable. With the exception of the period during which the Jesuits established their missions, ending in the mid-1770s, roughly the northern half of present-day Uruguay was a part of the Jesuit Estancias (pasture lands), worked by the sedentary and civilized Guaraní Indians. The natives of this area built no cities, did not know how to write, cultivated close to nothing and divided their time between hunting and warring.

There were vast numbers of wild cattle, descended from species introduced from Spain by Hernandarias. It is not difficult to see the spirit of the Charrúa Indians in the latter-day gauchos or in the farmhands that lived—some still live there today—in the large Estancias. Originally, these pasture lands were huge, fenceless tracts populated by wiry longhorns, which Indians and gauchos would lasso or "bowl" using the *boleadoras*. The latter was an instrument or weapon consisting of three stones attached by long leather straps. In the early days, the animals were caught and immediately slaughtered in the open

**FIGURE 4-1** Map of Uruguay

fields for their hides and meat which was cooked and eaten on the spot—including such delicacies as tongue. The rest of the carcass, being of no value, was left for predators.

Only much later did a primitive meat industry begin around Montevideo. The beef was salted to provision the ships in port and for military clients. Fencing and branding became mandatory in the 1870s.

Outside Montevideo and a few small towns scattered over the countryside, government and authority in general were generally absent, leaving ample scope to the individualism of Indians and gauchos and the greed of the Portuguese.

**TABLE 4-1:** Facts about Uruguay

| | *Uruguay* |
|---|---|
| Location | Southern South America, bordering the South Atlantic Ocean, between Argentina and Brazil |
| Geography note | Second-smallest South American country (after Suriname); most of the low-lying landscape (three-quarters of the country) is grassland, ideal for cattle and sheep raising |
| Area | Total: 176,220 sq km<br>Land: 173,620 sq km<br>Water: 2,600 sq km<br>Slightly smaller than the state of Washington |
| Land boundaries | Total: 1,564 km<br>Border countries: Argentina, 579 km; Brazil, 985 km |
| Population | 3.4 million (UN 2003) |
| Capital | Montevideo |
| Life expectancy | 72 years men; 79 years women |
| Natural resources | Arable land, hydropower, minor minerals, fisheries |
| Land use | Arable land: 7.21%<br>Permanent crops: 0.27%<br>Other: 92.52% (1998 est.) |
| Main exports | Meat, rice, leather products, vehicles, dairy products, wool, electricity |
| Average annual income | US$5,710 |

## INDEPENDENCE

Uruguay's struggle for independence was particularly protracted and complicated. Its beginnings, however, do not differ substantially from those of other South American colonies. In Montevideo, much as in Buenos Aires or Lima, the non-Spanish population (Criollos) increasingly resented the normative and socially discriminatory measures, which characterized the heavily bureaucratic, centralized and snobbish Spanish colonial system and society. Among other things, Criollos were barred from high, and lucrative, offices. This was a very important issue for caballeros, who, as such, were not supposed to work and yet had to spend according to their rank. The same Habsburg-spawned mentality toward trade resulted in a forest of paperwork, regulations and privileges, which not only added insult to injury with the Criollos, but also irritated even the local, pure-blooded peninsulares who engaged in commercial activities. This land, thus fertilized, was also intellectually irrigated by a combination of philosophical and ideological movements.

The ideas of the English liberals from Locke to Burke were known and endlessly discussed by many of the young Criollos, as were those of their American followers—mainly the Founding Fathers, through the Federalist Papers. This English thought intertwined with that of such pre-Revolutionary French luminaries as Rousseau, Voltaire, etc., and those who alternatively illuminated or directly set ablaze the various phases of France's revolutionary experience. Finally, in the same pot also stirred the freethinking and ratio-nalistic dogmas of Freemasons and other assorted anticlerical elements.

The first rumblings of revolt started as a side effect of Napoleon's invasion of Spain and his dethroning of the Bourbon king. If the monarch sitting in Madrid was illegiti-mate, then the colonies' ties to that king no longer held. As in Spain itself, the ancient rights of the local authorities (*cabildos*) came to the fore. Authority, vested in the crown, reverted to the people's delegates once the crown was lost to usurpers.

As in Buenos Aires, whose *pronunciamiento* (declaration of independence) happened shortly before, the revolutionary phenomenon was basically urban and aristocratic, that is, the Criolla upper class and intelligentsia. As also occurred else-where in both South and North America, all those who were in favor of the uprising did not share exactly the same views and goals. Among the revolutionaries, some were imbued with the ideas of the French Revolution and more precisely with the ideologues of its early stages. Others saw in the revolt the possibility of righting some of the wrongs attributed to the Spanish colonial system. Still others adhered strictly to the official justification, to wit that the colonies were reacting not against the king but against the usurper. Later, parties would trace some of their roots to these differences.

Uruguay's independence—or rather that of the Montevideo part of the River Plate viceroyalty—is intertwined with the evolution of its two neighbors, the viceroy-alty, then the United Provinces of the River Plate, and the Portuguese colony, then the Empire of Brazil. In fact, the better part of the struggle was against one or both of these neighbors.

In fact, loosening the Spanish yoke was the shorter and easier part. Once Buenos Aires dispensed with the viceroy, the citadel of Montevideo fell to the rebels and the Spanish practically vanished from the picture, giving lieu almost immediately to a rup-ture between the revolutionary authority in Buenos Aires and a part of the local forces in the then-named Oriental Province, that is, the province east of the Uruguay River. These were agitated, convulsive and recurrently chaotic times, which spilled over into the Civil War period. At one and the same time, the so-called United Provinces of the River Plate fought the Spanish in Chile and in the North (Alto Perú), wrangled among themselves as to what sort of government they should settle on (or should Buenos Aires wield power) and witnessed fierce infighting among factions. The last phenome-non produced a rapid succession of triumvirates and directorships, reminiscent of revolutionary France. In this process, the Oriental Province confronted Buenos Aires' centralism, favoring and fighting for a federality or confederate whose capital could be anywhere but Buenos Aires.

The Federalist forces, led by the Oriental José Artigas, were not successful. The Province, which had been the arena of confrontation with Buenos Aires, became the battleground for independence from the Portuguese.

Chased from the Iberian Peninsula by Napoleon, the Portuguese court moved to Río. From there the court watched how anarchy devastated the United Provinces and left the Oriental Province tantalizingly weakened. The old dream of the "natural" fron-tiers on the Uruguay-Plate rivers was impossible to repress. Portugal invaded the Oriental Province and occupied Montevideo. Buenos Aires declared war, but at the time could do little else, as it was bogged down partly by the war against the Spanish armies and partly by the differences among the provinces. These differences in the best of times meant no cooperation with the war effort, and the rest of the time signified direct military confrontation. In the Oriental Province, part of the local population, primarily Montevideanos, opted for collaboration with the lusitanos (Portuguese/Brazilians), while others emigrated to Argentina.

King Dom Pedro's decision to remain in Brazil when the court decided to return to Napoleon-free Portugal did not change the situation in the Oriental Province. Only after the Spanish threat had definitely vanished and a short period of relative harmony was enjoyed in the United Provinces did a combined army of Orientals and Argentinos defeat the Imperials of Brazil.

However, defeat in the field did not equate with independence. It did mean that a negotiating process could be initiated. This, too, was hard and complicated, with many conflicting interests at play. Argentina (actually only Buenos Aires at that time), wanted its Oriental Province back, but knew it would be very difficult to hold it over time. The Empire had lost its stomach for a fight, but was reluctant to give in to Argentina. Meanwhile, the Orientals, more and more distinct from both their neighbors and internally cohesive, after so many years of distrusting and battling both, had a growing nationalist party. They were strongly averse to the Montevideanos who had collaborated with the Imperials. Viewing this, Britain decided it had vital interests in the area that were not served by this never-ending succession of wars and guerrillas with constantly changing sides and issues. As it did a few years later in the Netherlands, and under the political guidance of Canning and the on-the-spot diplomacy of Ponsonby, Britain pushed for and obtained a solution through the recognition of the Oriental Province's political reality. The province became the República Oriental del Uruguay in a treaty signed by all the belligerents, including the Oriental army, which was guaranteed by Her Majesty's government.

Such was the end of a historical period, but not of the various strands which made up history.

## THE PERIOD OF THE CIVIL WARS

In 1830, under a new written constitution which included a centralized government and a strong, indirectly elected presidency, the Senate selected as its first president one of the two most important national military personalities, one who had been for a time a collaborator with the Imperials—General Rivera. A certain degree of bad blood was inevitable. Nevertheless, General Rivera ruled through the end of his term, albeit in a very individualistic and disorderly fashion. In the second election, the presidency fell to another general, this time of totally different personal and historical extraction. Manuel Oribe was a career officer, unlike his predecessor, and also unlike General Rivera had never bowed down before the Portuguese invaders. Democracy, alternation in office, political parties as opposed to factions—these were in the eyes of many in the young republic, although they were more theoretical concepts than accepted truths. This change was resisted by the former president. Revolution ensued with the exile of General Oribe to Argentina, which at the time was going through a bloody feud between Federalists and Unitarians. Uruguay was once more plunged into war in the crosscurrent of Argentinean and local factions.

The first phase of its history saw the birth of the country's so-called traditional parties: the Blancos who followed Oribe, and the self-proclaimed Defenders of the Law who allied with the Federalists of Argentina. Both parties had strong ties with the country's interior. Both were enemies of Buenos Aires' centralism under the Unitarios and of urban, European elitist culture. This culture was favored by the other party, the Colorados. This party was perceived by its opponents as opposed to the true national values which were preserved in the country and were free of foreign, liberal and frequently irreligious influences, all of which were present in the Colorado ranks.

Once again, Britain, this time aided by France, intervened in the local feuding to protect its interests. These interests were the free navigation of the rivers Plate, Uruguay, and Paraná, as well as the commercial ventures of some of its subjects, established in Buenos Aires and Montevideo. This time the powers went beyond persuasion, blockading the Argentinean ports held by the Federalists and aiding Montevideo, then in the hands of the Colorados and besieged by a Blanco army.

This first phase of the Civil Wars period ended, more out of exhaustion than from any other reason, in a peace treaty, which allowed for a relatively tranquil institutional interregnum. Unfortunately, the peace was of short duration. During the same period, Argentina continued to face fierce and frequently violent confrontations between Buenos Aires and a variable coalition of provinces, while Brazil, internally stable under the Empire, never missed an opportunity to influence events beyond its ever-expanding borders. In that context, another Blanco president tripped over a tangle of internal and geopolitical interests. Paraguay, under the absolute rule of Solano López, had interests and ambitions opposed to those of both Brazil and Buenos Aires. Buenos Aires was locked in its never-resolved struggle with the other provinces. A fraction of the Colorado party, linked to Brazil, coveted power. The immediate outcome was another revolution, the ousting of the constitutional president and a secret treaty between the Colorado revolutionary president, the Imperial government and the governor of Buenos Aires, to put a stop to the expansionist dreams of Paraguay's dictator, General Solano López. The next step was one of the most infamous episodes of the history of South America, the so-called War of the Triple Alliance, which devastated Paraguay to such an extent that the country is said to suffer still from its consequences.

By this time, the 1870s, some of Uruguay's political and cultural traits were distinctly in place. The small country was wedged between two giants that were a constant source of problems, forever trying to meddle in its internal affairs. The country was divided into two distinct realities. On the one hand, Montevideo was a port, cosmopolitan, modern and already bearing a strong presence of non-Peninsular Europeans. The city was the seat of government and of effective power in most of the country. The other Uruguay was the interior, sparsely populated, agrarian, more Spanish in its culture and more primitive. Here, authority was a personal condition dependent on courage and charisma. In Montevideo, the Colorado party was predominant, whereas the Blancos held sway in most of the rest of Uruguay. Economically, the country was also a juxtaposition of two realities: trade in Montevideo and extensive cattle raising in huge estancias in the interior. As mentioned, there was an incipient industry of salting and packing meat in and around Montevideo.

This turbulent period of Civil Wars had a hiatus in the form of three military regimes. These regimes were a result of reactions against the constant turbulence and disorder of partisan warring. During this calmer period, the country managed to advance in important areas such as the enclosing of lands, civil and commercial codes, the establishment of a system of public education, etc.

By this time, Montevideo was already on its way to becoming a cosmopolitan society, with the presence of citizens from many West and East European nations. In the interior, the Indian population had been almost entirely exterminated. The few tribes that had populated the vast countryside never adapted to the pace of progress, however slow it might be. Once their usefulness as warriors in the various wars of independence and civil strife was over, their indomitable ways moved them toward banditry. The last tribe was lured to a banquet by a senior officer and then, once duly plied with food and liquor, every single Indian was exterminated.

## ENTER MODERNITY

Toward the end of the nineteenth century Uruguay started to move into a new phase under the presidency of one of its more outstanding and polemical leaders, José Batlle y Ordóñez. He was very much the man of his age: modern, enlightened, a believer in progress. He identified with rationalism, invention, industry and education. Later, he was also an opponent of the Catholic Church, which had denied him the permission to marry a divorcée. Batlle y Ordóñez relied heavily on his party, the Colorados, and its grassroots militants, mostly located in Montevideo. The party had a heavy presence of immigrants, mostly of Italian and French origins.

Batlle pushed forward a full agenda of progressive reforms, which included labor legislation, favoring unions, protecting infant industries and unburdening the Church of some of its traditional vital activities, namely education and social activities in the area of health, old age and the like. Not to be outdone, leaders of the other party, by then named Partido Nacional, pushed in Congress for the first pieces of legislation in the area of social security which were to convert Uruguay to one of the earliest welfare states in the world. This modernism was completed with legislation on the family, rights of women, divorce, etc.

At the same time, President Batlle refused to countenance what had become a tacit status quo between the two parties. Under this arrangement, even if the presidency remained strong in the written constitution, the losing party, at that time the Blancos, protected themselves from excessive power of the opposition by holding a certain number of provincial governments. In effect, this system had evolved into a sort of barony in certain parts of the country.

Batlle decided to stop this practice, a decision which—predictably—provoked the Partido Nacional to take up arms, first in 1897 and then, virtually for the last time, in 1904. By then, the relatively stable balance of forces between the government's regulars and the Blanco irregulars was breaking under the influence of progress and differences in economic potential, the main factor being the railway, which was no match for the mounted armies of the Nacionalistas.

Even though there were some further attempts after 1904, the era of the Civil Wars was over, but not before having marked very strongly and for many years the different paths of the two traditional parties. The Colorados were confirmed as a mostly urban party, with their power base in Montevideo and adjacent cities. With a bent toward the interests and ideas of the city and of industry and its unions, the Colorados were the party of government and power, having won the elections steadily for many years. They were the party of modernism and positivism, of anticlericalism and freemasonry. On the other hand, the Blancos, generally out of government, with their power base in the interior, were the party of tradition, closer to the old Spanish roots and to the interests of the ranchers—which were frequently at odds with those of Montevideo.

In spite of such well-defined differences and an ill-disguised antagonism, this was an era of political deal making between them, or, more precisely, between factions of each party, as frequently internal feuds were stronger and more bitter than party differences. This was also the time of progress in electoral legislation and of dabbling with constitutional engineering. The Partido Nacional had made of the former its main banner in the later uprisings. They campaigned for electoral honesty and against fraud and gerrymandering. The divisions within the parties finally led to legislation that guaranteed free, clean elections. In fact, the legal structure was so well designed that not only has it been substantially the same since, but it has also served as an inspiration for other countries in South America and outside. As for the constitution, a combination of realpolitick by the leading groups within the parties and the optimistic rationalism of the times produced a number of constitutional changes, some more felicitous than others, many short-lived. This is a national weakness the political classes have not entirely shed to this day.

## ON TO THE WELFARE STATE

By the second decade of the twentieth century, Uruguay was a vigorous country, sought after by young, hard-working immigrants, with a flourishing agricultural sector. It was progressive in certain areas like genetics and possessed a budding industry, thriving trade and a battery of modern legislation. All of this legislation concerned the state: public health, public education, public works, state companies (monopolies in most cases), preferential financing by state banks (including a housing mortgage bank), labor legislation, and a widespread social security system covering retirement (at 55 and 60) and a constellation of pension causes. Everything added up to an almost ideal country, by then politically stable. And so it was, while it lasted. Or, rather, while agricultural income sufficed to pay for both industrial protection and distribution policies.

## SLIPPING BACKWARD

The decades covering the two World Wars—with the exception of the black 1930s—were boon times for Uruguay, with a very favorable equation in terms of trade. They were the times of Grand Tours, things French (from furniture to food, clothes and authors), English commercial and financial houses and, most of all, the consolidation of a numerous and solid middle class. Beef and wool fabrics easily paid for all of it. By the mid-1950s, the Korean War was barely a shot in the arm and signs of exhaustion started to show.

The writing appeared on the wall in November 1958, when the Colorado Party lost the elections for the first time in over 90 years. By then, Uruguay, the "Switzerland of America" as it so proudly repeated, had gone Swiss all the way, having modified the Constitution once again, creating collegiate executives both at the national and regional levels (20 mini parliaments plus a two-chamber Congress). As for patronage, bickering and blocking became the main features of Uruguayan politics.

## STAGNATION AND CRISIS

As terms of trade deteriorated and infant industries skipped adulthood to go straight into old age, Uruguay was caught with a huge state structure and an overly mature culture. It was rights-oriented, distributive, classically French and encyclopedic. The social blanket was no longer big enough to cover everybody, and the times changed to continuous pulling by just about everybody.

Successive governments were either unwilling or unable, or a combination of both, to grapple with reality and lead the country through necessary but painful reforms. Wise enough to drop the democratic snag of collegiate executives through yet another constitutional change, Uruguay failed to produce results through the mirage of planning and development policies, the fad in Latin America during the 1960s. Enlightened rational planning was prolific in literature but produced scant results in reality (beyond a further increase in costs for a country already living beyond its means).

As the novelty of government in other hands than the Colorados faded and inflation became chronic, the political system got bogged down, offering public opinion the image—sometimes exaggerated—of inefficiency, petty corruption and bickering. Then, late into the sixties a new phenomenon emerged in Uruguayan reality: the left's overcoming its traditional infighting to create a united front (Frente Amplio) and Uruguay's contagion by another Latin-American disease: guerrilla movements. Unbelievable at first, then Robin Hoodesque and later bloody and extreme, the Tupamaros disrupted both the functioning of the political system and national traits of peaceful coexistence.

The elections of 1971 were held in a climate of strong confrontation and fear, and resulted in the victory of the government's candidate (a former minister campaigning as an honest non-politician), with a strong showing by the left.

Continuing economic stagnation, a polarized situation due to the then apparently invincible Tupamaros and a dialogue of the deaf between the government and the leader of the Blancos led to a coup by the military, which had—surprisingly—wiped out the Tupamaros shortly after the new government took office. Initially backing the President, then substituting others more to their liking for him, the military ran the country for 11 years in a rather unique way.

With a semi-democratic structure among the top officers of the three branches which granted relatively greater weight to the army, an agreed-upon division of national wealth (i.e., the oil refinery had Air Force presidents; electricity and telephones went to the Army, the Port went to the Navy, etc.) and a certain internal balance of power that effectively barred any one man from either absolute power or perpetuation in office, the military tried—initially with great self-confidence—to do what the supposedly inept and corrupt politicians had been unable to accomplish. Accompanied by a group of either like-minded or servile civilians, they wavered between their centralized, planned, and structured mentality and alternative economic advice—that is, between planning and free marketing.

Initially, a large number of the population watched with a passive but expectant attitude. As time went by with no improvement emerging and amid signs of harsh repression, expectation turned to a silent but solid opposition.

Mindless omnipotence and the impossibility of dismantling a State structure to which they belonged plunged the military regime into a deep economic crisis. Once again, Uruguay, believing itself to be different from the other Latin American countries, was dragged with everyone else into the debt crisis of the 1980s. In 1982 the peso, artificially pegged to the dollar through the sheer stubbornness of the government, had to be released and immediately jumped from 13 to 43 pesos per dollar in a week.

Long and difficult negotiations made way for an orderly and peaceful, though tutored, return to democracy, with new elections in 1984.

## THE PRESENT

The return to democracy has seen three governments and is now into the fourth.

Politically, the first election showed Uruguay's inclination to predictability with the election of Julio María Sanguinetti, an intelligent political pro who promised no surprises. With the backing in Parliament of the Blanco party, thanks to the generous attitude of its leader (who had watched the elections from a military prison, where he was barred from running), Sanguinetti concentrated on sorting out the pitfalls inevitably produced by the 11-year break in democracy and confrontation in Uruguayan society. Political refugees and émigrés returned. Parties and unions were legitimized. Tupamaros were freed and amnestied and an antimilitary backlash was avoided by a clever legal gimmick. A law was enacted declaring that the State's opportunity to chastise the delinquent military had expired. It was touch-and-go for while, as the law was subsequently put to a plebiscite, but finally—though not definitively—a formal burying of the hatchet took place.

Economically the government's performance was far less successful. Governing in a de facto coalition, necessary to obtain parliamentary majorities, with a president schooled in the old Batllista (New Deal type) culture, the country barely struggled through the first few years. It then stumbled through a severe drought, finally counting the days to the next inauguration, throttled by a huge external debt, high fiscal deficits, recession and runaway inflation.

The 1989 elections were a landside for the Blancos, although not enough to win a majority. The left again moved forward, winning the capital city of Montevideo for the first time in history. The other bad piece of news for the incoming government was a plebiscited modification of the Constitution—which virtually no politician dared oppose in the teeth of almost 500,000 retirees—making pensions and retirements automatically adjustable for inflation. The budget deficit, already at 6 percent of GDP, in the first year of the new administration jumped another two points, and every point more of inflation meant higher social security costs.

President Lacalle's government, which had campaigned on a liberal (in the European sense of the term) platform, set out to tackle, at the same time, the debt-deficit-inflation front and the much-needed modernization of the economy. It basically took two directions: opening up trade and tackling state direct and regulatory activities. This was a tough battle, for which it at first had scant backing from the Colorados and then outright opposition. The lowest point came in December 1992 with yet another plebiscite, called by the left and backed by former President Sanguinetti, abrogating certain pieces of privatizing legislation. The government was soundly beaten and forced to go it alone for the remaining two years, trying to keep its policies in line.

The outcome was perhaps better than expected: though much of its reforming agenda could not be pushed through and although the Blancos lost the elections (albeit by a small margin), a considerable degree of transformation was achieved.

The year 1995 saw Sanguinetti back in office and another government coalition, with the Blanco party offering decisive support, but again with a Mitterandist president who showed little faith in market-oriented transformations. The left had again increased its voting, retaining Montevideo for the third consecutive time.

A partial modification of the overburdensome social security system was voted and the Constitution (again!) modified: initially to introduce a two-round runoff system for the presidency (to allow both traditional parties to block the left, by then the biggest third of the electorate) and to force parties to hold primaries and file for only one candidate. (The former multi-candidate system made very efficient vote-getting machines, but were impossible to discipline in government once the myriad of chieftains had secured their bit of power spoils.)

Dr. Sanguinetti's second presidency mirrored the first in economic terms, passing on a very sticky baton, this time to a man of his own party. In December 1999 on the second ballot, the third (his father being the second) Batlle attained the presidency on his sixth try.

Enfant terrible–cum–maverick, brilliant to some, dilettante to others, with the backing of the Blanco party (and the tremors of Sanguinetti's faction of the Colorados) and with the Frente Amplio established as the leading party in votes, Batlle started what everybody expected was going to be a seismic presidency.

Contrary to all expectations, what shocks have since taken place have been due to external causes. It is fair to say President Batlle has had an unbroken string of bad luck. There was devaluation in Brazil, foot-and-mouth disease passed on from Argentina and structural problems untouched by the second Sanguinetti administration. The Argentinean meltdown and a banking crisis that also originated in Argentina have crippled Uruguay without even the relative hope of seeing the government seize on any of those misfortunes to try and galvanize the still very conservative country into the overdelayed structural reforms.

Once again stuck in recession, with huge deficits, growing indebtedness, 16 percent unemployment and a pall of pessimism, acute even by Uruguay's ever gloomy cultural standards, the country faces three more years of this government and the crossroads of an attractive utopia-peddling left versus two other barely distinguishable parties, one whose president has offered nothing of what he stood for, the other who feels let down in his backing but dares not walk out.

## URUGUAY'S ECONOMIC HIGHLIGHTS DURING THE TWENTIETH CENTURY

During the twentieth century Uruguay's economic behavior was a continuum of stop-and-go events. This evolution falls into several distinct phases: (a) the period up to the mid-1930s was one of rural predominance with growth generated by expansion of agricultural and livestock production for the European markets; (b) the time of rapid industrialization, which covered some two decades—from the mid-1930s to the end of the Korean War—and first emphasized the processing of agricultural and livestock products for export but subsequently became subordinated to import substituting industry, mainly for the domestic market; (c) since 1957 the lapse of the coexistence of economic stagnation and rampant inflation which lasted for almost 20 years after the mid-1950s; a period—1974–1984—in which certain economic liberalization policies began—mostly on administered prices and financial transactions followed by a deep economic and banking crisis; and (d) finally after 1985, a period of certain rehabilitation, following the military government during which political and administrative changes were introduced to lay the foundation for the resumption of economic growth. This lapse ended with a sharp deterioration in economic conditions and a banking crisis stemming from domestic imbalances backed with negative external shocks from the region, particularly Argentina.

## THE TWENTIETH CENTURY: BEGINNINGS (1900–1930)

The rural predominance époque was in large measure an extension of colonial times, the major difference being that the benefits of export trade accrued to the national economy instead of the colonial power. The export-led model designed in colonial times in which raw wool, beef exports (dried meat) and hides were the export backbone was present throughout the nineteenth century.

In that regard, the British Empire and in second place other European countries (Germany, Holland and France) were the main customers for the country's exports. Their presence in the country through direct investment (railways, slaughterhouses, gas) was the main way to channel technological change. Until 1930, that growth paradigm held, despite some changes in the economic structure. A growing urban population called for industrialization policies and a timid but growing participation of the State took place.

Also, external conditions began to change fast: the decline of the British Empire, the successive European crises and the upsurge of the United States as the new world power drastically affected market conditions for the country's exports.

With the passage of time and especially under the influence of the dominant political figure of the period, President Jose Batlle Ordonez, the country began to move toward a welfare state, which subsequently became the central element in national economic life. The welfare state survived the Great Depression surprisingly well, and by the mid-1930s, Uruguay's per capita income compared favorably with that of a number of countries in Western Europe.

Moreover, as a portion of the agricultural and livestock surplus (with the land tenure structure and the low input-output system of production remaining unaltered) was being transferred to the urban population in Montevideo and its surroundings, a less skewed income distribution began to emerge. This transfer of income occurred through direct government action, with the public sector expanding its functions in the fields of education, public health, social security and infrastructure.

The authorities encountered only moderate resistance from the rural sector. Output was growing and the economic and social power remained in their hands, while political power was increasingly transferred to the emerging urban middle class .

The world crisis of the 1930s and the degradation of European export markets generated negative effects on the economy. The Ottawa Convention was the final blow, when preferential access to the United Kingdom's markets was granted to its former colonies, putting additional downward pressure on Uruguay's export prices. These facts together with the international crisis tainted economic performance. Conditions for change in economic policy strategy were mature and policy makers did not waste time in implementing them.

## THE POST–WORLD WAR II PERIOD (1945–1955)

The inauguration of the industrialization period coincided with shortages of imported raw materials due to foreign exchange problems in the 1930s and supply limitations during World War II. Therefore, the industrial growth that occurred during those years was based almost exclusively on industries using domestic inputs. With the end of the war, imported supplies of capital and intermediate goods were no longer a constraint and the development of export industries, especially the livestock industry, came almost to a halt. Industrialization assumed the familiar pattern of progressive substitution of imports by means of controls and subsidies, largely facilitated by a multiple exchange rate system.

The resulting industrial structure was highly vulnerable in the light of its high costs and limited market. Moreover, the lack of fuels and industrial raw materials rendered Uruguayan industry almost completely dependent on imported inputs and, therefore, on the performance of the export sector. Although by the end of the industrialization period in the mid-1950s Uruguay was probably the most urban and prosperous country in Latin America, its prosperity and great social progress rested on shaky foundations.

Having neglected the development of its export sector, especially livestock, it was singularly unprepared to cope with the precipitous drop in international meat and wool prices following termination of hostilities in Korea. Although some economic growth took place during this period, its imbalance served as a prelude to the long and painful decade of stagflation. As a consequence, import substitution policies would be the linchpin of the country's economic strategy until the early seventies, through the use of different mechanisms.

The Uruguayan economy in the immediate post-war period gave cause for satisfaction due to the high ratio of export value to population together with import substitution policies, which promoted a decade of rapid industrial growth. In fact, Uruguay in 1956 enjoyed the highest per capita income of any Latin American country. That phenomenon eroded the beneficial perception of the economic model of export-led growth, which broadly fitted the Uruguayan economy before 1930.

However, these benefits were not lasting because the model was not sustainable. Moreover, stagnation was already in place in the form of a closed economic model that taxed exports in favor of industrial policies and the financing of a glutted public sector. High export values were achieved during the period, but this resulted from a sharp rise in export prices during the Korean War period rather than an increase in volume production.

In fact, the annual rate of growth of per capita income during 1945–1955 of about 3.4 percent was achieved mainly on the basis of domestic market dynamics. Product diversification and import substitution were characteristic of agriculture as well as of industry in this period.

Under the stimulus of high guaranteed prices, the average area under cereal production increased from 1.0 million hectares in 1944–45 through 1948–49 to 1.4 million and 1.6 million in succeeding five-year periods. The objective of the greatly increased farming area was met to an unprecedented degree. Additionally, those policies were accompanied by the further extension of labor and social security legislation, notably the institution of wages councils from 1943 and family allowances (1950). Nonetheless, the performance of the Uruguayan economy in the post-war decade was itself far from convincing. It depended on favorable, but temporary, external conditions.

Their erosion and the accumulating distortions that accompanied the process of expansion and diversification were already evident in Uruguay in the early 1950s, an experience shared with other Latin American countries that adopted the strategy of import-substitution industrialization. The central characteristic of the period after the mid-1950s was stagnation of production and rising fiscal disequilibrium financed with foreign reserve losses and increased indebtedness. Following that rapid growth in the post-war years, deceleration was already evident during 1954–1957.

This extraordinary record indicates very clearly the marked deterioration that began in the second half of the 1950s, and which resulted in a negative rate of growth of per capita income for the period 1955–1970.

Stagnation was accompanied by shifts in the sector composition of production. During the period of rapid industrial growth up to the mid-1950s, the secondary sector increased its GDP's share dramatically. Primary and tertiary activities both grew at the annual rate of 4 percent in this decade, but during 1955–1960, when GDP showed no growth at all, the primary sector contracted still further. (See Table 4-2.)

| TABLE 4-2: GDP growth erratic after WW II | | |
| --- | --- | --- |
| | *Total* | *Per Capita* |
| 1945–1950 | 5.4 | 4.0 |
| 1950–1955 | 4.2 | 2.7 |
| 1955–1960 | 0.0 | −1.5 |
| 1960–1965 | 0.8 | −0.6 |
| 1965–1970 | 2.2 | 0.9 |
| 1945–1955 | 4.8 | 3.4 |
| 1955–1970 | 0.9 | −0.3 |

The components of the primary sector are agriculture and livestock production. Their growth up to 1955 was 4 percent annually, but this was succeeded by a five-year period of equally sustained and rapid contractions. The 1960s were marked by substantial fluctuations, from the low level of the late 1950s to a peak in 1966.

## THE ECONOMIC DECLINE (1956–1975)

Throughout the 1950s there was no major revision of the economic strategy, which began to be implemented in the late 1940s. The distortions in the economy that were evident by 1955 were not so pressing that demand for change was irresistible, nor so severe that ad hoc measures could not contain their adverse effects.

Expansionary income policies and production promotion (subsidies) generated rising fiscal deficits, which caused rising price trends and erosion of international reserves.

Since then, a long period of inflationary trends, recursive balance of payments crises, failed adjustment programs and lack of growth has held sway.

If growing unemployment was one of the main indicators, a process of rapid inflation was certainly the other. The index of consumer prices demonstrates a rising trend.

Three phases of inflation can be detected. The first reached a peak in 1959 and 1960 with annual increases in the price level of about 40 percent. The rate then fell to 10 percent in 1962, but thereafter accelerated steadily to a peak of 125 percent in 1968.

The external situation was dominated by four factors: the failure of export earnings to regain the level achieved in the early 1950s, a persistent tendency to run a deficit on the balance of payments current account, the loss of gold and currency reserves and the growth of international indebtedness. The evolution of exports earnings up to 1970 shows three distinct phases.

During the early 1950s export receipts averaged US$244 million. The second phase was of decline to 1957–1960, when average receipts fell to US$132 million, and during the decade 1960–1970, which saw a slow but sustained recovery, with export receipts in excess of US$200 million for the first time since the mid-1950s. The commodity boom export prices at the time of the Korean War represented the culmination of a rising export price trend, which had begun at the end of the 1930s.

However, to suppose that the rapid decline of export earnings after 1954 merely resulted from the loss of exceptionally favorable world prices is wrong, because there was in addition a dramatic fall in the volume of exports. This fact stemmed from the exhaustion of promotional agricultural policies.

A sophisticated—and costly—multiple exchange rate regime was one of the main channels to pursue promotional industrial policies and subsidize domestic consumption. This was complemented with tariffs, quotas, reference prices (aforos) and other equivalent protectionist tools.

The chronic tendency to run a current account deficit on the balance of payments was supported in part by the reduction in gold and currency reserves, and in part by increased borrowing abroad. During World War II, current account surpluses and an inflow of foreign capital created a strong currency reserve that was not seriously weakened until the mid-1950s, but deterioration thereafter was rapid. In addition, the level of external obligations increased very greatly, particularly in the decade 1955–1965.

| TABLE 4-3: Prices increase after WW II | |
|---|---|
| 1946–50 | 5.5 |
| 1951–55 | 11.1 |
| 1956–60 | 23.4 |
| 1961–65 | 30.7 |
| 1966–70 | 66.1 |

*Sources:* DGEC, Indice de los Precios del Consumo; BCU. Boletin Estadístico Mensual.

Summing up, economic stagnation dealt a blow to the Uruguayan import substitution model that eventually was to prove fatal.

The policy orientation of the Colorados was finally abandoned with the Exchange and Monetary Reform Law of December 1959, overcome by opposition by the rural exporting sector.

In any case, the Blanco party, after the liberalization efforts of its first administration (1958–1962), succumbed to the old batllista model in a different guise. After 1962, expansionary credit policies through the Banco de la Republica ignited a new round of inflationary pressures and a balance of payments crisis. A banking crisis swept through a large part of the domestic financial sector, generating losses close to 10 percent of the GDP. New disguised protectionist measures were enforced (quotas, deposits in advance) without positive results on economic growth and employment.

The Reform Law was, in a sense, an inevitable development. It was clear by the late 1950s that the import-substituting industrialization strategy implemented by the Colorados had played out. Further manipulation of trade and exchange controls could only be effective in the very short run.

The decline in prices for Uruguay's exports was not the sole cause of the economic stagnation and severe inflation. Throughout this period economic policy-making by improvisation brought about a gradual transfer of resources from the low-cost agricultural and livestock sectors to the high-cost industry and social services.

This process also developed an inefficient agricultural sector due to the subsidies to noncompetitive activities, which indirectly taxed those who were more efficient, such as cattle raising. This development discouraged investment in agriculture and livestock whose output actually declined. This decline compounded the economic problem stemming from the deterioration in the terms of trade.

The inflation that accompanied economic stagnation for over two decades can be attributed to several interrelated factors: the reluctance of a population accustomed to a high level of consumption to accept austerity, the unbearable cost of established welfare programs, the huge budgetary and public enterprise deficits and the excessive wage increases extracted by powerful groups of well-organized urban workers. Toward the end of the stagflation period the country became deeply aware of the predicament created by the "well-intentioned experiment that became a total failure" and searched for a more viable approach. Desperation became manifest in the rise of urban political terrorism.

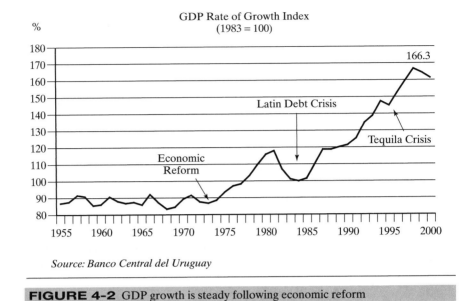

Source: Banco Central del Uruguay

**FIGURE 4-2** GDP growth is steady following economic reform

The outcome was the unraveling of the political fabric, giving place to successive failed stabilization programs within a mounting political crisis, whose overtone was the appearance of urban guerrillas. This factor led to a coup d'etat, which inaugurated 15 years of military rule and also the beginning of liberalization experiments in economic policy.

## ECONOMIC LIBERALIZATION AND CRISIS AGAIN (1974–1985)

Given the country's failure to curb inflation and retain growth through a drastic adjustment program coupled with a wage and price freeze, economic liberalization began to gain adherents.

In fact, in response to its poor economic performance, which was aggravated by a worldwide recession, Uruguay launched a series of timid reforms designed to reduce the government's role in quotas, price controls and price subsidies. The administration eliminated personal income taxes and increased the emphasis on indirect taxation through value-added taxes. Most importantly, the government liberalized international financial transactions. (See Figure 4-2.)

Beginning in 1974, Uruguayan residents were permitted to hold foreign assets without restriction and exchange controls were eliminated, in effect making the peso a fully convertible currency. Free repatriation of profits and capital from Uruguay was instituted shortly thereafter.

In response to the liberalization policies pursued from 1975 to 1980, Uruguay's economy grew at an average annual rate of 4.5 percent for the period. Rapid growth, however, was accompanied by double-digit inflation. Uruguay's exchange rate management, which set the monthly rate of devaluation of the Uruguayan currency vis-à-vis the U.S. dollar in accordance with inflation differentials between Uruguay and its main trading partners, contributed to the persistence of high and variable monthly inflation rates.

Seeking to reduce inflation, in 1978 the government abandoned its passive crawling peg policy and introduced an "active" crawling peg policy. A surge in private bank lending led to an increase in aggregate demand and to even greater inflation rates, which resulted in the overvaluation of the Uruguayan currency.

The result was a heightened lack of competitiveness and debt overhang, coupled with a number of negative external developments (including the 1979 oil crisis, rising international interest rates, reduced external demand resulting from the worldwide recession and policy adjustments undertaken by Brazil and Argentina). All these facts led to a loss of confidence, which resulted in massive capital flight.

In November 1982, the government allowed the peso to float. The sharp peso depreciation weakened enterprises and banks' balance sheets, mostly in dollars, further worsening the position of debtors and increasing the number of nonperforming assets of the banking system. This situation resulted in the failure of many private banks, the de facto nationalization of some of them and swap operations to help reestablish their liquidity, including those pertaining to international banks. This evolution resulted in heavy losses to Banco Central and the overall deterioration of the public sector's fiscal accounts. The consolidated public sector deficit reached 12.2 percent of GDP in 1983. The deficit of Banco Central alone was 8.1 percent of GDP.

A severe recession followed this financial crisis, with real GDP falling by 16.0 percent in the 1982–1984 period. Moreover, heavy public sector borrowing, an unanticipated rise in international interest rates and the global economic slowdown during the period resulted in a deterioration of Uruguay's external debt situation. In 1982, Uruguay's ratios of external indebtedness were relatively low: its debt-to-GDP (measured at current prices) ratio was 45 percent and its debt service–to-exports ratio was 50 percent. By 1985, its debt-to-GDP (measured at current prices) ratio had risen to 104 percent and its debt service–to-exports ratio had reached 70 percent.

Notwithstanding the size of Uruguay's external debt, the Republic maintained its long-standing tradition of prompt debt service throughout the 1980s. The country did, however, negotiate a rescheduling of its maturing debt obligations to commercial bank creditors twice during the early 1980s. External factors, including the worldwide recession and the economic difficulties of Uruguay's neighbors, clearly played an important role in the economic deterioration in 1982. However, a large part of the responsibility was borne by domestic policies

These policies included the deliberate slowing of the pre-announced depreciation of the currency with a view to containing inflation, while at the same time maintaining the de facto indexation of wages and social security benefits to past inflation. The substantial real appreciation of the peso that resulted from these policies had a particularly depressing effect on the traded goods sector. Over the same period, there was also a considerable weakening in financial policies.

Democracy returned in 1985. Together with regaining political stability, growth creation was the second imperative goal, a goal imperiled by the recent economic crisis that placed a heavy burden on external accounts due to the meltdown in exports and the high public indebtedness. In spite of these facts, a modest economic recovery began in 1985, followed by two years (1986–1987) of GDP growth rates of 8.9 and 7.9 percent, respectively.

During 1988 and 1989, however, Uruguay's real GDP growth slowed to an annual average of 0.6 percent due to limits in the operating capacity of the manufacturing sector and a severe drought from late 1988 through 1989.

This period (1985–1989) at least had the merit of re-knitting the economic and social fabric after the long night of dictatorship. In fact, difficult legislation was passed in order to facilitate economic development, which consumed great political capital in introducing needed economic reforms. In any case, wages and social indicators improved with the expectation of sustainable growth.

However, the specter of the generous but unsustainable social security system, which consumed at that time more than 10 percent of total GDP, a percentage that increased substantially in the coming years, haunted the economy. The social security issue became a central factor in the political and macroeconomic issues of the next decade. Inflation and persistent fiscal deficits continued, reaching annual average levels close to 70 percent.

The high degree of price indexation to past inflation, together with an active exchange rate policy—the crawling peg—assured inflation's persistence. The authorities sought to regain economic growth rather than price stabilization. The debt was wisely managed, using available financing mechanisms such as the Baker Plan and later the MYRA (Multi-Year Restructuring Agreement). During all these episodes, regional and local investors, coupled with multilateral financial institutions (IADB, World Bank), became the country's main lenders.

## THE ROARING NINETIES (1990–2000)

Anti-inflationary policies, reforms and a desperate search for economic growth were the main issues during this decade. The Lacalle government inherited an economy for which rampant inflation due to persistent fiscal imbalances was the main plague to fight, coupled with high external indebtedness. That administration tried to correct these imbalances with mixed results. The debt issue was promptly solved in 1991 and inflation began to decrease slowly.

Only in the second half of the decade did the inflation level decrease to one digit. In its efforts to transform the economy in the early 1990s, the government took steps to open it further to market forces and reduce the public sector's size and burden on the private sector. In this way, the Lacalle administration tried to pursue a reformist agenda by the introduction of structural reforms through privatizations. (See Figure 4-3.)

The public telephone company ANTEL was first in line in that process. However, a referendum was called for the left and then backed by a portion of the Colorado party, opposing privatization. The popular vote was overwhelmingly against privatization. This fact sent a powerful signal to the political parties in regard to privatizations: Uruguayan society was quite reluctant to accept drastic reforms. In fact, the vote maintained the status quo. As a consequence, during the Lacalle administration, reforms in the social security system were timidly pursued and in consequence failed.

A new recovery began in mid-1991, and GDP increased steadily between 1991 and 1994 at an average cumulative annual rate of 5.2 percent.

The Mexican crisis (1994) had a direct and indirect adverse impact on the economy of Uruguay, in particular on Uruguay's exports of manufactured goods. As a result, the contraction in aggregate demand in neighboring countries, particularly Argentina, was coupled with a decrease in domestic private demand and public sector investment. In 1995 following the Mexican crisis, GDP contracted by 1.5 percent compared to the 1994 GDP.

During the second Sanguinetti administration, Uruguay's economy recovered (GDP growth of 5.4 percent in 1996, 4.9 percent in 1997 and 4.6 percent in 1998). This improvement was mainly a result of increased exports and growth in gross fixed investment, particularly private sector investment, which in turn stimulated private consumption. Inflation decreased sharply thanks to the happy mix of adequate economic policies, which took advantage of an exceptional period of regional and world growth coupled with high liquidity in international financial markets.

In light of all these factors, a reform on the social security system was finally passed. Accordingly, a new privately-funded regime was substituted for the old pay-as-you-go system. The savings obtained assured fiscal consolidation.

The liberalization of international financial transactions allowed Uruguay to develop a strong reputation as a regional financial center, notwithstanding the financial crisis of the early 1980s. As of December 31, 1999, approximately 87 percent of deposits in the private banking system were denominated in foreign currencies (primarily U.S. dollars), more than half belonging to nonresidents or related to offshore activities. In 1997 the sovereign external debt was rated "investment grade."

Uruguay has also become an important regional tourist center with more than two million people (equivalent to more than two-thirds of Uruguay's population) visiting the country each year. In 1999, when approximately 2.3 million tourists visited the country, gross tourism receipts represented one of the most important sources of

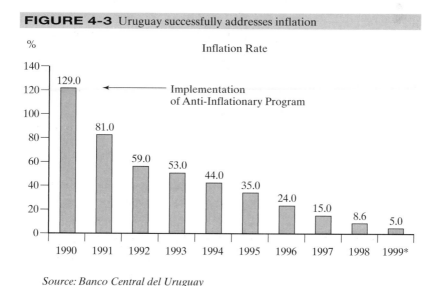

**FIGURE 4-3** Uruguay successfully addresses inflation

Inflation Rate

*Source: Banco Central del Uruguay*

*estimated

exchange earnings, surpassing wool and meat, Uruguay's traditional exports. Regional events began to deteriorate in early 1999. Brazil sharply devalued its currency (January 1999), followed by a plummeting of exports to that country. Argentina was also negatively impacted and a new wave of contractive regional forces shadowed Uruguay's economic performance. This situation also was reinforced by the first signal of decreasing world activity, first perceived as a deterioration in terms of trade.

As a result, economic activity decreased by 3.2 percent in 1999. Private consumption declined 1.8 percent, fixed private investment fell by 12.9 percent and exports of Uruguayan goods and services dropped by 7.3 percent.

All these facts, together with incomplete medium-term fiscal solvency generated by the inflexible burden of the public expenditure, posed a challenge difficult to surmount in a crisis period. Again, the new millennium was inaugurated with a deep crisis stemming from internal aspects, but reinforced by structural fragilities that Uruguay's society was not yet able to solve.

## POVERTY AND INCOME DISTRIBUTION

Poverty levels in Uruguay have decreased significantly since 1986, and there has been a trend toward redistribution of income from the top 10 percent of the population to the bottom 40 percent. CEPAL, an agency of the United Nations, estimates that in 1994, 6 percent of urban households of Uruguay could be defined as poor, living on an income that is below the minimum amount needed to purchase essential food and nonfood requirements, as compared to 8 percent in 1992 and 12 percent in 1990. Nearly 90 percent of Uruguay's population resides in cities. (See Table 4-4.)

While Uruguay has disparities in the distribution of wealth and income, such disparities are not of the same magnitude as those of certain Latin American countries such as Brazil, Colombia, Chile, Argentina, Mexico and Venezuela.

Poverty in Uruguay has been attributed to unemployment and underemployment and the increasing disparity in income between skilled, educated workers and the unskilled and relatively less-educated workers. Since one of the principal causes of poverty is poor education, Uruguay has taken steps to improve the country's educational system. To address these problems, recent governments launched several plans to modernize and extend the educational structure of the country at the primary and secondary level.

**TABLE 4-4:** Toward greater economic equality

| Income Group | 1990 | 1994 | 1997 |
|---|---|---|---|
| Lowest 40% | 20.1% | 21.6% | 22.0% |
| Next 30% | 24.6 | 26.3 | 26.1 |
| Next 20% | 24.1 | 26.7 | 26.1 |
| Highest 10% | 31.2 | 25.4 | 25.8 |
| Total | 100.0% | 100.0% | 100.0% |

Problems relating to poverty have also been addressed through health care accessibility and other measures. Uruguay has a public health system that gives access to services on a sliding-scale basis, where fees are based on a citizen's ability to pay, and guarantees medical care for workers. The government also maintains funds for the extraordinary medical expenses of the needy.

## MERCOSUR AND BEYOND

Geography is one of the dynamic forces shaping history among neighboring countries. The same argument applies to regional trade, mainly for the smaller economies. Uruguay is a case in point. The region has an overwhelming presence over Uruguay, a fact that sometimes is camouflaged by the international economic cycle. However, in the end, the region always has an impact through numerous and sometimes unexpected channels. In fact, beef and wool exports—the backbone of the export-led strategy—were and are largely linked to extra-regional markets.

However, despite all efforts to diversify its export customer matrix, Argentina and Brazil remain as important markets through formal or informal channels. More than that, some goods—defined traditionally as nontradable—become tradable when exposed to the light of regional trade. The explanation is that Uruguay is located in the crossroads of the two largest South American countries.

This is one of the challenges that Uruguay faces vis-à-vis the region, which has a powerful effect on its economic evolution. Trade is one of the dimensions influenced by the region. In spite of all efforts made to disentangle the country from regional events, they continue to have powerful effects on economic and political decisions.

Mercosur was created in 1991 as a regional agreement to formalize and strengthen trade regional flows. Argentina and Brazil were the creators of the bloc, as a way to take advantage of and reinforce their productive structures. Uruguay did not have a chance to reject the idea of the free trade agreement, in spite of the risks involved, such as increasing its dependence on regional events. (See Figure 4-4.)

Mercosur established a free-trade zone among Argentina, Brazil, Paraguay and Uruguay, with the exception of certain remaining trade barriers subject to a transitional regime. In this regard, import quotas were eliminated, export procedures were simplified, the use of anti-dumping devices was curtailed and domestic content and compensatory export requirements that protected the domestic industry were removed.

Additionally, import tariffs were reduced from a range of 0–55 percent (with five different tariff positions) in 1990 to 0–20 percent (with four different positions) in 1994, and the import surcharge of 5 percent was eliminated. Since January 1, 1995, duties on imports of most products from outside Mercosur are set under a common external tariff (CET) ranging from 0 to 20 percent. However, changes in protection levels as a result of the CET will not take place fully until early in the twenty-first century and are product specific.

Some doubts have arisen concerning the effects of tariffs on small economies such as Uruguay's. Trade diversion costs were the most important issue, as second-rate import suppliers—in price and quality—would displace better options. Trade creation gives full access to a bigger market in sensitive items such as rice, dairy products, chemicals, garments and textiles—which favored joining the agreement.

- Dynamic economy
- Sophisticated regional financial and service center
- Strong economic indicators
- Social and political stability

| Selected Facts | |
|---|---|
| Population | 3.1 Million |
| 1998 GDP (est.) | $21.3 Billion |
| Literacy Rate | 97.3% |
| Ratings (Investment grade) | |
| Moody's/S&P | Baa3/BBB– |
| Duff & Phelps/IBCA | BBB–/BBB– |

*Source: Banco Central Del Uruguay*

**FIGURE 4-4**  A portrait of Uruguay

In the beginning, regional trade catapulted trade flows with Argentina and Brazil forward. (See Figure 4-5.)

This initial trend coincided with an upsurge in regional economic activity stemming from a virtuous worldwide cycle. Therefore, linking this fact with the positive results of the treaty is still a question of further analysis. Events during the late 1990s

**FIGURE 4-5**  Brazil and Argentina dominate Uruguay's trade structure

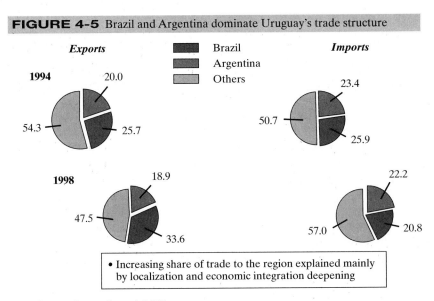

- Increasing share of trade to the region explained mainly by localization and economic integration deepening

*Source: Banco Central del Uruguay*

**TABLE 4-5:** Mercosur: A major trade partner for Uruguay

| | Argentina | | | | Brazil | | | |
|---|---|---|---|---|---|---|---|---|
| | Exports | | Imports | | Exports | | Imports | |
| | US$ | %* | US$ | %* | US$ | %* | US$ | %* |
| 1995 | 267.1 | 12.6 | 608.6 | 21.2 | 700.0 | 33.2 | 698.6 | 24.3 |
| 1996 | 271.5 | 11.3 | 703.1 | 21.1 | 831.0 | 34.6 | 745.5 | 22.3 |
| 1997 | 354.3 | 13.0 | 801.4 | 29.4 | 940.2 | 34.5 | 801.9 | 29.4 |
| 1998 | 513.2 | 18.5 | 841.6 | 22.1 | 935.2 | 33.8 | 793.4 | 20.8 |
| 1999 | 369.0 | 6.4 | 796.0 | 23.7 | 557.0 | 24.9 | 652.0 | 19.4 |

* As percentage of total.

show that as the economies of the main partners began to decline, Mercosur went into a deep crisis. First, the ambitious goals to formalize a customs union for the year 2000 were delayed. Second, exceptions in trade were put into place for sensitive items as a way of protecting local activities. (See Table 4-5.)

Also, Mercosur's spirit was tainted with several administrative actions curtailing trade flows, which disguised tensions and imbalances among its partners. The crucial issue was that some kind of common playing field on macroeconomic issues had to be in place. This forgotten fact nested further imbalances. Exchange rate policy coordination became a paramount challenge.

All existing regional agreements, by choice or by default, have an exchange rate currency as anchor. The NAFTA agreement has the dollar, and the European Union (EU) had first the deutsche mark and later the euro. Thus, macroeconomic coordination among partners becomes crucial. Mercosur had none of this, and all efforts to resolve the problem failed. A second aspect highlighted by events was the lack of a common goal linking Mercosur to other regional agreements.

In this regard, Brazil tends to think of Mercosur as a negotiating platform by which to engage in talks with the EU and NAFTA. Argentina and Uruguay take a more pragmatic stand. They believe that Mercosur does not limit bilateral trade agreements with other countries. Therefore, more general agreements could be negotiated under the umbrella of treaty talks between Mercosur and other regional trade entities. In fact, in 1996, Uruguay negotiated a Free Trade Agreement with Mexico, and it may negotiate another with the United States.

In short, Mercosur could be characterized as an effort to engage the southern cone countries in a common external trade policy. In this context, Brazil is the leading force.

After the decline of the world economic cycle, which began in the late 1990s, Mercosur evidenced clear failures in design. This failing highlighted major differences and structural frailties among the partners. A revamping of the agreement is doubtful in the near term.

Perhaps the status of regional trade flows will be the reverse of the starting situation in the early 1990s. This was another failed experience, as a result of improvisation, wishful thinking about the virtue of this kind of agreement and the substantively different views of the primary partners. In these stormy waters, a small country like Uruguay faces enormous challenges. The goal is for economic policy—mainly as relates to foreign trade—to compensate for the determinism of geography, country size and direction of external flows. To date, Mercosur has not fully achieved any of these goals.

A full revamping of the treaty is necessary if the treaty is to continue as a suitable vehicle to balance trade flows among regional partners and to fully exploit the benefits of trade globalization. In this regard, a much lower, flat external tariff has to be instituted to lower trade diversion, which most benefited Brazil. Macroeconomic coordination, mainly in exchange rate policies, must be enforced.

Finally, more flexibility is needed for member countries to negotiate bilateral agreements with other regional blocs and/or individual countries in order to facilitate the transition toward a fully integrated regional trade area whose final objective is to become an economic union within which goods, services and persons can circulate freely.

## BIBLIOGRAPHY

Abdala, W. and S. Maciel. *Manual de Ciencia Política.* Fondo de Cultura Economica.

Aguilera de Prat, C. R. and P. Vilanova. *Temas de Ciencia Política.* Barcelona: PPU, 1987.

Almond y O. *Diez Textos Básicos de Ciencia Política.* Ariel.

Arendt, H. *Crisis de La República.* Taurus.

Aristóteles. *Obras.* Aguilar.

Aron, R. *Introduction a la Philosophie Politique.* Livre de Poche.

_____. *Une Histoire du XXe. Siecle.* Plon.

Arthur, J. (1992) *Democracy.* Belmont CA: Wadsworth Publishing.

Barber, B. (1988) *The Conquest of Politics.* Princeton, NJ: Princeton University Press.

Baran, P. A. *The Political Economy of Growth.* Modern Reader.

Berlin, I. *The Sense of Reality.* Pimlico.

Bobbio, N. *The Future of Democracy.* University of Minnesota Press.

_____. El *Filósofo y la Política (Antología).* F.C.E.

Braud, P. *Science Politique, L'Etat.* Du Seuil.

_____. *Science Politique, La democracie.* Du Seuil.

Brittan, S. (1983) *The Roles and Limits of Government.* Minneapolis, MN: University of Minnesota Press.

Broadie, A. (1997) *The Scottish Enlightenment.* Edinburgh: Canongate Books.

Bronner, S. E. *Twentieth Century Political Theory.* Routledge.

Brown, B. E. and R. Macridis. *Comparative Politics.* Harcourt Brace.

Buchanan, J. M. *The Limits of Liberty.* University of Chicago Press.

_____. *Freedom in Constitutional Contract.* Texas A & M University Press.

Burke, E. and T. Payne. *Reflections on the Revolution in France.* Anchor.

_____. *The Rights of Man.* Anchor.

Burns, J. M. *The Crosswinds of Freedom.* Vintage Books.

_____. *The Vineyards of Liberty.* A. Knopf.

_____. *The Workshop of Democracy.* Vintage Books.

Caminal Badia, M. *Manual de Ciencia Política.* Tecnos.

Cappella, J. N. (1997) *Spiral of Cynicism.* New York: Oxford University Press.

Chilcote, R. H. *Theories of Comparatives Politics.* West University Press.

Cohen, J. L. and A. Arato. *Civil Society and Political Theory.* M.I.T. Press.

Cohen, M. and N. Fermon. (1996) *Princeton Readings in Political Thought.* Princeton, NJ: Princeton University Press.

Collin, D. Les *Grands Notions Philosophiques La Justice et Le Droit.* Seuil.

_____. *La Societe, Le Pouvoir, L'Etat.*

Crick, B. *In Defense of Politics.* Penguin.

Crozier, M. *Etat Modeste, Etat Moderne.* Fayard.

Dahl, R. A. (1989) *Democracy and Its Critics.* New Haven: Yale University Press.

Dahl, R. A. and C. A. Lindblom. *Politics, Economics and Welfare*. Ed. Transactions Publishers.

Denquin, J. M. *Introduction a la Science Politique*. Hachette.

_____. *Science Politique*. Presse Universitaire.

Desai, M. *Marx's Revenge*. Verso.

Diamond, Larry. *Politics in Developing Countries*. Lynne Pienner.

Díaz, R. *Historia Económica del Uruguay*. Taurus.

Doyenart, J. C. *El Problema está en Nosotros*. Fin de Siglo.

Durkheim, E. *Les Regles de la Metode Sociolique*. Flammarion.

Duverger, M. *Sociología de la Política*. Ariel.

_____. *Métodos de las Ciencias Sociales*. Ariel.

Easton, D. *Enfoques Sobre Teoría Política*. Amorrortu Editores.

Etzioni, A. *The Communitarian Thinking*. University Press of Virginia.

_____. *New Communitarian Thinking*. University Press of Virginia.

Franco, R. *Democracia 'A la Uruguaya*. El Libro Libre.

Friedman, M. *Capitalism and Freedom*. University of Chicago Press.

García Hamilton, J. I. *El Autoritarismo y la Improductividad*. Sudamericana.

Gaus, G. F. *Justificatory Liberalism*. Oxford University Press.

George, R. P. *Natural Law, Liberalism and Morality*. Clarendon Press.

González, L. B. *Political Structures and Democracy in Uruguay*. University of Notre Dame Press.

Gordon, S. *Historia y Filosofía de las Ciencias Sociales*. Ariel.

Gorosito, R. *El Nacimiento de la Política*.

Gray, J. *Endgames*. Polity.

_____. *Liberalism*. University of Minnesota.

_____. *Las Dos Caras del Liberalismo*. Paidós.

Grompone, A. M. *La Ideología de Batlle*. Arca.

Hall, J. A. *Powers and Liberties*. Penguin Press.

Hamilton, A., J. Madison, and J. Jay. *The Federalist Papers*. Menthor.

Hayeck, F. A. *Camino de Servidumbre*. Alianza.

_____. *Law, Legislation, and Liberty*. Routledge.

_____. *The Constitution of Liberty*. University of Chicago.

Heilbroner, R. L. *The Worldly Philosophers*. Clarion.

Hofstadter, R. *The American Political Tradition*. Vintage.

Horowitz I. L. and Lipset S. M. *Dialogues on American Politics*. Oxford University Press.

Jacobs, L. A. *An Introduction to Modern Political Philosophy*. Prentice Hall.

Joyce, P. *Politics*. Teach Yourself.

King Gamble, J. *Introduction to Political Science*. Prentice Hall.

Keynes, J. M. *Teoría General de la Ocupación, el Interés y el Dinero*. Fondo de Cultura Económica.

Khon, J. *Le Contral Social Liberal*. Ed. Presse U.

Kung, H. *Economics*. Oxford University Press.

Kymlicka, W. *Contemporary Political Philosophy*. Clarendon Press.

Lijphart, A. (1992) *Parliamentary Versus Presidential Government*. New York: Oxford University Press.

Lijphart, A. and C. Waisman. (1996) *Institutional Design in New Democracy*. Boulder CO: Westview Press.

Locke, J. *Two Treatises of Government*. Mentor.

Marquand, D. *The New Reckoning*. Polity.

_____. *The Unprincipled Society*. Jonathan Cape.

Marx, K. *El Capital*. E.D.A.F.

McClelland, J. S. *A History of Western Political Thought*. Routledge.

Meynaud, J. *Introducción la Ciencia Política*. Tecnos.

Mill, J. S. *Politics and Society*. Fontana.

Montesquieu, C. *Persian Letters*. Penguin.

_____. *The Spirit of the Laws*. University of California.

Mulhall, S. *Liberals and Communitarians*. Blackwell.

North, D. C. *Institutions, Institutional Change and Economic Performance*. Cambridge University Press.

Oliveria, A. C. (1997) *Marco Regulador de las Organizaciones de la Sociedad Civil en Sudamérica*. Washington DC: PNUD.

Ophulus, W. *Requiem for Modern Politics*. Westview Press.

Panizza, F. E. *Uruguay: Batllismo y Después*. De la Banda Oriental.

Pilar del Castillo e Ismael Crespo. *Cultura Política*. Tixrant Blanch.

Platon. *La República*. Tesoro Literario.

Porter, R. *Enlightenment*. Penguin Press.

Prieto, F. (1989) *Lecturas de Historia de las Ideas Políticas*. Unión Editorial.

Putnam, R. O. (1993) *Making Democracy Work*. Princeton NJ: Princeton University Press.

Rama, G. *La Democracia en Uruguay*. Latinoamericano.

Rauch, J. (1994) *Demosclerosis*. New York: Times Books.

_____. (1999) *Government's End*. New York: Public Affairs.

Real de Azúa, C. *La Clase Dirigente*. Nuestra Tierra.

_____. *Partidos, Política y Poder en el Uruguay*. Universidad de la República.

Rosanvallon, P. *Le Crise de L'Etat Providence*. Du Seuil.

_____. *La Démocratie Inachevée*. Gallimard.

Rothschhild, E. (2001) *Economic Sentiments*. Cambridge MA: Harvard University Press.

Runciman, W. S. *Weber Selection*. Cambridge University Press.

Sabine, G. *Historia de la Teoría Política*. Fondo de Cultura Económica.

Sahakian, W. and M. L. Sahakian. *The Ideas of the Great Philosophers*. Barnes and Noble.

Sartori, G. *Comparative Constitutional Engineering*. New York University Press.

_____. *Teoría de la Democracia*. Alianza.

_____. *Elementos de Teoría Política*. Alianza.

Schmitt, K. *El Concepto de lo Político*. Alianza.

Schumpeter, J. *Capitalism, Socialism and Democracy*. Allen and Unwin.

Serrano, N. P. *Tratado de Derecho Político*. Civitas.

Shunway, N. *The Invention of Argentina*. University of California Press.

Smith, A. *The Wealth of Nations*. University of Chicago.

_____. *Theory of Wordly Sentiments*. Clarendon Press.

Tawney, R. H. *Religion and the Rise of Capitalism*. Penguin.

Taylor, P. B. *Government and Politics of Uruguay*. Tulane University.

Touchard, J. *Historia de las Ideas Políticas*. Tecnos.

Touraine, A. *Qué es la Democracia*. Fondo de Cultura Universitaaria.

Valadier, P. *L'Anarchie des Valeurs*. Albin Michel.

Van Parijs, P. *Real Freedom for All*. Clarendon Press.

Zakaria, F. *The Future of Freedom*. W. W. Norton.

# CHAPTER 5
# CHILE

DR. HERNÁN FELIPE ERRÁZURIZ

## INTRODUCTION

Chile's capital is Santiago, and its official language is Spanish. Chile's monetary unit is the peso (represented as $), whose value is determined freely against the U.S. dollar and other currencies. It is in the GMT-4 time zone (GMT-3 in the summer). To call Chile, use telephone code +56.

### KEY ECONOMIC INDICATORS

During 2002, total GDP was $64.1 billion, reflecting an estimated 1.9 percent yearly growth. In 2001 GDP had grown by 2.8 percent. Chile's economy is estimated to have grown by around 3 percent in 2003, mainly due to the recovery of the economy of the United States and to expanding total trade.

### FINANCIAL INDICATORS

Inflation lightly increased from 2.6 percent in 2001 to 2.8 percent in 2002, in part due to the depreciation of the Chilean peso.

### FISCAL POLICY

During 2002, the central government ran a limited deficit equivalent to 1.5 percent of the GDP. This was the fourth consecutive deficit, and the 2003 projection is for a deficit close to 1.8 percent of GDP. This fiscal imbalance forced the government to issue new national debt.

### EXTERNAL DEBT

The Chilean external debt on November 30, 2002, was $41,088 million, equivalent to 64 percent of the GDP. Public external debt is equivalent to 18 percent of the total external debt. Finally, 80 percent of the total external debt is scheduled in the long term.

### POPULATION

The latest census (2002) indicates that Chile's population totals 15,328,467 inhabitants with a population growth rate of 1.13 percent. Women total 7,646,856 and men total 7,403,485 inhabitants; therefore, 50.8 percent of the population is women and 49.2 percent is men. This share has remained constant between 1992 and 2002.

**FIGURE 5-1** Map of Chile

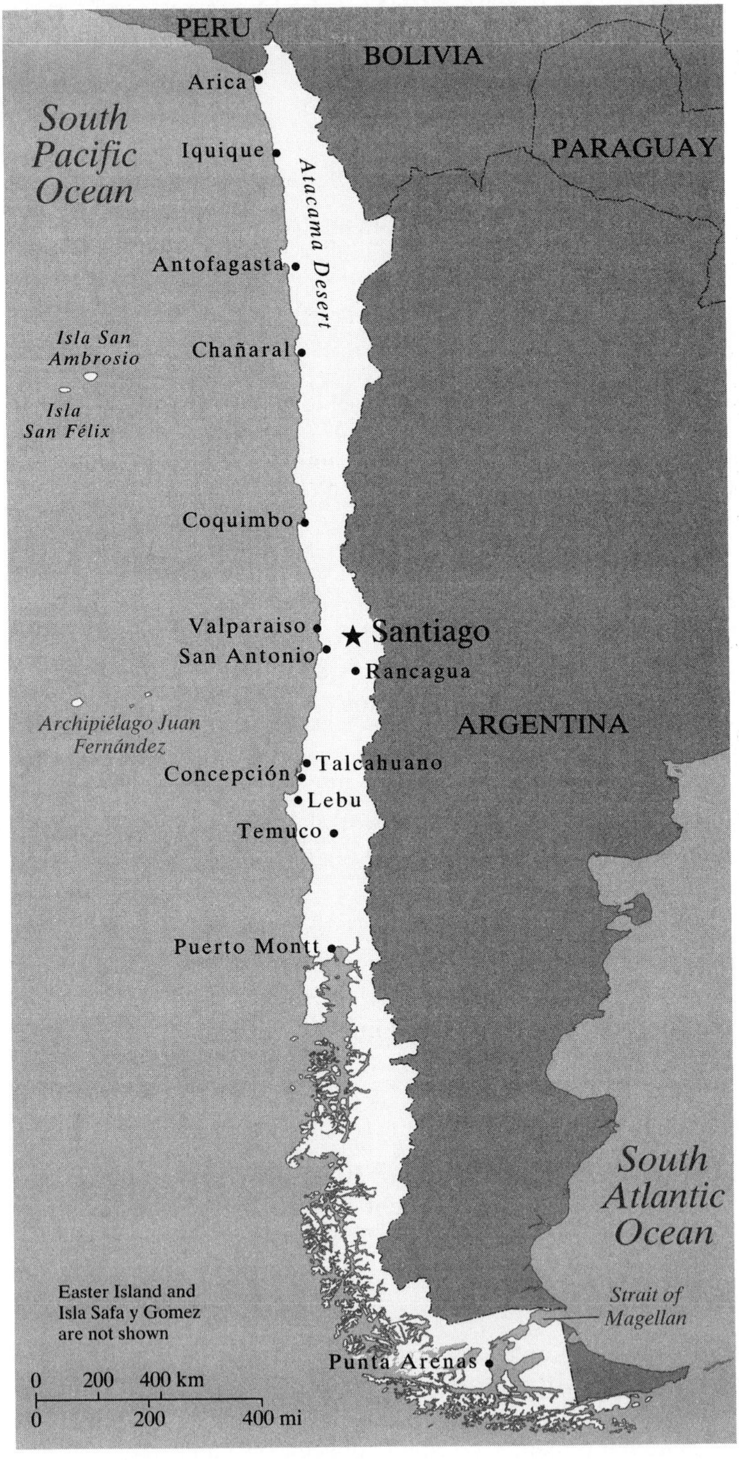

**TABLE 5-1:** Indicators of housing and basic infrastructure

|  | 1970 | 1992 | 2000 |
|---|---|---|---|
| Permanent housing | 79.0% | 91.0% | N.A. |
| Owners of a house | 54.0% | 68.0% | 85.3% |
| Access to urban drinking water | 67.0% | 97.0% | 99.6% |
| Access to rural drinking water | 34.0% | 86.0% | N.A. |
| Access to sewage system | 31.0% | 83.0% | 93.1% |

**TABLE 5-2:** Chile's health indicators

|  | 1970 | 1980 | 1990 | 1995 | 2000 |
|---|---|---|---|---|---|
| Life expectancy at birth (in years) | 62 | 67 | 72.2 | 73 | 75.25 |
| Infant mortality rate (per 1,000 live births) | 79.3 | 31.8 | 16 | 12 | 10.1 |
| Undernourished | 15.5% | 11.5% | 7.4% | 5.3% | N.A. |

**TABLE 5-3:** Chile's evolution of educational system (% of children being enrolled under six years old)

|  | 1970 | 1990 | 1994 | 1996 | 2000 |
|---|---|---|---|---|---|
| Average of years in school (years) | 4.5 | 9 | 9.2* | 9.5 | 9.8 |
| Years in school of the 20% low income (years) | N.A. | 7.4 | 7.3 | 7.3 | 7.8 |
| Children in high poverty without access to primary education | 43.0% | 4.5% | 3.8% | 3.5% | 2.3% |
| Secondary education access | 40.0% | 80.3% | 84.2% | 86.0% | 90.0% |
| Access to secondary education to 20% of low income | N.A. | 73.0% | 73.3% | 75.3% | 82.3% |

*For 1992.

The urban population represents 86.7 percent, the largest concentration being in the capital, Santiago. In absolute terms urban and rural populations total 13,044,221 and 2,006,120 inhabitants, respectively. Between the 1992 and 2002 census, the urban population increased 17.1 percent, while the rural population decreased 9.1 percent. In 1992, the share of urban and rural population was 82.45 and 16.55 percent, respectively.

The average population density according to the 2002 census was 19.9 inhabitants per square kilometer, while in 1992 this figure was 17.7 inhabitants per square kilometer.

Regarding age structure, 28.5 percent of the population is between 0 and 14 years old, 64.4 percent is between 15 and 64 years old and 7.2 percent is 65 years old and over. In 1992, this age structure was as follows: 30.1 percent was between 0 and 14 years old, 63.8 percent was between 15 and 64 years old and 6.1 percent was 65 years old and over.

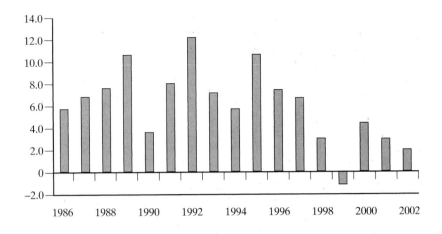

*From 1986 to 1995 statistics considered input-output matrix of 1986. Since 1996 statistic are elaborated in base of an input-output matrix of 1996.*

**FIGURE 5-2** Chile's annual gross domestic product

**TABLE 5-4:** GDP per capita growth (in percent)

| Country | 1900–1950 | 1950–73 | 1973–2000 |
|---------|-----------|---------|-----------|
| Argentina | 1.2 | 2.1 | 0.4 |
| Brazil | 1.7 | 3.8 | 1.3 |
| Chile | 1.4 | 1.2 | 3.3 |
| Mexico | 1.2 | 3.1 | 1.8 |

**FIGURE 5-3** Chile's gross domestic product per capita growth

Selected Periods

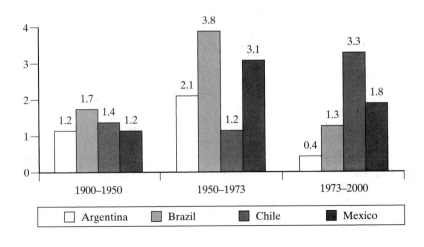

Life expectancy at birth is 72.6 years for men and 79.4 years for women. The birth rate is 16.8 per one thousand people and the death rate is 5.5 per one thousand people. The total population's literacy rate is 95.2 percent. Chile's infant mortality rate was estimated to be 9.36 deaths per one thousand live births in 2001.

The vast majority of Chileans are of European or mestizo ethnic origin. Aboriginals represent only 3 percent of the population.

From 1987 to 2001, the workforce expanded at an annual average rate of 2.1 percent, well above demographic trends. Over the same period, jobs increased by an average annual 2.3 percent and unemployment dropped steadily from 10.9 percent in 1987 to 6.3 percent in 1998. As activity slowed and firms sought to counteract a contraction of domestic demand through productivity gains, unemployment rose to a peak of 11.5 percent in the winter of 1999. In 2001, it dropped to an average of 9.1 percent and in 2002 it rose to 9.6 percent as economic activity remained weak.

## BUSINESS

Chile has undergone substantial economic and social change since the mid-1970s, and the country has currently one of the most liberal, market-based economies in Latin America. Major structural reforms have been completed over the past decades. Further changes in tax laws were introduced in 2001. Corporate income tax is currently 16.5 percent, but it will be increased gradually to 17 percent, effective 2004. Such income tax is treated as a credit toward the additional 35 percent tax for profit remittances abroad. Personal income tax was reduced from 45 percent (top marginal tax) to 40 percent.

In addition, a reform to the labor law was approved, introducing additional restrictions to the regulation of labor contracts. Chile is also the most open economy to foreign trade and investment in Latin America. There are no restrictions for capital flows and foreign investment. Non-tariff trade barriers are rare and customs duties are low (as an average, less than 5 percent) and nonselective. During 2002 Chile agreed to the terms of a free trade agreement with the United States and in November of that year signed an Association Agreement with the European Union, which also eliminates most tariffs on bilateral trade.

## POLITICAL SYSTEM

The country's official name is the Republic of Chile. Organized as a republic, executive powers are invested in the president of the republic, legislative authority in the National Congress (bicameral: Senate and House of Representatives) and judicial power in the courts of law.

The head of state is Ricardo Lagos (2000–2006), who was elected Chile's president in a closely contested election in January 2000. Congressional elections were last held in December 2001 and increased the percentage of the opposition coalition Alianza por Chile to 44 percent.

## LOCATION

Chile borders the South Pacific Ocean to the west and south, Argentina and Bolivia to the east and Peru and Bolivia to the north.

## TOTAL AREA

Excluding claimed Antarctic territory and including Easter Island, San Fernandez and other islands, Chile has a land area of 756,566 square kilometers.

## CAPITAL

Chile's capital is Santiago, with a population of 6,038,000 (2002). Administratively, Chile is divided into thirteen regions and its principal seaports are Valparaíso, San Antonio, Iquique, Antofagasta, Talcahuano, San Vicente, Valdivia, Puerto Montt and Punta Arenas.

## NATURAL RESOURCES

Chile is the largest exporter of copper in the world and its natural resources include timber, iron ore, nitrates, precious metals and molybdenum. The central valley is very fertile and suitable for a wide variety of crops and fruit. Forestry, wines, fresh fruits, fish farming and ocean fisheries are relevant sectors of the local industry. Domestic production of oil and natural gas is almost irrelevant.

## GEOGRAPHY

Chile is located in southwest South America It is a narrow strip some 100 to 445 kilometers wide and 4,200 kilometers long, located between the Pacific Ocean and the peaks of the Andean chain, running from the 17th parallel of southern latitude to Cape Horn. It covers 756,566 square kilometers. It is bordered by Peru to the north, Bolivia and Argentina to the east, the Drake Sea to the south and the Pacific Ocean to the west, in which it also possesses several islands and archipelagos. Chile also claims rights to over 1,200,000 square kilometers on the Antarctic continent, where it maintains a number of bases.

Chile's national territory was formed by the elevation of the South American landmass through ongoing pressure from the Nazca plate in the Pacific, making it highly subject to earthquakes. It displays extremely diverse geographical and climatic characteristics. In Chile's far northern reaches, called the *Norte Grande* or Great North, an arid climate prevails, with mountain ranges, salt flats and the Atacama Desert, the world's driest desert. Below this area is the *Norte Chico* or Little North, with more abundant vegetation thanks to a greater number of rivers and streams.

Further south, the traveler reaches Central Chile, also known as the Central Valley. This zone includes numerous transverse valleys, extending between the Andes chain and the coastal mountain range, carved by rivers surging from the high Andes to the sea. These rivers contribute to the creation of a moderately rainy Mediterranean climate, suited to a broad range of agricultural products. Below the Central Valley, the area known as the South begins, with its rainy and moderately cold climate, suitable for livestock ranching. Finally, in the continent's extreme southern reaches, toward Cape Horn and Tierra del Fuego, lie the Austral Regions, presenting a rugged mixture of mountain and coastal landscapes, including the cold and windy Patagonian plains, massive forests and torrential rivers, as well as numerous lakes, channels, ice fields and glaciers.

## POPULATION

Upon the arrival of the first Spanish conquistadores in the mid-sixteenth century, indigenous people in the area numbered an estimated 500,000 and were distributed among more than fifteen distinct ethnic groups.

The political and military influence of the Inca Empire predominated in the north, extending to the Maule River deep in central Chile. This Peruvian empire dominated numerous ethnic groups, the Picunches being the most prominent among them. The Picunches also occupied the lands southward to the Bío Bío River. After the Spanish conquest, they were assimilated within a short time, becoming the largest element of the colonial economy's workforce.

The Mapuches or Araucanos populated the lands between the Bío Bío and Toltén rivers. A few centuries before the European discovery of America, they had invaded Chilean territory from the east over the Andes Mountains. With their warlike spirit, they continued to resist the Spanish invaders until the second half of the nineteenth century. Their descendents, although partly intermixed, make up Chile's only numerically significant original ethnic group today, comprising 3 percent of the population.

In the Austral Regions south to Tierra del Fuego, small groups of indigenous peoples such as the Onas, Chonos and Alacalufes roamed the islands and channels, fishing and hunting the llama-like guanaco. These groups are extinct today.

A special case is the Polynesian ethnic group, which colonized Easter Island or Rapa Nui in the Pacific, 3,000 kilometers from the South American coast, in approximately A.D. 500. This territory was incorporated into Chile in 1888. Today, some 3,000 people live on the island, mainly engaged in the tourist industry and with little agriculture, since most of the land remains under State control.

The surviving indigenous peoples have not been exempt from difficulties. The Andean communities (aymaras) in the country's north, estimated at 45,000 people, have been affected by water extraction by mining enterprises, as well as the urban and industrial enclaves that have sprung up in the great northern desert. The Mapuches continue to struggle for recognition of their culture and ownership rights to their ancestral lands. During the past 10 years, Chile has created an institutional structure to address the problems of indigenous peoples, a long-term challenge which will involve measures to reduce poverty and improve health care and education.

## IMMIGRATION

The first Spanish settlers in Chile were single men, mostly soldiers. In 1541, 154 Europeans arrived. The number of European inhabitants was estimated at 25,000 in 1700 and 50,000 in 1800. A census in 1813 calculated the total population to be 521,175 whites, mestizos and other mixtures; 80,000 peaceful Indians; and 150,000 rebellious Indians.

During the colonial period, Spanish legal barriers blocked immigration by other European nationalities. However, with the advent of the House of Bourbon to the Spanish throne in 1700, French settlers began to arrive in Chile. With independence (1810–1818) a free trade policy was decreed, paving the way for new waves of immigration from England, North America and Italy. In the mid-nineteenth century, the government promoted the settlement of German and British immigrants in the southern Central Valley, Croats in Antofagasta and Punta Arenas and finally Christian Arabs. In the Great North, a significant number of Peruvians and Bolivians became Chilean with the country's incorporation of the Tarapacá region after the War of the Pacific (1879–1883).

## POLITICAL DEVELOPMENTS

### DISCOVERY

Chile was "discovered" from the north by the frontier governor Diego de Almagro in 1536, who returned to Peru with the intention of organizing a new expedition. Earlier, in 1510, Chile had been "discovered" in the extreme south by the Portuguese explorer Ferdinand Magellan in the service of Spain.

### CONQUEST

In 1541, Captain Pedro de Valdivia led an expedition into Chile and settled there on order of the viceroy of Peru and in the name of Philip II of Spain. Valdivia was designated governor, founding Santiago as well as numerous forts and cities further south. Indigenous resistance began, during which the governor was killed. The Spanish retreated north of the Bío Bío River, which constituted a sort of frontier, although it was not recognized by either side since the conquistadores extended as far south as Chiloé. The governors who succeeded Valdivia continued the war in sporadic battles; the area of La Araucanía was not pacified until 1860–1880. Meanwhile, the port of Valdivia and the main island of Chiloé remained under the direct control of the viceroyalty of Peru.

### THE COLONIAL PERIOD

The Spanish royal government of Chile, under the authority of the viceroy of Peru, was organized in the late sixteenth and early seventeenth centuries. Executive authority was vested in the governor and the commander-in-chief of the armed forces, with legislative and judicial powers exercised by the Royal Tribunal and the city councils of the leading settlements, all dependencies of Peru and Spain. The Church retained great influence, although with significant intervention on the part of the political authorities, who were authorized by the Pope to appoint the highest ecclesiastical offices.

Chile's economic importance in this period was based partially on its deliveries of agricultural products to the viceroyalty and Spain, but more importantly on metals, including gold, silver and copper. Its strategic significance derived from its possession of the only passage between the Atlantic and Pacific Oceans (the Strait of Magellan and Cape Horn) and from its status as the most intense focus of indigenous resistance, demanding constant reinforcements from Spain. Until the late eighteenth century, Chile covered not only the territory between the Pacific and the Andes, extending from the Atacama Desert in the north to the Strait of Magellan in the south, but also territories that are important provinces of Argentina today; the governor of Chile also controlled Tucumán, Mendoza and other regions.

## INDEPENDENCE

In 1700, the Spanish crown had passed from the Habsburgs to the House of Bourbon. In 1809, Napoleon installed his brother Joseph as king of Spain, replacing the Bourbon king Ferdinand VII. As in Spain itself, councils were organized in the Americas, which pledged their allegiance to the Bourbon king. Chile formed its first governing council in 1810, installed its first National Congress in 1811 and attempted self-government on the basis of various constitutional texts. This gave the people of the New World an opportunity to gain their own experience in political affairs and promoted the spread of ideas of independence. When the Bourbon crown was restored in Spain, Ferdinand VII set out to recover his overseas dominions and sent ships and troops to Chile, sparking the wars of independence. In 1814, Spain re-conquered Chile and reestablished European authority. It lasted only until late 1818, however, when final independence was declared under the authority of General Bernardo O'Higgins as Supreme Director.

## THE PERIOD OF ANARCHY

Chile attempted to reorganize its political system under several constitutions (those of 1818, 1822 and 1823), which did not adequately reflect the prevailing ideas and were unable to bring order to the country. After some attempts at federalism and the promulgation of a very liberal constitution for the time (1828), Joaquín Prieto was elected president of the Republic in 1831. With the help of his minister Diego Portales, Prieto spearheaded the constitutional reform, which culminated in the establishment of the 1833 Constitution.

## THE REPUBLIC

Under the 1833 Constitution, the government was successfully organized, exercising strong authority within established limits. Further attempts to overthrow the government by force fell into disrepute and ceased. The country's new political cohesiveness permitted the waging of two significant armed conflicts: against the Peruvian-Bolivian Confederation in 1837 and against Peru and Bolivia in 1879–1883.

The country's executive authority remained rooted in the president of the Republic. Legislative power was vested in two parliamentary bodies, the Chamber of Deputies and the Senate. Judicial power was exercised by the court system, including lower courts, appeals courts and the Supreme Court.

## THE RISE OF THE PSEUDO-PARLIAMENTARY SYSTEM

In the 1860s, parliamentary rules allowed a certain number of Deputies or Senators to summon ministers of government for questioning. This led to the Congressional demand that a minister or cabinet subject to a vote of censure by the legislature should be dismissed, since the government must have the confidence of Congress. This practice gave rise to periodic disputes and a high turnover of ministers. The president found himself obliged to recall censured ministers, since if he did not, Congress would refuse to approve recurring measures such as those relating to the budget, taxes and the armed forces. The president did not have the power to dissolve Congress and allow the voters to settle conflicts. This style of government became known as "pseudo-parliamentary."

## THE 1891 CIVIL WAR

Because of disagreements over President Balmaceda's political and economic proposals, Congress refused to approve the national budget for 1891. The president, supported by the armed forces, responded by decreeing that the previous year's budget would remain in force for the current year. The Congress accused the president of legislating by decree, declared him a dictator and, calling upon the Navy for support, formed a parallel government in the north, financed with the proceeds from the area's rich nitrate mining operations. Hostilities broke out, and the war culminated in September 1891 with 10,000 dead. Although Balmaceda was victorious, the parliamentary interpretation was reestablished, with Congressional interference in executive affairs increasing until 1924, when the problem of ministerial turnover was exacerbated by social tensions, chiefly arising from the decline of the nitrate industry after the invention of synthetic nitrates.

## THE 1925 REFORM

In 1924, the military declared the political system inoperative and incapable of resolving the country's urgent social problems and forced Congress to approve social legislation such as the Labor Code. President Arturo Alessandri was deposed, but the military requested his return in 1925. He accepted on the condition that the Constitution should be reformed to allow ministers to serve solely at the president's discretion, to eliminate the need for recurring approval of some laws and to provide that the previous year's budget would remain in force if a new one was not approved in a timely manner. The new Constitution was approved through a plebiscite.

## TOWARD SOCIALISM

Between 1925 and 1932, popular protests and the country's economic crisis led to the dissolution of several governments. Two presidents were obliged to resign and were constitutionally replaced by military ministers; the country was even governed during a short period by military councils proclaiming a "socialist republic."

In 1932, President Arturo Alessandri again took office and established a fully constitutional government. In 1938, the Popular Front, which originally included the Communist Party, was elected to power. It launched an economic policy aimed at industrialization, autarky and the protection of domestic industries, achieved through the creation of public enterprises, price fixing, exchange rate controls and limits on imports and exports.

In 1958, Jorge Alessandri became president with the backing of a center-right coalition, pledging to introduce liberal reforms into the economy. However, he failed to achieve fulfillment of his program due to lack of support in Congress. In 1964, the Christian Democrats came to power and again increased State intervention in the economy, promoting their plans as a third option between the right and Marxism. Their policies included agrarian reform with land expropriations, State purchase of shares in the big privately owned copper mining companies and the extension of State interference in all economic spheres.

In 1970, socialist President Allende took office and quickly nationalized all of the country's mining, agricultural, manufacturing and financial activities, establishing fixed prices for products in all sectors. Many of these initiatives were contrary to law and the

Constitution, even violating the rulings of the courts. The country entered a state of crisis, with shrinking production levels, industrial paralysis, high inflation, shortages, exchange rate and balance of payments crises and other difficulties. Allende tried to relieve the country's paralysis by designating active admirals and generals as ministers, but he sparked conflict with the judicial branch due to State officials' reluctance to abide by court decisions, as well as with Congress for his attempt to push through a constitutional reform creating three areas of the economy—State-held, mixed and private—without the approval of the legislature.

In August 1973, the Chamber of Deputies declared the government unconstitutional and called upon the military leaders serving as ministers to put an end to the illegalities, signaling that failure to do so would compromise the armed forces' professional and constitutional status. Days later, Allende declared that the country's food supply was sufficient for only three days.

## THE PINOCHET GOVERNMENT

In September 1973, in the midst of a full-fledged production crisis and with serious threats of civil unrest, a military council took power after a violent coup d'état. The aim of the military council was basic economic reorganization: reestablishment of the legal framework, the return of banks and businesses to their owners, price deregulation and implementation of an economic policy allowing resources to be assigned by the market. In 1982 and 1983, the balance of payments crisis came to a head, and Chile maintained a fixed exchange rate for four years, leading to an acute banking crisis and the renegotiation of the country's external debt. The country confronted this crisis by liberalizing currency markets, negotiating with foreign creditors to extend repayment periods, taking over and liquidating several banks and strongly supporting exports, all of which led to a turnaround in the situation by 1986.

Starting in that year the country's GDP began to rise to unprecedented levels, thanks to far-reaching economic and social reforms, including tax and tariff reductions; the privatization of state-owned companies; the encouragement of international investment, capital and trade; privatization of the social security system through individual savings accounts; the founding of private universities; the transfer of primary and secondary education to the municipalities, supported with subsidies; and administrative decentralization and regionalization, along with overall reductions in the size of the State. With moderate alterations, the country has continued to follow the main thrust of these reforms.

The government of Augusto Pinochet faced a hostile international climate, both within the Communist orbit—since it had deposed the first popularly elected Marxist head of government—and also in the Western world, which accused it of disrupting democracy and of serious human rights violations and restrictions on individual liberty.

Additional difficulties included tensions with Peru and Bolivia at the centennial of the Pacific War and disputes with Argentina over the Picton, Lenox and Nueva Islands in the eastern mouth of the Beagle canal, south of Tierra del Fuego, which were finally resolved through the mediation of Pope John Paul II. Under the military regime, Chile withdrew from the Andean Pact, which had fixed common external tariffs for its members (Chile, Peru, Bolivia, Ecuador, Colombia and Venezuela) and regulated foreign trade and investment.

## THE 1980 CONSTITUTION

The new Constitution, approved in a plebiscite in 1980, reestablished a strong presidency, a bicameral legislature and an independent judiciary. It also extended and strengthened individual rights; created new mechanisms for their protection; and accentuated the autonomy of the Constitutional Tribunal, the office of Comptroller-General and the Central Bank.

## THE TRANSITION PERIOD

The 1980 Constitution gradually took hold in the political system during a long transition period in which the military council approved the basic laws complementary to the Constitution, in contrast with the country's experience in 1925 when the Constitution did not take full effect until 1932, since the laws established by Congress in the interim distorted and even contradicted constitutional provisions. The 1980 Constitution established a transition period lasting until 1989, when elections would be held to install the new National Congress. The presidency would be established through a plebiscite on General Pinochet's leadership in 1988, or if the result was negative through a presidential election in 1989. The negative result of the 1988 plebiscite led to free presidential elections in 1989, where Patricio Aylwin was elected president.

## THE BINOMIAL SYSTEM

The new electoral provisions established a so-called binomial system, in which all voting districts simultaneously elect two representatives. This system tends to favor moderate, centrist politics, both in the designation of candidates and the election of representatives. Extreme positions are rejected, resulting in the formation of two great coalitions or political movements, favoring the search for consensus and compromise.

## THE TRANSFER OF POWER

In March 1990, in fulfillment of the Constitution's political plan, the military handed over legislative power to the new National Congress and executive authority to President Aylwin, who was elected by a majority of the parties opposed to the military regime, united in the Concertación coalition.

## THE CONCERTACIÓN ADMINISTRATIONS: AYLWIN (1990–1994), FREI RUIZ-TAGLE (1994–2000) AND LAGOS (2000–2006)

With the advent of democracy, the country reestablished political normality under President Patricio Aylwin without crises. The armed forces were gradually subordinated to civilian authority, and the country earned favorable recognition abroad.

Aylwin's economic policies maintained the growth rate, budgetary discipline and economic reforms achieved by the military government, and the new administration designated a special commission (the Rettig Commission) to investigate human rights violations during the previous government. Aylwin also initiated negotiations for free trade agreements with Canada and Mexico, which were concluded successfully by his successor.

Arbitration commenced to resolve the outstanding border disputes with Argentina in the far south (at Laguna del Desierto and Campo de Hielo Sur). Diplomatic relations were normalized with Cuba and Russia, as they had been with Poland, Czechoslovakia, Hungary and other Central European countries at the end of the military government, after the fall of the Berlin Wall.

During the administration of President Eduardo Frei Ruiz-Tagle, the trade negotiations initiated by Aylwin resulted in final agreements, and the border disputes with Argentina were resolved. Chile also became an associate member of Mercosur. President Frei's economic policies continued the trend initiated in the mid-1970s and achieved further advances in privatization with the sale of the State's minority shares in an electric company, the transfer to foreign investors of the principal State-held water utilities, the privatizing of the country's ports and the initiation of roadway concessions to private enterprises. However, moderate budget deficits, higher taxes and growing pressure for intervention in the labor market, combined with the Asian financial crisis, contributed to a gradual decline in the country's growth rate.

The presidential term of Ricardo Lagos began in March 2000, after a narrow victory over the mayor of Santiago, Joaquín Lavín. The new president began negotiations with the opposition for Constitutional reforms to the electoral system, to increase the number of Senators and eliminate the non-elected "institutional" Senate seats. Such negotiations continued in 2003. The unfavorable repercussions of a labor reform that added costs to the hiring or firing of workers, combined with slow economic growth, led Lagos, by the end of 2001, to announce measures favoring employment and private investment. At the beginning of President Lagos' term and the end of U.S. President Clinton's, negotiations were initiated for a free trade agreement (FTA) between both countries. In December 2002, an FTA was agreed to with the United States, while in November an Association Agreement was signed with the European Union. President Lagos has maintained economic reforms and market-oriented policies although he has stopped privatizations.

## ECONOMIC POLICIES

The protectionism imposed by the Spanish colonial authorities was gradually eased during the establishment of the Republic. The period from 1860 to 1897 saw significant trade liberalization. In the late nineteenth century, however, Chile's industries pressed for higher tariffs, organizing themselves into the SOFOFA (*Sociedad de Fomento Fabril*, or Federation of Chilean Industry), which remains the country's leading industrial association. They pushed through a law empowering the president of the Republic to raise tariffs up to 35 percent by decree. In spite of the increasing restrictions on international trade, however, the export sector represented 70 percent of GDP—thanks to the income from nitrate and copper mining—and continued to drive the country's economic growth until the 1930 crisis, which led to expanded State ownership and intervention in productive activities, as well as a new wave of trade protectionism. Both trends continued, until virtually all industries were in State hands and external trade was shut down in the 1970–1973 period. The situation has been reversed since that time through privatization and trade liberalization.

To confront the 1930 crisis, the authorities opted for selective manipulation of the economy, with import reductions through higher trade barriers and the stimulation of internal demand in favor of domestic production. This policy continued unbroken until its fatal unraveling in 1973. Populist forces, industrial cartels and labor organizations pressed for rising State intervention in manufacturing and service industries, reinforcing protectionist impulses and rejecting the trade liberalization opportunities arising from the creation of General Agreement on Tariffs and Trade (GATT) at the end of World War II.

## IMPORT SUBSTITUTION

Protectionism received strong support from the Economic Commission for Latin America and the Caribbean (ECLAC), created by the United Nations after a petition by Chile in 1950. ECLAC laid the conceptual basis for protectionism as a tool to confront falling prices for raw materials and to promote domestic manufacturing industries with a protected market.

Discrimination against the export sector led to export stagnation, the monopolistic domination of domestic markets by obsolete industries, increased external vulnerability, recurring balance of payments crises, currency devaluations and high inflation rates. Chile's GDP growth rate for the period between 1930 and 1973 was approximately 1.2 percent per annum.

## REGIONAL INTEGRATION

An attempt was made to correct the failures of the import substitution policy with the expansion of the limited internal market through planned regional integration, which would permit economic competition on a larger scale.

The first integration initiatives were undertaken in late 1960. The ALALC (*Asociación Latinoamericana de Libre Comercio*, or Latin American Free Trade Association), which included 15 countries, did not achieve significant advances, and the product-by-product tariff reduction negotiations, with producers in each member country enjoying voting rights, paralyzed the process. Meanwhile, through the Andean Pact, Chile, Peru, Bolivia, Ecuador and Venezuela hoped that their relative similarities would permit a more rapid advance toward economic integration, but again, interminable discussions on the location of various industries, the application of protectionist measures and trade barriers and discrimination against foreign investment led to the failure of the Pact, from which Chile withdrew in 1976. In the mid-1970s, ALALC was transformed into Asociacion LatinoAmericana de Integracion (ALACI), which favored the more modest objective of bilateral accords, rather than free trade among all its members. By refraining from insisting on the extension of bilateral accords to all other members, ALADI permitted moderate advances in integration.

## UNILATERAL TRADE LIBERALIZATION

Between 1974 and 1991, Chile opted for a strategy of unilateral trade liberalization, reducing its tariffs on all products from an average rate of 100 percent to some 10 percent, without negotiating reciprocal agreements. Its across-the-board tariff of 7 percent, with very limited exceptions (automobiles, milk, wheat, cooking oils and sugar) would continue to fall each year, dropping to 6 percent in 2003.

## BILATERAL AND REGIONAL FREE TRADE AGREEMENTS

Since 1991, Chile has continued its unilateral trade liberalization process while promoting bilateral and regional free trade agreements. Over the past ten years, it has concluded bilateral trade agreements setting tariffs at zero for nearly all commercial transactions with Bolivia, Peru, Mexico, Canada, Ecuador, Venezuela and Colombia, and it is currently negotiating a similar accord with Costa Rica and Central America.

## MERCOSUR

The high and variable external tariff levels (ranging between 0 and 20 percent during a ten-year period) of the Southern Common Market (Mercosur) treaty, to which Argentina, Brazil, Uruguay and Paraguay were parties, along with the macroeconomic instability of its members and their policy of negotiating collectively with the European Union and the United States, led to initial resistance on Chile's part to joining this association. However, it entered into the special status of associate member in 1998, without applying the common external tariff, and with an agreement to reduce tariffs within the group and gradually eliminate other trade barriers, resulting in free trade for most transactions by 2008.

## ASSOCIATION AGREEMENT WITH THE EUROPEAN UNION

In November 2002 the EU–Chile Association Agreement (the "EU Agreement") was signed. Although trade is an important part of the EU Agreement, it goes far beyond this. The EU Agreement is based on three pillars—a political dialogue, cooperation and trade—thus covering the broad range of EU–Chile relations.

The trade part of the EU Agreement establishes a free trade area in goods through the progressive and reciprocal liberalization of trade in goods over a maximum transitional period of ten years. At the end of the transitional period, full liberalization will have been reached for 97.1 percent of bilateral trade of $7,387 million (average 1999–2001), with, per sector, 100 percent full liberalization of industrial trade, 80.9 percent full liberalization of agricultural trade and 90.8 percent full liberalization of fisheries trade. In addition, for a number of agricultural and fisheries products other forms of tariff preferences are granted, such as tariff quotas, leaving only 0.4 percent of total bilateral trade not covered by any form of liberalization.

**TABLE 5-5:** Chile's imports and exports for 2001

| Country | EXPORTS | | IMPORTS | |
|---|---|---|---|---|
| | Mil. of $ FOB | % | Mil. of $ CIF | % |
| Mercosur | 1,520 | 8.2 | 3,093 | 17.1 |
| Argentina | 727 | 3.9 | 2,022 | 11.2 |
| Brazil | 688 | 3.7 | 968 | 5.4 |
| Other LA (excl. Mexico) | 1,277 | 6.9 | 838 | 4.6 |
| NAFTA | 3,886 | 21 | 4,012 | 22.2 |
| European Union | 4,224 | 22.3 | 2.849 | 15.7 |
| Asia | 4,476 | 24.2 | 2.314 | 12.8 |
| Others | 631 | 3.4 | 1,438 | 7.9 |
| TOTAL | 15,914 | 100.0 | 14,544 | 100.0 |

Liberalization of trade in goods will thus take place consistently with Article XXIV of GATT, that is, involving substantially all trade liberalization and not excluding any sector.

The tariff elimination schedules are as follows:

- Industrial products: The European Union eliminates 100 percent of its tariffs, for most imports from Chile at the entry into force (99.8 percent) and the rest in 2006. Chile equally eliminates all its industrial tariffs, for most imports at entry into force (91.7 percent) and the rest in 2008 (4.5 percent) and 2010 (3.8 percent). Average EU industrial imports from Chile (1999–2001) amount to €3,229 million, whereas average Chilean industrial imports from the European Union over the same period amount to €2,886 million.

- Agricultural products (including processed agricultural products): On the European Union side, tariffs will be eliminated for 97 percent of agricultural imports from Chile, relating mostly to full elimination of tariffs and in certain cases to elimination of ad valorem duties only. This will be done at entry into force (33 percent), in 2007 (55 percent), in 2010 (12 percent) and in 2012 (0.2 percent). In addition, certain products will benefit from other forms of preferential treatment, including tariff quotas for products such as meat, cheese, certain fruits and sugar confectionary. Agricultural products not benefiting from any form of liberalization represent 0.9 percent of total Chilean imports into the European Union. Chile eliminates tariffs for 81.9 percent of EU agricultural exports to Chile, at entry into force (61.5 percent), in 2008 (16.6 percent) and in 2012 (3.8 percent). In addition, Chile grants the European Union preferential treatment under tariff quotas for products such as olive oil and cheese.

  Average EU agricultural imports from Chile (1999–2001) amount to €866 million, whereas average Chilean agricultural imports from the European Union over the same period amount to €117 million.

- Fish and fisheries products: The European Union eliminates tariffs for 90.8 percent of fish imports from Chile, at entry into force (34.3 percent), in 2007 (39.6 percent), in 2010 (2.4 percent) and in 2012 (14.5 percent). Chile eliminates its tariffs for 97.6 percent of fish imports from the European Union at the entry into force of the EU Agreement. Both sides grant each other reciprocally tariff quotas for products such as tuna and hake.

  Average EU fisheries imports from Chile (1999–2001) amount to €283 million, whereas average Chilean fisheries imports from the European Union over the same period amount to €5 million.

The tariff elimination programs will start from the tariffs as applied at the entry into force of the Agreement (the so-called base rates). In the case of Chile, this applied tariff will be 6 percent for basically all products [an exception is information technology (ITA) products for which the applied tariff is already at zero]. In the case of the European Union the tariffs applied to Chile vary, depending on the product. As part of an overall package, the European Union agreed to start its tariff elimination from the rates effectively applied to Chile instead of the MFN (most-favored-nation) duties. In practical terms, these rates are those which the European Union unilaterally grants to Chile under the Generalized System of Preferences (GSP).

In order to benefit from preferential treatment under the Agreement, a product when exported must be considered as originating either in the Community or in Chile. For this purpose, it must comply with the origin rules established in a specific annex to the EU Agreement. In this respect, when the product exported is not entirely manufactured ("wholly obtained") in one of the two parties, goods imported from third countries must undergo sufficient working or processing in compliance with the specific origin rule set out for the final product to be exported.

The EU Agreement includes a standstill clause ensuring that neither side will increase its tariffs vis-à-vis the other party as from the entry into force of the EU Agreement.

## FREE TRADE AGREEMENT WITH THE UNITED STATES

The United States and Chile began bilateral negotiations on a free trade agreement (FTA) in December 2000. In December 2002, the United States and Chile reached an agreement on an historic and comprehensive FTA (the "U.S. Agreement") designed to strip away barriers and facilitate trade and investment between both countries. U.S. Trade Representatives and the Chilean Foreign Minister signed the U.S. Agreement and submitted it to their Congresses for approval in 2003. The U.S. Agreement is the first comprehensive trade agreement between the United States and a South American country.

The United States has only four FTA partners: Canada, Mexico (within the North American Free Trade Agreement, or NAFTA), Israel and Jordan. In November, Ambassador Zoellick announced conclusion of the substance of an FTA with Singapore. U.S. firms may offer financial services to participants in Chile's highly successful privatized pension system.

The U.S. Agreement establishes a secure, predictable legal framework for U.S. investors in Chile. Among the most important features of the U.S. Agreement is that both parties commit to effectively enforce their domestic labor and environmental laws. An innovative enforcement mechanism includes monetary assessments to enforce commercial, labor and environmental obligations. Cooperative projects will help protect wildlife, reduce environmental hazards and promote internationally recognized labor rights.

State-of-the-art protections and non-discriminatory treatment are provided for digital products such as U.S. software, music, text and videos. Protections for U.S. patents, trademarks and trade secrets exceeds past trade agreements.

## GROUND-BREAKING ANTI-CORRUPTION MEASURES IN GOVERNMENT CONTRACTING

U.S. firms guarantee a fair and transparent process to sell goods and services to a wide range of Chilean government entities, including airports and seaports.

Traditional market access to services is supplemented by strong and detailed disciplines on regulatory transparency. Regulatory authorities must use open and transparent administrative procedures, consult with interested parties before issuing regulations, provide advance notice and comment periods for proposed rules and publish all regulations.

## PROPERTY RIGHTS

Under Chile's Constitution, expropriation can take place only where there is a law authorizing expropriation in that specific case; compensation is determined by mutual agreement or, in its absence, by the Chilean courts.

In general, property rights are strongly enforced. The Constitution expressly states that "in no case may anyone be deprived of his property, assets, or any of the essential faculties or powers of ownership, except by virtue of a general or a special law which authorizes expropriation for the public benefit or the national interest, duly qualified by the legislator."

The expropriated party may contest the legality of the expropriation before the ordinary courts of justice and, at all times, has the right to indemnification for patrimonial damage actually caused, to be fixed by mutual agreement or by a decision issued by the courts in accordance with the law. In the absence of an agreement, the indemnification must be paid in cash.

Material possession of the expropriated property will take place following full payment of the indemnification, which, in the absence of an agreement, must be provisionally determined by experts in the manner prescribed for by law. In the case of contestation regarding the justifiability of the expropriation, the court may, on the merit of the information adduced, order the suspension of the material possession.

Therefore, expropriation requires indemnification on the basis of market value. In the event of a dispute, the Chilean government cannot take possession of the property until the courts issue a final decision on indemnification. As this may necessitate a long trial, the administration usually prefers to pay prices similar to the market value, or even higher.

## ENVIRONMENTAL REGULATIONS

The Chilean Constitution of 1980 grants to all citizens the right to live in an environment free of pollution. It further provides that other constitutional rights may be limited in order to protect the environment. One of the prime objectives of Chile's environmental policy concerning the introduction and development of investment projects hinges on reconciling the strategy for economic growth with proper environmental protection in the arena of public and private investment processes.

The Chilean Environmental Act, Law No. 19,300, was promulgated in March 1994. The regulatory framework for its enforcement—in terms of considering environmental concerns in investment projects—includes, among other things, the Environmental Impact Assessment System (EIAS). The purpose of the Environmental Impact Assessment, applied to projects and/or activities performed by the public and private sectors, is to assure the environmental sustainability of such undertakings.

Certain projects or activities prone to generating environmental impact must be subjected to an Environmental Impact Assessment System. Their specific effects, characteristics or circumstances will determine whether an Environmental Impact Statement or an Environmental Impact Study should be filed.

The Environmental Act is to be conceptualized as a set of procedures designed to identify and evaluate positive and negative environmental impacts to be generated or presented by a given project or activity. The EIAS will then assist in designing measures aimed at abating the negative impacts and enhancing any positive effects. An important part of these procedures depends on the involvement of State entities with environmental jurisdiction and/or in charge of issuing specific sector environmental permits associated with the project or activity.

The Environmental Act has placed the burden of implementing and administrating the EIAS on the National Environmental Commission (CONAMA). Within this institutional framework, the CONAMA and the Regional Environmental Commissions (COREMAs) are in charge of coordinating the process whereby ratings are assigned to the Environmental Impact Study and Environmental Impact Statements are reviewed. The various State bodies with environmental competence participate actively in this process.

The Environmental Act provides that the projects or activities under its purview and further specified in the Regulations may only be executed or revised following an assessment of their environmental impact. Further, it stipulates that the environmental contents of all the permits and dictums to be issued by State entities must be analyzed and settled through the EIAS.

## FOREIGN INVESTMENT, CAPITAL MOVEMENTS AND EXCHANGE RATES

Starting in 1974, as trade liberalization progressed, restrictions on capital movements and transactions in foreign currency were also gradually eliminated. Currently, Chile places no restrictions on the entry and exit of capital, and the nondiscrimination principle is applied to foreign investors, who may invest in all areas of the economy. Foreign investment, chiefly from the United States, Spain, Canada and England, is concentrated in manufacturing, mining, electricity, fisheries, banks and financial services.

Foreign investors are subject to a tax of 35 percent on the repatriation of their profits. Exchange rates are fixed freely by the market and without interference by the Central Bank. Capital movements to or from Chile do not require prior authorization. However, amounts over US$10,000 must be remitted through commercial banks, who must inform the Central Bank about the remittances.

## PRIVATIZATIONS

The State has privatized nearly all public enterprises, with the exception of BANCOESTADO, ENAMI and CODELCO (Chile's largest company and the world's largest copper producer) in the copper mining sector, along with ENAP, the National Oil Company, which maintains a monopoly in the area of fuel refining and oil extraction. (The country's oil reserves are nearly depleted, and more than 90 percent of oil and gas supplies are imported.) The State also holds shares in water and sewer utilities.

## BILATERAL INVESTMENT TREATIES

In 1991, Chile became a signatory of the Washington Convention of 1965 that created the International Centre for Settlement of Investment Disputes (ICSID). Since then, Chile began to negotiate bilateral investment treaties (BITs), agreements through which Chile provides additional protection both to inward and outward foreign investment flows. As of January 2002, Chile had negotiated 51 BITs, of which 35 were in force.

**TABLE 5-6:** Bilateral investment treaties

| Country | Status | Country | Status |
| --- | --- | --- | --- |
| Argentina | In force since February 27, 1995* | Honduras | Approved by Congress in September 2001 |
| Austria | In force since November 17, 2000 | Hungary | Signed on March 10, 1997 |
| Belgium | In force since August 5, 1999 | Italy | In force since June 23, 1995 |
| Bolivia | In force since July 21, 1999 | Nicaragua | In force since December 10, 2001 |
| Brazil | Approved by Congress on December 14, 1994 | Norway | In force since November 4, 1994 |
| Colombia | Signed on January 22, 2000 | Panama | In force since December 21, 1999 |
| Costa Rica | In force since July 8, 2000 | Paraguay | In force since September 16, 1997 |
| Croatia | In force since July 1, 1996 | Peru | In force since August 11, 2001 |
| Cuba | In force since September 30, 2000 | Poland | In force since September 22, 2000 |
| Czech Republic | In force since December 2, 1996 | Portugal | In force since February 24, 1998 |
| Denmark | In force since November 30, 1995 | Romania | In force since August 27, 1997 |
| Dominican Republic | Signed on November 28, 2000 | Spain | In force since April 27, 1994 |
| Ecuador | In force since February 21, 1996 | Sweden | In force since February 13, 1996 |
| El Salvador | In force since November 18, 1999 | Switzerland | Signed on September 24, 1999 |
| Finland | In force since June 14, 1996 | The Netherlands | Signed on November 30, 1998 |
| France | In force since December 5, 1994 | Turkey | Signed on August 21, 1998 |
| Germany | In force since June 18, 1999 | Ukraine | In force since August 29, 1997 |
| Greece | Signed on July 10, 1996 | Uruguay | In force since April 22, 1999 |
| Guatemala | In force since December 10, 2001 | Venezuela | In force since May 17, 1994 |

*Signed treaties need to be ratified by Congress before they can be in force. Treaties are in force in Chile after they are published in the Official Gazette.

Under these agreements, each contracting State commits itself to providing fair and equal treatment to investments legally materialized in its territory by investors of the other contracting State. It also guarantees the principles of national treatment, nondiscrimination and most-favored-nation status.

Moreover, BITs usually grant private property rights through the establishment of basic principles and minimum standards in case of expropriations. Likewise, they guarantee that any expropriation or measure with similar effect is adopted in accordance with a law based on public good or national interest, in a nondiscriminatory manner.

Through BITs, the contracting States guarantee the free transfer of capital, of profits or interest generated by foreign investments and, in general, any transfer of funds related to investments.

Additionally, these agreements establish a dispute settlement mechanism in case of controversies that might arise between an investor of a contracting State and the other contracting State. Basically, this mechanism assures that controversies will be settled through friendly consultations. If no agreement is reached, the investor will be entitled to submit the case to the domestic jurisdiction of the host State of the investment or to international arbitrage. This jurisdictional option is definitive.

As an additional guarantee for foreign investors, BITs allow access (if not full access, at least access with reasonable premiums) to insurance coverage against noncommercial risks offered by multilateral or governmental agencies such as Multilateral Investment Guarantee Agency (MIGA) and The Overseas Private Investment Corporation (OPIC).

The aforementioned guarantee is reinforced by the principle of subrogation granted in BITs. This means that if one contracting State—or an agency authorized by it—grants any kind of insurance against noncommercial risks to an investment in the territory of the other contracting State, the latter shall recognize the rights of the former to subrogate for the rights of the investor in case it has paid the insurance.

The protection provided by these agreements applies both to investments made after the agreement comes into force as well as to those made before that date.

## CONCLUSIONS AND LATEST EVENTS

Chile's trade agreements and reforms make its economy the most open to international competition in Latin America. To this is added some twenty years of conservative balanced budgets, increased monetary stability with a current annual inflation of less than 3 percent and its status as the world's fourth fastest-growing economy in recent years, although the growth rate has since declined. For more than a decade, Chile's GDP grew at an annual rate of 7 percent, although it rose by only 1.9 percent during 2002 and is projected to expand 3 percent in 2003. Thanks to these successes, a broad consensus prevails among both the governing and opposition parties to maintain Chile's policies of openness to international trade, avoid budget deficits, keep inflation under control and promote private investment.

From a political perspective, during the last decade democracy and the rule of law have been expanded and stability is well established. Military subordination to the government has been reached and an independent judiciary is ruling without government intervention.

Freedom of expression has been increased after a new press law was published. Latest events on minor cases of administrative corruption have created an agreement between the government and the main political party, Unión Democrata Independiente

(UDI), to improve transparency and to modernize the governmental institutions. UDI, a center right opposition party, has also agreed to legislate in order to finance campaigns with public monies. After twelve years the government coalition, Concertación (center left), is beginning to exhibit internal divisions and a relevant part of the society is looking for a change in the political authorities in future elections. Concertación has a tight majority in both houses of the Congress, while the opposition (center right) is increasing its representation.

According to different opinion polls taken in the last two years, opposition leader Joaquín Lavín, Mayor of the Municipality of Santiago, appears to be the most likely successor to President Lagos. Public agenda is concentrated in reforms of the education and public health system and in constitutional changes in order to change the electoral system, increase the number of members of the Senate, eliminate the non-elected senators and reform the national security council.

## BIBLIOGRAPHY

### Periodicals publications

Banco Central. Boletín Mensual (Monthly)

Banco Central. Cuentas Nacionales (Annual)

Banco Central. Documentos de Trabajo

Banco Central. Indicadores de Comercio Exterior (Monthly)

Centro de Estudios Públicos CEP. Estudios Públicos (Quarterly)

Centro de Estudios Públicos CEP. Puntos de Referencia (Monthly)

Instituto Nacional de Estadísticas INE. Compendio Estadístico (Annual)

Libertad y Desarrollo. Serie Informe (Económica; Política; Social) (Monthly)

Libertad y Desarrollo. Temas Públicos (Semanal)

Universidad Católica de Chile. Cuadernos de Economía (Quarterly)

Universidad de Chile. Centro de Economía Aplicada CEA. Documentos de Trabajo. Serie Economía

Universidad de Chile. Centro de Economía Aplicada CEA. Análisis económico descriptivo de las regiones chilenas. Documentos de Trabajo. Serie Economía Agosto 2002

Universidad de Chile. Instituto de Estudios Internacionales. Estudios Internacionales (Quarterly)

Universidad de Chile. Facultad de Ciencias Físicas y Matemáticas. Perspectivas en política, economía y gestión (Biannual)

Universidad Gabriela Mistral. Report of Chile (Annual)

### Books

Büchi Buc Hernán. La Transformación Económica de Chile, del Estatismo a la libertad. Editorial Norma. 1993.

Comité Inversiones Extranjeras. Chile Inversión Extranjera en Cifras. Período 1974–1999. Comité de Inversiones Extranjeras.

French-Davis, Ricardo; Stallings, Bárbara. Reformas; crecimiento y políticas sociales en Chile desde 1973. CEPAL. 2001.

Góngora, E.; Robertson, R.; Vial, C. Gonzálo y otros. Dimensión histórica de Chile. Revista Dpto. de Historia y Geografía de la Academia de Ciencias Pedagógicas. 1984.

Holt, Jocelyn; Correa, Sofía y Figueroa Consuelo. Historia del siglo XX chileno. Editorial Sud Americana Chilena. 2002.

Lavín, Infante Joaquín. Chile a quiet revolution. Editorial Zig Zag. 1988.

Libertad y Desarrollo. Cristián Larroulet ed. Soluciones Privadas a Problemas Públicos. Quebecor World Chile S.A. 1991 1ª edición; 2003 2ª edición.

Lüders, Rolf; Ibañez, Pedro. Hacia una economía de mercado: diez años de Política económica. 1983.

Márquez de la Plata, Alfonso. El salto al futuro. Editorial Zig Zag. 1992.

Méndez, Juan Carlos. Chilean Economy Policy. Calderón y Cia. Ltda. 1979.

Piñera Echeñique, José. Chile 2010 Libertad, libertad mis amigos. Economía y Sociedad Ltda. 1997.

Piñera Echeñique, José. La Revolución Laboral en Chile. Editorial Zig Zag. 1992.

Piñera, Echeñique José. Camino Nuevo. Economía y Sociedad Ltda. 1993.

Rojas Sánchez, Gonzalo. Chile escoge la libertad. La presidencia de Augusto Pinochet. Editorial Zig Zag. 1998.

Wisecarver, Daniel; Williamson, Carlos; Lüders, Rolf; Desormeaux, Jorge y otros. El Modelo Económico Chileno. CINDE Centro Información para el Desarrollo Económico. 1992.

## Public Policies

Libertad y Desarrollo. Cristián Larroulet. Las Tareas de Hoy. Políticas Sociales y Económicas para una Sociedad Libre. Editorial Zig Zag. 1994.

Libertad y Desarrollo. Cristián Larroulet. Chile 2010: el desafío del desarrollo. Quebecor World Chile S.A. 2002.

# CHAPTER 6
# COLOMBIA

DR. JOSE MANUEL CARDENAS

## INTRODUCTION

Colombia has stood out because of its long democratic tradition and its sustained economic development. Its geographic position and its natural and human resources place Colombia in a privileged situation on the continent. However, its development has slowed in the last few years, partly because of the international recession and partly because of armed internal conflict. Nonetheless, the situation is not as desperate as one may imagine from viewing the international news.

The new Alvaro Uribe administration, which began August 7, 2002, has, with the support of the United Nations, proposed international mediation to search for dialogues with the subversive groups on the basis that they abandon terrorism and facilitate the cease of hostilities. Colombia needs to continue its national integration process and, under the principles of open regionalism, integrate more closely with the international community. In reality, these are two faces of the same coin. This chapter examines the situation and perspectives the country has concerning the future, especially as concerns regional integration.

## THE LAND AND THE PEOPLE

Colombia is strategically located at the midpoint between North and South America. It is the only country within South America with coastlines on both the Atlantic and the Pacific Oceans. This favorable geographical position allows Colombia to have easy access to the U.S., European, Latin American, African and Asian markets. The country's location and geography, with vast lowlands and mountainous areas, explain the sharp variations in climate and the abundance of natural resources. In fact, Colombia holds between 14 and 15 percent of the world's total biodiversity, slightly less than Brazil, while covering only 0.77 percent of world's surface.

The population is located mainly in the Andean highlands, which consist of three major ranges that extend like fingers from the Ecuadorian border, northeast of the Caribbean Sea. To the southeast of the Cordillera Oriental lie the vast and thinly populated lowlands, which consist of the Llanos (Orinoquia) and Amazonian regions. Together, they account for three-fifths of the country's area. This vast region is waiting to be integrated into the national economy. Thus, Colombia comprises many regions (the Caribbean, Pacific, Andean, Orinoquia and the equatorial tropics) that demand a new political-administrative dimension as Colombia enters the twenty-first century.

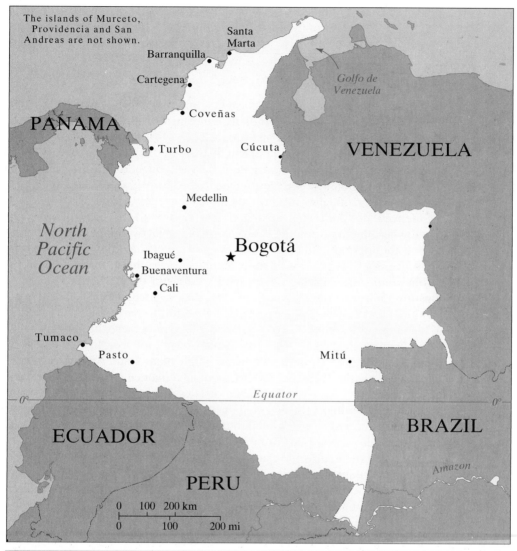

The islands of Murceto, Providencia and San Andreas are not shown.

Santa Marta

Barranquilla

Cartegena

Coveñas

PANAMA

Turbo

Cúcuta

VENEZUELA

*Golfo de Venezuela*

Medellin

*North Pacific Ocean*

Ibagué

Buenaventura

Cali

Bogotá

Tumaco

Pasto

Mitú

*Equator*

ECUADOR

BRAZIL

*Amazon*

PERU

0    100   200 km

0         100      200 mi

**FIGURE 6-1** Map of Colombia

In terms of population, Colombia ranks third in Latin America after Brazil and Mexico. The current population of 42 million people, which accounts for 8 percent of the region's inhabitants, is estimated to expand to 46 million by 2005. Unlike other Latin American countries, Colombia's urban population is not concentrated in the country's capital but is widely distributed among various cities.

Bogotá, the capital city, has approximately 6.4 million inhabitants, or 15 percent of the total population. The cities that follow are Cali and Medellin, with nearly 2 million each, and Barranquilla, with over 1 million inhabitants. Almost 90 percent of the people are under the age of 50. There has also been a significant shift from rural to urban areas over the last thirty years. Colombia's cities have experienced a large increase in inhabitants, moving from 57 percent of the total population in 1970 to 71 percent in 2001.

## HISTORY

There is little recorded history of pre-Spanish Colombia. When the Spaniards arrived, they found mostly Chibchan-speaking Indians, concentrated in the western mountainous regions and without firm political institutions.

The Spanish conquest of Colombia began in 1525; by 1559 the Audiencia of Santa Fé de Bogotá, part of the viceroyalty of Peru, was established and the colonial era begun. After 1740 the Audiencia was transferred to the newly created viceroyalty of the Nueva Granada (comprising present-day Colombia, Venezuela, Ecuador and Panama).

Independence came following Spain's defeat at Boyacá in 1819. In 1821, when Nueva Granada became the Republic of Greater Colombia, two major political parties were organized: the Liberals and the Conservatives. One or the other of these two parties governed over various periods of time. Finally, in 1958, both parties agreed on a plan that consisted of alternating governments between them. Beginning in 1974, under a constitutional amendment passed in 1968, the president and all legislative bodies at the national level were to be elected without regard to party.

Colombia is the oldest and one of the most solid democracies in South America. During the last century, all of Colombia's presidents, except for during the military regime period of 1953–1957, were elected democratically. While many Latin American countries suffered dictatorships in the 1970s and 1980s, Colombia remained a bastion of democracy on the continent. This tradition has been maintained despite the constant threats posed to the country's stability by almost fifty years of the existence of left-wing guerrillas and the rise of right-wing private justice groups, commonly known as *paramilitares,* in the 1980s.

In recent years, however, politics have become more complicated as these two groups have financed their subversive activities with money based on drug trafficking. In order to solve the country's political and economic problems, the Pastrana administration launched a peace-building strategy, commonly known as Plan Colombia, that gained wide international support. Unfortunately, the peace process has not shown positive results and the obligation of redefining the process fell on the Alvara Uribe administration beginning on August 7, 2002.

## THE ECONOMY

The Colombian economy has traditionally stood out due to its firmness, stability and orthodox management of political economics. From 1932 until 1996 there was stable, positive economic growth. In the 1980s Colombia was the only country in South America that did not suspend payments of its external debt; the country's inflation was under control and did not present the volatility of other countries in the region. These factors allowed the country to grow at a satisfactory level that allowed diversification of the productive structure and an improvement in the standard of living of the population.

Today, Colombia is the world's largest exporter of soft coffee, emeralds and green bananas; the world's second largest exporter of flowers; the fourth largest Latin

American exporter of petroleum; the world's fourth largest exporter of coal and the world's sixth largest exporter of gold.

Only in the last four years, due to the international crisis, the downfall in the prices of its principal exports (coffee, petroleum, coal, nickel and manufactured products—especially textiles, leather and graphic arts) and the diminishing domestic demand caused by the armed conflict, did the country enter a period of recession, which is expected to end by 2003.

The Pastrana administration introduced measures to stop and reduce the impact of the downturn in the economy and put the economy back onto a sustainable growth track. These measures, known as the Macroeconomic Adjustment Program, targeted, through structural reforms, the main weakness factors of the public sector budgetary system (pension system, income structure, regional and local finance) aiming at fiscal balance. They also provided tools for private sector recovery. The reforms that were approved and implemented are the following:

### Tax Reform Program (Law 633/00)

This includes the expansion of the value added tax (VAT) base through the inclusion of products and services formerly excluded on the list, an increase in the VAT rate from 15 to 16 percent and the inclusion of a tax on financial transactions of 0.3 percent. The reform would allow the government to collect approximately $3.6 billion Colombian pesos.

### Reforms in the Financial Sector

To address the difficulties faced by the financial sector, the government implemented economic emergency measures beginning in 1998, including the imposition of the 0.2 percent tax on bank withdrawals which was later made permanent by the Tax Reform Law and increased to 0.3 percent. The proceeds of this tax were used to alleviate mortgage debts, restructure financial institutions and strengthen the National Financial Guarantees Fund (FOGAFIN).

FOGAFIN is the public sector entity instructed to provide credits for capitalization purposes to financial institutions. Likewise, the government implemented other measures to raise the capitalization requirements of private as well as public financial institutions and to put in order the financial status of the main public banks before privatizing them.

### Economic Recovery Law (Law 550/99)

This law was passed to establish a regime that would promote and facilitate the reactivation of corporations (excluding those in the financial sector) and territorial entities. Basically, it provides the necessary measures to prevent the bankruptcy of corporations and territorial entities that have been struck by the economic recession. It enables debt restructure agreements between internal and external creditors and the debtors in ways that preserve the existence of the firm. It also creates special conditions for renegotiation of financial sector debt and pending taxes, as well as new instruments to provide capital for productive endeavors.

### Regional Expenditure Rationing Program (Law 617/00)

As the Colombian administrative system is not federal but decentralized, this law aimed at imposing fiscal discipline on regional and local governments with serious fiscal imbalances. It was expected that as a consequence of its implementation, it would generate net savings in public expenditure of approximately 0.11 percent of GDP in the years 2001 and 2002.

### Lottery and Games of Chance Law (Law 643/01)

This law aimed at guaranteeing profitability and economic feasibility to lotteries and games of chance as a source of public income. Also, the 2000 budget (Law 547/00) and the 2001 budget (Law 628/00) reflected the planned expenditure cuts by the government to improve the fiscal balance of the economy.

### Social Support Network

An historically high unemployment rate is one of the biggest challenges for Colombian economic authorities. According to DANE (National Statistics Department), as quoted by the National Planning Department (DNP), the national unemployment rate as of December 2001 was 16.7 percent and 19.7 percent for the seven main cities alone. To tackle this problem the government launched a two-tier strategy for the short and long term. In the short run, the creation of a Social Support Network (RAS) was to generate 91,000 jobs in 2001.

In the medium and long run, the strategy comprises three elements: sustained economic growth; an increase in secondary education enrollment, including an aggressive loan program to finance tertiary and technical education; and reforms to introduce flexibility into the labor market. Unemployment for the year 2002 was expected to be at 14 percent.

The new Uribe administration has the purpose of continuing the monetary and financial stabilization policy of its predecessor, but due to the difficult social situation, it seeks, among other things:

- To revise and extend the agreement of the International Monetary Fund, which expires in September of the present year.
- To maintain the Central Bank's financial independence but to demand political responsibility in the fulfillment of its goals and a greater coordination with the social policies.
- To pass into a second stage of structural reforms, which include the pension system, to increase the retirement age and decrease benefits, the reduction of bureaucracy and a tributary reform which increases taxes.
- To maintain the international financial commitments and convoke the multilateral credit organizations to understand the difficult situation of indebtedness in virtue of which the foreseeable flow in the next few years will be negative.
- To advance a political reform to fight against corruption, which implies a state reform to reduce expenses and deepen the decentralization process.
- To provide a firm hand against violence and crime through an integral, democratic and transparent citizen security policy, which implies the increase of the public force.
- To continue the struggle against drug trafficking.
- To apply the military component of Plan Colombia and destine the resources of the social component to concrete programs of eradication of illicit farming.
- To create a vigorous program of productive employment, which implies the construction of 100,000 homes per year, public work programs, massive city transport, national food production protection and support towards small and medium businesses.
- To start an educational revolution that will allow the country to increase the educational offerings for 1,500,000 students, to provide a permanent evaluation of teachers and students to guarantee their quality and to ensure the enrichment of technical development and scientific investigation.

**TABLE 6-1:** Socioeconomic indicators

| | |
|---|---:|
| **Land area** (sq km) | 1,141,748 |
| **Population** (millions, 2002 projection) | 43.04 |
| **Annual growth rate** (2002) | 1.8% |
| **Density** (people per sq km, 2001 projection) | 37.8 |
| **Rural population** (percentage of total population, 2002 estimate) | 26.3 |
| **Access to** | |
|   **Safe water** (1997) | 75.1% |
|   **Sanitation** (1997) | 85% |
| **Public expenditure in health** (% of GDP) | 2.1 |
| **Population per physician** (1997) | 992 |
| **Life expectancy at birth** (1995–2002) | 70.66 years |
| **Cost of living, 1999** (based on a ranking with New York = 100) | 79.44 |
| **Human development index (HDI)** (1997) | 0.77 |
| **Illiteracy rate** (1999) | 8.3% |
| **Public expenditure on education** (1999, % of GDP) | 2.7 |
| **Distribution of graduates by** specialization areas (1999) | 106.755 |
|   **Educational Sciences** | 18,964 |
|   **Health Sciences** | 10,993 |
|   **Economics/Administration/Accounting** | 34.998 |
|   **Engineering/Architecture** | 23.127 |
|   **Mathematics/Natural Sciences** | 1.582 |
|   **Others** | 17.091 |
| **Participation of women** (as a % of the total 1999) | |
|   **Administrators and managers** | 38.8 |
|   **Professional and technical** | 45.6 |
| **Gini coefficient** (1999) | 0.56 |

| **Main cities' population** (2001) | Thousand People | Percentage of Total |
|---|---:|---:|
| Bogotá | 6,573 | 15 |
| Medellin | 2,004 | 5 |
| Cali | 2,212 | 5 |
| Barranquilla | 1,279 | 3 |
| Bucaramanga | 540 | 1 |
| Cartagena | 927 | 2 |
| Others | 29,500 | 69 |
| **Currency** | Peso (COP) | |

*Sources:* DANE, DNP, ICFES, The World Competitiveness Yearbook 1999, Human Development Report 1999 and IMF Statistical Appendix 1999.

## THE ROAD TOWARD INTEGRATION

Simón Bolívar proposed early on the necessity of creating a Confederation of American States not only to build an offensive and defensive alliance toward the European powers but as a true and permanent entity. It would have its own powers and would express common interests and establish the directives to follow in the political, economic and social fields. These ideas gave birth to the Panama Congress in 1826, which suggested both political and economic integration across the region. Even though on this occasion Colombia proposed the establishment of free maritime traffic, the rest of the delegates would not agree to it.

The United States, following President Washington's[1] political legacy, kept itself alienated from the outside world in order to consolidate the Union. In 1886, having terminated its industrialization process, the United States changed this attitude and during the First International Conference of American States proposed to the Latin American countries a series of measures to free commerce. These measures were not accepted by the latter for fear that the commerce would be one way only and would favor the interests of the United States.

From that time until the Sixth International Conference of American States, the Latin American countries rejected the proposals made by the United States to endorse economic and commercial agreements. This situation changed with the political ideas of the New Deal designed by Franklin D. Roosevelt to fight against the bilateral course Nazi Germany had given to world commerce.

The basis of these new political ideas are found in the Reciprocal Trade Agreement, proclaimed in 1934 by the U.S. Congress. This law authorized the president to sign free trade agreements based on the most favored nation's clause with the purpose of assuring equity in commercial relations and to avoid discrimination. The United States signed these agreements with a large number of countries, but many agreements were abrogated because they were inconvenient for the United States. Such was the case for Colombia.

When the United States and its allies won World War II, U.S. trade policy, which had been bilateral, became multilateral. This climate allowed the General Agreement on Tariffs and Trade (GATT) to be signed. Initially the GATT was considered to be a club of rich countries. Developing countries only entered it when a special and differential treatment was established.

Following Bolívar's ideas, in 1948 Colombia proposed the establishment of the Gran Colombian Customs Union, made up of Colombia, Ecuador and Venezuela. Such was also the purpose of the 1948 Quito Charter. Nonetheless, this initiative was unsuccessful.

With the Montevideo Treaty signed in 1960, the Latin American Free Trade Association (LAFTA) was created. Colombia signed the treaty in 1962. The goal of this agreement was to create, over a period of twelve years, a free trade zone. Initially, LAFTA functioned satisfactorily, but it quickly lost its dynamics and the small and medium countries started to show their dissatisfaction.

This led to the 1966 Declaration of Bogotá, signed by Presidents Eduardo Frei of Chile and Carlos Lleras of Colombia. This Declaration gave birth to the Cartagena

---

[1]Farewell Speech. Sept. 17, 1796.

Agreement between Colombia, Chile, Ecuador, Peru and Venezuela. The member countries wanted to be part of a more advanced integration process than that allowed by LAFTA and established a customs union. This agreement was not limited only to commercial aspects but also covered a development process for investment. Thus, an industrial program was established as the pivot of regional development and a wider market was sought to favor the goods and services of national origin.

As a consequence of globalization, this closed model of integration, which did not give satisfactory results, changed at the beginning of the 1990s into an open model. This change of direction was a result of the beginning of a unilateral opening process by the Latin American countries, especially the Andean countries, and the search for a greater integration with the world economy. It started from the so-called open regionalism defined by the Economic Commission for Latin America and the Caribbean (ECLAC) as the process that results from the consolidation of the nascent interdependence of the preferential agreements and the markets resulting from trade liberation in general. In this way, the goal of open regionalism is to obtain explicit integration policies compatible with, and to complement, the policies that enhance competition.[2]

This new direction of the Andean process of integration, initiated in May 1987 with the approval of the Quito Protocol, was later widened and deepened through political decisions [Acts of Galapagos (1989), La Paz (1990), Barahona (1991), Quito (1995) and Sucre (1997)—which became legal agreements; and Protocols of Trujillo (1996) and Sucre (1997)]. Recently, the presidents at the Andean Presidential Summit, held in Santa Cruz de la Sierra (January 29, 2002), signed the Declaration that carries the name of this city, in which they set out the way in which they planned to accomplish some of the integration agreements.

## QUITO PROTOCOL

This Protocol preserved the philosophies and objectives of the Cartagena Agreement, extending the social and external coordination aspects and introducing important modifications related to the flexibility, complementarity and amplification of the integration instruments.[3]

### Harmonization of Policies

This compromise was made gradual and more flexible. The industrial and agricultural regimes were replaced by general programs as were the physical infrastructure and social planning.

### Industrial Development Programs

As a consequence of the preceding and with the purpose of giving more importance to market forces, the chapter based on industrial programming was completely replaced by simpler mechanisms, such as complementary agreements and industrial integration projects, resulting from private sector initiatives.

---

[2]Manuel Jose Cardenas. Implications of the Open Regionalism in the Legal System of the Cartagena Agreement. "The Andean Court of Justice in the Andean Community Law" Seminar. Bogotá, July 28–29, 1994, page 5.

[3]Hector Maldonado Lira. 30 Years of Andean Integration: Balances and Perspectives. Andean Community. General Secretary. Icon. Ediciones Integrales. Lima. 1999, page 66.

### Customs Union

The liberalization program was made automatic and irrevocable. The terms and other aspects, for example, the rules for the Common External Tariff, are to be established by the Commission. Previously, they had always been established in the Agreement's text.

Simultaneously with the gradual changes agreed upon in the Cartagena Agreement and in the Quito Protocol, the countries were advancing rapidly in the adoption of internal financial liberation policies as well as exchange and external trade. This process was known as unilateral opening. In many cases, it led to internal liberalization decisions that were more advanced than those agreed upon at a subregional level. In many decisions, because of this, the Commission was forced to accelerate the terms agreed upon in the tariff liberalization to create a free trade zone.

### TRUJILLO PROTOCOL

This Protocol, signed in March 1996, introduced changes in political and institutional material. The Andean Community was created and the Andean Integration System institutionalized. The Andean Group already had an independent legal system of supranational character. With these changes, not only were these functions reinforced, but the Community also acquired a political dimension and international legal representation.

The Trujillo Protocol was included in the legal system of the Andean Presidential Council. Before it was expanded to fields other than that of trade, decisive powers were granted to the Andean Council of Ministries of Foreign Affairs, therefore reducing the competition of the Commission in the areas of trade and investment. The board of three members was replaced by a General Secretariat, and coordination among all the institutions of the Andean Integration System was encouraged.[4]

The Protocol amending the treaty creating the Court of Justice of the Cartagena Agreement, through which new challenges were assumed and others reinforced, was signed on May 28, 1996.

### SUCRE PROTOCOL

This Protocol, signed in June 1997, introduced changes to the Cartagena Agreement in relation to Peru's special situation to facilitate its participation in the integration process. These changes also updated the agreement on the internal evolution of the process and globalization, particularly as concerns external relations, trade in services and social integration.

Due to the preceding, the Andean Presidential Council, in the Acts of Guayaquil (April 1998) and Cartagena (May 27, 1999), the latter corresponding to the celebration of the 30th anniversary of the signing of the Cartagena Agreement, created guidelines

---

[4]The Andean Integration System is composed of the Andean Presidential Council, the Andean Council of Ministers of Foreign Affaires, the General Secretariat, the Court of Justice, the Andean Parliament, the Business and Labor Advisory Council, the Andean Development Corporation, the Latin American Fund, the Simón Rodríguez Agreement, the Simón Bolívar Andean University, the Advisory Councils established by the Commission and the rest of the bodies and institutions created within the framework of Andean subregional integration.

to deepen economic integration and to advance the integration politically and socially. Of these guidelines, it is important to emphasize the following:

- Create a Common Market in the year 2005, for which work should be completed on the four liberties of movement—of people, capital, goods and services—to improve the laws on competence and enhance competition, advance in the harmonization of macroeconomic policies, complete the community regime on investments and define a common agricultural policy.
- Enhance physical integration, through viable road projects.
- Establish a community policy to stimulate integration and border development.
- Advance in a program aimed at liberalizing intra-subregional trade in telecommunications to create a common market (except for radio broadcasting and television), which should be finished by the year 2002.
- Implement the Andean Community's Common Foreign Policy in a gradual, integral and flexible manner, in the three major fields of the international agenda: political, economic and sociocultural.
- Develop a Social Agenda and participation in the civil society, which implies actions in educational, cultural, scientific and technological fields, relations with the society, the coordination of job policies and the creation of an investment fund and social compensation, to alleviate the negative sectorial and territorial impacts caused by economic integration. In the declaration of Santa Cruz de la Sierra the accomplishment of some of these aspects were specified.
- Completion of the Free Trade Area by June 30, 2002.
- The Common External Tariff should be valid for all member countries and in place no later than December 30, 2003. It will have four levels: 0%, 5%, 10% and 20%.
- Establish a common agricultural policy and definition of macroeconomic convergence.
- Reiterate foreign policy material, and participate as a group in the negotiations of the FTAA (Free Trade Area of the Americas).

## MEDIUM- AND LONG-TERM VISION

The Andean presidents have given priority to political themes. They seek a medium- and long-term vision of the integration process that takes into account the realities and characteristics of the present world.

This position is all the more important if you take into account that contemporary international politics are essentially characterized by globalization. This is a long-term process that develops in different ways in the different societies. Globalization generates commercial and investment opportunities, cultural change, the possibility of using technological development and greater human contact. It also generates risks and ambiguities, not just order, stability and certainty.

To understand the nature of these difficulties and their possible solutions, the causes of globalization have to be taken into account. To do so, let us examine the changes happening in the world. The former industrial economy has evolved into a digital economy, based on knowledge in a society of information. This development has brought new problems and challenges.

There will be even greater changes when the human genome is deciphered. With this, the development of biotechnology will take place in the next few years. It is well known that when societies change their paradigms, those best prepared obtain advantages most quickly. In these circumstances, societies with a strong social and economic structure can advance on the road toward a creative and long-lasting insertion in the world economy.

The Andean Community has to simultaneously confront and resolve two great challenges. Not only must it advance on the road to social cohesion and growth but it must also dynamically incorporate into the new knowledge-based economy. When passing from an industrial economy to a digital one, it is easy to stay within the principles of open regionalism.

However, Colombia must be more efficient and competitive to prevent the gap that separates it from the developed countries from widening.[5] It is important to take into account that there is a horizon of opportunities in the new economy. Everything is new and great skills are required. This is why the Andean Community needs to find its course and have the capacity to confront successfully the challenges that the twenty-first century brings; it has to take priority actions internally as well as externally.

Externally, the Community and its member countries should take a series of actions to enter the networked society in a competitive and connective way, seeking closer relations among themselves, focusing primarily on infrastructure.

The possibilities for the creation of a Common Market and of maintaining an open model of integration as a step in the globalization process and the formation of the Free Trade Area of the Americas (FTAA) depends on Colombia being able to carry out concrete actions in these areas.

Externally, the Andean Community must advance in the coming years, until 2005, through four important negotiations of great significance for its member countries:

- Development of a free trade area between the Andean Community and Mercosur, for which negotiations ended in January 2002.
- Participation in a new round of multilateral trade negotiations, which were launched in November 2001 in Doha (Qatar) by the World Trade Organization (WTO).
- The defining of a possible Association Agreement with the European Union at the Summit between the European Union and Latin America and the Caribbean, which was scheduled for May 17 and 18, 2002, in Madrid.
- The creation of the Free Trade Area of the Americas (FTAA), which shall become effective by December 2005.

While the first three negotiations involve traditional negotiations between trade partners, in which each of the countries maintain their individuality and autonomy, the negotiations for the development of the FTAA may imply the partial absorption of the Andean Community by the latter. In these circumstances a negotiation strategy must be established which involves the following assumptions and negotiation lines.

---

[5]Manuel Jose Cardenas. Present and Future of the Andean Integration in the Latin American and global context with views towards the twenty-first century. Intervention in representation of the Andean countries in the Extraordinary Reunion of ALADI Committee of the Representatives to celebrate the thirtieth anniversary of the signing of the Cartagena Agreement. Montevideo. May 19, 1999.

## ASSUMPTIONS

The Free Trade Area of the Americas (FTAA) represents opportunities as well as risks—opportunities because of the dimensions of the market, number of inhabitants, gross domestic product and trade dynamics; and risks because of the large differences between the stages of development of the 34 countries that form it, particularly because of the presence of the United States and Canada.

For the countries forming the Andean Community, the FTAA is nowadays the number one destination for their exports and the main source of their imports. The FTAA is also an important source of foreign investment.

## NEGOTIATION LINES

The strategy must be founded on three fundamental pillars: (1) Strengthening of the production and service sectors in order to make them more competitive within an economy based on innovation, knowledge and technology; (2) defining, with the participation of the private sector, a national negotiating position that allows the identification of opportunities not just for existing production, but for new sectors as well; and (3) achieving an adequate coordination within the Andean Community.

In relation to the first strategy, the modernization process of the production and service sectors is obviously not easy. It requires a growth process and demands the allocation of considerable financial and human resources. A medium- and short-term program has to be designed to generate competitive sectors capable of getting the maximum benefit from an opening market just as soon as the FTAA liberalization process begins in the year 2005.

In relation to the second strategy, the participation of the private sector and of the society itself is crucial, requiring the adoption of new mechanisms.

In relation to the third strategy, if the presidents agree that the countries of the Andean Community should act together with a common voice in the FTAA negotiations, the coordination should not be done only at a technical level by the representatives of the Andean Community in the different negotiating groups. Instead, a clearly defined political orientation is required by the Commission in order to give coherence to the negotiation and to establish priorities in the different subjects they manage.

Even though it's true that the Andean Community must not just negotiate to maintain its status quo, a thorough examination of the trade trends that are worth preserving is necessary. This examination should highlight the implications of the subregional preservation agreement clause and the aspects related to a forum created to resolve trade disputes, which would take shape as the substantial negotiations of the FTAA agreement advance.

One of the immediate aspects of the establishment of mechanisms is the definition of terms and rules limiting the FTAA, such as the special and differentiated treatment of the member countries. Negotiations on market access, services, governmental purchases and investments are fundamental.

To conclude, it is important to emphasize that in the past presidential elections the Colombian people ratified their democratic will in choosing Alvaro Uribe with 53 percent of the votes. Uribe has received a clear term of office to re-establish the peace, reaffirming authority and guaranteeing democratic security with respect for human rights and international humanitarian law, and likewise to advance in its economic and social process, and fully insert the country in the international community.

One has to keep in mind that the solution to the armed conflict and drug trafficking is linked to the economic outcome, which does not depend only on internal measures but on a favorable international environment. Due to this Colombia needs to intensify its commerce with its neighboring countries and strengthen the integration agreements, which will permit the adoption of joint positions in the negotiations of the peace process, especially with the United States, to pinpoint the Free Trade Area of the Americas. Colombia must also insist on deepening its relationships with Europe, somewhat abandoned in recent times, and with the Pacific Basin countries, having overcome the effects of the past decade's crisis.

## BIBLIOGRAPHY

Banco de la Repúlica www.banrep.gov.co Información económica. (2001)

Banco de la Repúlica www.banrep.gov.co Acuerdo de Colombia con el Fondo Monetario sobre Facilidades

COINVERTIR (www.coinvertir.org) Colombia: Outlook and Investment Potential. Coinvertir. Bogotá. 2001

COINVERTIR (www.coinvertir.org) Economic information: Talking points on Economy. Coinvertir 2001

Departamento Nacional de Planeación, www.dnp.gov.co, Plan de Desarrollo para Construir la Paz (1998–2002)

# CHAPTER 7
# ECUADOR

DR. LUIS VALENCIA RODRIGUEZ

## INTRODUCTION

The Republic of Ecuador is situated in the northwestern part of South America, bordering the Pacific Ocean to the west, Colombia to the north and Peru to the east and south. The coordinates are 1 latitude north and 5 latitude south and 75th meridian west. Its total area is 256,370 square kilometers. Its total land boundaries are 2,010 kilometers, with the following borders: Colombia, 590 kilometers; Peru, 1,420 kilometers; and the coastline, 2,237 kilometers.

The present main concern of the government and people of Ecuador relates to the economic situation, which in recent years has suffered several setbacks. Ecuador's economy traditionally has been based on the export of agricultural products, mainly cocoa, coffee and bananas, with little or no aggregated value, until the discovery of petroleum in the eastern part of the country during the 1970s. The economy tends now to be diversified, relying on the export of petroleum but extending to other primary and nontraditional products. In June 2001, a National Plan for Exports 2001–2010 was adopted with the purpose of promoting and increasing new exports, taking into account the impact of dollarization on the economic and social conditions of the country. It is now possible to see some improvements in these areas.

## THE LAND AND THE PEOPLE

The country is divided into three continental regions—the Costa, Sierra and Oriente—and one insular region—the Galapagos Islands. Costa, located between the Pacific Ocean and the Andes mountains, consists of coastal lowlands and small mountains. Sierra is composed of two major chains of the Andes mountains—Cordillera Occidental (Western Chain) and Cordillera Oriental (Eastern Chain)—and intermountain basins or plateaus between the two chains. Cordillera Occidental contains Ecuador's highest peak, Mount Chimborazo (6,310 meters). Oriente (eastern region) consists of Andean piedmont, eastern lowlands and flat to rolling tropical jungle. The archipelago of the Galapagos is islands of varied sizes located 1,000 kilometers west of the Ecuadorian coast.

Costa's climate is tropical, although variations (between 25° to 31°C) in temperature and rainfall result from proximity to warm and cool ocean currents (e.g., the Humboldt current). Sierra's climate ranges from tropical (in the lowlands and valleys) to freezing, depending on altitude; notable rainfall variations also occur. Tropical climate and abundant rainfall prevail in Oriente (around 25°C). The Galapagos' climate varies from tropical and desert-like at sea level to cool and wet at the highest point.

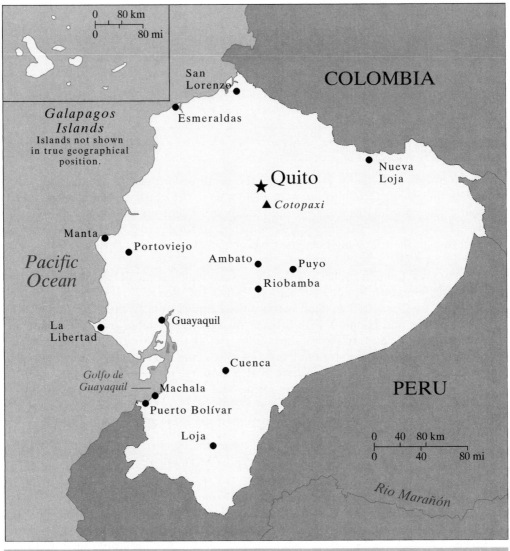

**FIGURE 7-1** Map of Equador

Natural hazards are frequent earthquakes, landslides, volcanic activity and periodic droughts. Current environmental issues are deforestation, soil erosion, desertification and water pollution from oil production wastes.

Ecuador's highways amount to 43,197 kilometers, of which 5,444 are paved and 37,753 unpaved (2001 estimate). Railways (not all of them in use at present) amount to 812 kilometers (single track). Ports and harbors are Guayaquil, Esmeraldas, La Libertad, Manta, Puerto Bolívar and San Lorenzo. There are 182 airports (1999 estimate), of which 57 have paved runways and 125 have unpaved runways.

Administratively, Ecuador is divided into 22 provinces with Quito as the capital of the Republic. Its national holiday is August 10, commemorating the day in 1809 when Quito proclaimed its independence.

The total population of Ecuador (provisional data of the national census, November 25, 2001) is 12,090,804; population per square kilometer is 47.16. The population growth rate is 2 percent (2001 estimate). Life expectancy is 70.8 years. The infant mortality rate is 34.08 per 1,000 births (2001 estimate). The GNP per capita is US$1,310 and GDP is US$37.2 billion (2000 estimate).

Ecuador's population is ethnically mixed. The largest groups are indigenous, around 25 percent, and mestizos or *cholos* (persons of mixed Spanish and Indian ancestry), 55 percent. Caucasian and others represent 10 percent of the population, and African comprises 10 percent. Although Ecuadorians were heavily concentrated in the mountainous central highland region a few decades ago, today's population is divided about equally between that area and the coastal lowlands. Migration toward cities—particularly larger cities—in all regions has increased the urban population to about 55 percent. The tropical forest region to the east of the mountains remains sparsely populated and contains only about 3 percent of the population. Quito has about 1.5 million inhabitants and Guayaquil, the main port, about 2 million. The workforce is 4.8 million, of which agriculture represents 42 percent; trade, 20 percent; services, 19 percent; manufacturing, 11 percent; and other, 8 percent. The main industries are petroleum, food processing, textiles, metalwork, paper products, wood products, chemicals, plastics, fishing and lumber. The industrial production growth rate is 2.4 percent (1997 estimate).

The predominant religion is Roman Catholic (95 percent), but religious freedom is recognized and other religions are practiced peacefully. Spanish is the official language, but indigenous languages are recognized, especially Quichua, Shuar and others.

The 1998 Constitution states that social policy should be directed primarily toward the poor in order to reduce the high percentage of Ecuadorians in poverty and to correct growing social inequalities derived, for example, from the fact that the poor have access to public education of low quality, while the rich can attend private institutions that offer better services. The public education system is tuition-free, and attendance is mandatory from ages 6 to 14. In practice, however, many children drop out before age 15, and in rural areas only about one-third complete sixth grade.

The government is striving to create better programs for the rural and urban poor, especially in technical and occupational training. In recent years, it also has been successful in reducing illiteracy (literacy now runs at 85.8 percent). Enrollment in primary school has been increasing at an annual rate of 4.4 percent—faster than the population growth rate. According to the 1998 Constitution, the central government must allocate at least 30 percent of its revenue to education. In practice, however, due to budgetary constraints, it allots a much smaller percentage. Public universities have an open admission policy. In recent years, however, large increases in the student population, budget difficulties and extreme politicization of the university system have led to a decline in academic standards.

## THE SOCIETY AND ITS ENVIRONMENT

Spanish social structures and values took hold most completely in the sixteenth century in the Sierra. Not coincidentally, the Sierra was also the Ecuadorian region where the conquerors of the Inca had been most successful fifty years earlier. Spanish officials adapted the prevailing Inca hierarchical social system and established a tripartite, semifeudal structure consisting of small numbers of white elites (both *peninsulares,*

Spanish-born persons residing in the New World, and *criollos,* persons of pure Spanish descent born in the New World), a somewhat larger group of mestizo artisans and a large Indian underclass. Since Ecuador lacked the mineral riches found in other Spanish colonies, such as Peru and Mexico, land became the critical commodity. Through the *encomienda* system, elites received tracts of Sierra land along with the right to extract labor from Indians living on that land. Colonists also adapted the Inca concept of obligatory public service (*mita*) and required Indians to toil in textile sweat-shops scattered through the highlands. Debts incurred through the Spanish *mita* often transformed what was supposed to be a transitory labor obligation into a peonage system passed across generations.

The Sierra, the region of earliest European settlement, was ruled for most of its history by a narrow rural oligarchy whose power base lay in the sizeable haciendas they controlled. The haciendas dominated both social and economic relations. Most of the population depended to a greater or lesser extent on the largess of the white elite who controlled the land. This elite ruled virtually without challenge until the mid-twentieth century. Between this white elite and the mass of Sierra Indians were the mestizos or *cholos*. In values and identity, they were closer to the dominant whites. The Sierra Indians, who stood at the bottom of the social pyramid, had limited opportunities for economic security or social advancement. Both mestizos and whites regarded Indians as immutably inferior. The latter's only hope for improvement lay in assimilating the norms and values of the dominant ethnic groups, thereby changing ethnic affiliation.

Like the hacendados of the Sierra, the elite of the Costa (coastal region) also had their roots in agriculture and the control of land, but their attention focused primarily on export crop production and commerce. Ethnically more diverse than the Hispanic elite of the Sierra, the Costa upper class included successful immigrant families drawn over the years by the region's expanding economy. Most of Ecuador's blacks, the descendants of the small numbers of African slaves who came to work on the region's plantations, were also *costeños* (residents of the Costa).

The successful struggle for independence in the 1820s resulted in the transfer of power from *peninsulares* to *criollos*. It did little, however, to change other aspects of the social system, which by then had become dominated by haciendas with a resident Indian labor force. These residents, known as *huasipungueros,* typically worked the hacienda fields for four days per week in exchange for the right to own a small plot of land (*minifundio*). The *huasipungo* system survived in isolated pockets of the Sierra until finally being abolished by the 1964 Agrarian Reform Law. This law and a successor measure in 1973, however, did not affect the basic distribution of landownership, which remained highly inequitable.

The twentieth century saw the rise of an Ecuadorian middle class whose interests were genuinely distinct from the narrowly-based rural oligarchy, and the demise of the self-contained, autonomous hacienda. Changes in the hacienda economy created a mobile, rural-based labor force, and by the end of the 1980s, society consisted of a small, privileged elite; a more numerous, diverse and politically active middle class; and the mass of impoverished small-scale peasants, artisans and wage earners. The middle class transformed Ecuadorian politics.

Like many other Latin American nations, Ecuador had enacted agrarian reform legislation in the 1960s and 1970s. These laws brought little substantive improvement in the lives of most peasants. In the early 1980s, only 5 percent of all farms exceeded fifty hectares, yet these same farms represented over 55 percent of land under cultivation. By contrast, 80 percent of all farms encompassed fewer than ten hectares and accounted for only 15 percent of farmland.

This situation afforded Costa and Sierra landlords an impetus and an opportunity to replace their resident and permanent laborers with temporary workers. In the Sierra this trend, coupled with increased population pressure on land, continued a pattern of migration to the Costa and the Oriente that had begun in the 1950s. The volume of rural-urban migration grew in both the Costa and Sierra until, in the early 1980s, nearly half of all Ecuadorians lived in cities.

Profound regional, ethnic and social divisions continued to characterize Ecuadorian society in recent history. The country's three main geographic regions, differing in their histories and economies, provided one of these divisions, and there were also ethnic and social cleavages within the regions.

The Oriente traditionally was a neglected backwater, isolated geographically and culturally from the rest of the nation. Its population was limited to dispersed groups of indigenous tropical forest Indians who lived by slash-and-burn agriculture or by hunting and gathering. European intrusion was limited to the occasional missionary or trader. Beginning in the 1960s, however, the Oriente experienced colonization by land-poor peasants from the Sierra and exploration by oil companies. Both colonization and exploration had a devastating impact on the indigenous population.

## COMBATING CORRUPTION

Corruption, in addition to causing serious moral harm, constitutes an obstacle to the progress of Ecuador. It increases the cost of goods purchased and of public works, drives away investment, weighs negatively on the national budget and causes serious damages to the national economy. Some first signs of corruption, public and private, were present with the discovery of petroleum and the following increasing indebtedness.

These considerations led to the inclusion of severe provisions in the constitutional text in order to prevent, fight and punish corrupt acts. Some worth mentioning are that incompatibilities are established between economic interests and the performance of public functions, and authorities (including police and the military) are required to present sworn declarations of their material possessions before taking public posts and upon concluding their functions. Furthermore, the Constitution has established a Commission for Control of Corruption, autonomous and politically and economically independent, which receives information and complaints about illicit acts committed by State institutions or officials. The Commission is in charge of investigating these situations and, if they are founded, it submits them to the decision of the Courts. There are many cases under the consideration of the judiciary, among them some involving high-ranking officials. The Supreme Court has already pronounced some sentences on these matters.

## A BRIEF HISTORY

Advanced indigenous cultures flourished in Ecuador long before the area was conquered by the Inca Empire in the fifteenth century. The most ancient artifacts—remnants of the Valdivia culture found in the coastal region—date from as early as 3500 B.C. Other archaeological sites in the Sierra date from 2,000 years ago. Pre-Columbian Ecuador is reflected in the persistence of native languages, customs and economic activities among a considerable, though diminishing, number of communities in the Sierra and the Oriente. The Inca expansion met with fierce resistance by several Ecuadorian tribes. The influence of these conquerors based in Cuzco (modern-day Peru) was limited to about a half century, less in some parts of Ecuador. The invading Incas recognized the technological advancement of the people they were conquering and many Cañaris (one of the ancient populations of southern Ecuador) were taken to the Inca center of Cuzco with the goal of producing what we might today call "technological transfer."

In 1534, the Spanish arrived and defeated the Inca armies, and Spanish colonists became the new elite. The indigenous population was decimated by the Spanish forces and by disease in the first decades of the new rule—a time when the natives also were forced into the *encomienda*, the labor system for the Spanish landlords. In 1563, Quito became the seat of a royal *audiencia* (administrative district) of Spain. The legacy of three centuries of Spanish colonial rule is also pervasive and includes a social inequality that largely coincides with race, rural land tenure patterns and the nation's dominant European cultural expressions.

After independence forces defeated the royalist army in 1822, Ecuador joined Simón Bolívar's Republic of Gran Colombia, only to become a separate republic in 1830. Independence did little, however, to change other aspects of the social system, which by then had become dominated by haciendas with a resident Indian labor force (*huasinpungueros*). The nineteenth century was marked by instability, with a rapid succession of rulers. The conservative Gabriel Garcia Moreno unified the country in the 1860s with the support of the Catholic Church and with the fierce imposition of his will in all the domains of the public and even private life of Ecuadorians. In the late 1800s, world demand for cocoa tied the economy to commodity exports and led to migrations from the highland to the agricultural frontier on the coast.

A coastal-based liberal revolution in 1895 under Eloy Alfaro reduced the power of the clergy and opened the way for capitalist development. The removal of the religious issue did little to alter regional tensions. The end of the cocoa boom produced renewed political instability and a military coup in 1925, which resulted in important reforms in the political and social life. The 1930s and 1940s were marked by populist politicians such as five-time president Jose M. Velasco Ibarra. In January 1942, Ecuador signed the Rio Protocol to end a brief war with Peru begun the year before. Ecuador agreed to a border that conceded to Peru much territory Ecuador previously had claimed in the Amazon. After Word War II, a recovery in the market for agricultural commodities and the growth of the banana industry helped restore prosperity and political peace. From 1948–1960, three presidents—beginning with Galo Plaza—were freely elected and completed their terms.

Recession and popular unrest led to a return to populist and domestic military interventions in the 1960s, while foreign companies developed oil resources in the Ecuadorian Amazon. In 1972, a nationalist military regime seized power and used the new oil wealth and foreign borrowing to pay for a program of industrialization, land reform and subsidies for urban consumers. With the oil boom fading, Ecuador returned to democracy in 1979, but by 1982 the government faced a chronic economic crisis, including inflation, budget deficits, a falling currency, mounting debt service and uncompetitive industries.

On three occasions in the twentieth century—1925, 1963 and 1972—the military seized direct political control. They tried to carry out espoused socioeconomic reforms. The last period of military rule—1972 to 1979—was both the most ambitious and disappointing of the three. Although one of the motivations for intervention was to prevent civilian politicians from dissipating the new-found petroleum wealth, the military's principal legacy was that of ever-increasing foreign debt obligations.

In 1984 the presidential election was narrowly won by Leon Febres-Cordero of the Social Christian Party (PSC). During the first years of his administration, Febres-Cordero introduced free-market economic policies and took strong stands against drug trafficking and terrorism. His disdain for the give and take of the democratic process led to bitter wrangling with other branches of government and his own brief kidnapping of elements of the military. A devastating earthquake in March 1987 interrupted oil exports and worsened the country's economic problems.

Rodrigo Borja of the Democratic Left (ID) party won the presidency in 1988. His government was committed to improving human rights protection and carried out some reforms, notably an opening of Ecuador to foreign trade. The Borja government concluded an accord leading to the disbanding of the small revolutionary group "Alfaro Lives," whose declared objectives were to promote better living conditions to the impoverished masses. However, continuing economic problems undermined the popularity of the ID, and opposition parties gained control of Congress in 1990.

In 1992, Sixto Duran-Ballen, a rightist politician, won in his third run for the presidency. His government's popularity suffered from tough macroeconomic measures, but it succeeded in pushing a limited number of modernization initiatives through Congress. A war with Peru erupted in January–February 1995 in a small region where the boundary prescribed by the 1942 Rio Protocol was in dispute.

Abdala Bucaram, a populist politician from the Guayaquil-based Ecuadorian Roldosista Party (PRE), won the presidency in 1996 on a platform that promised populist economic and social reforms and the breaking of what Bucaram termed the power of the nation's oligarchy.

During his short term of office, Bucaram's administration drew criticism for corruption. Bucaram was deposed by the Congress in February 1997 on grounds of alleged mental incompetence. In his place, Congress named interim President Fabian Alarcon, who had been President of Congress and head of the small Radical Alfarist Front party. Alarcon's interim presidency was endorsed by a May 1997 popular referendum.

On August 10, 1998, Jamil Mahuad of the Popular Democrat Party (center-left) took office as president. He won the election by a narrow margin. On the same day, Ecuador's new constitution came into effect.

Mahuad concluded a general peace agreement with Peru in October 1998, but increasing economic, fiscal and financial difficulties drove his popularity steadily lower. This situation deteriorated continuously. To avoid a banking collapse, large amounts of public funds were transferred to certain private banks as an emergency measure with no positive results. President Mahuad then resorted to an unpopular measure for trying to stop the transfer of funds abroad: freezing banking deposits for one year, which was later prolonged to three years. The president's popularity and image were worsened when it was disclosed that one of the banks in crisis had given an important sum of money to the presidential electoral campaign.

On January 21, 2000, during demonstrations in Quito by indigenous groups, the military and police refused to enforce public order. Demonstrators entered the National Assembly building and declared a three-person junta in charge of the country. During a night of confusion and negotiations President Mahuad was obliged to flee the presidential palace for his own safety. Vice President Gustavo Noboa took charge. Congress met in emergency session in Guayaquil on January 22 and ratified Noboa as president of the Republic in constitutional succession to Mahuad. The new administration was scheduled to complete the remainder of Mahuad's term, due to expire on January 15, 2003.

## GOVERNMENT

As a consequence of the constant political instability, Ecuador has had nineteen constitutions since the establishment of the Republic in 1830 until the present date.

A Constitutional Assembly gathered at the beginning of 1998 to create a new constitution. The two major objectives that guided the work of the Assembly were (1) a political reform aimed at resolving the governance problems of the democratic system, and (2) an economic reform directed toward the creation of institutions capable of responding to a new international environment and to the needs of national development.

Ecuador is a democratic and unitary state with a republican, presidential, elective, responsible and representative government. The constitution provides for concurrent four-year terms of office for the president, vice president and members of Congress. Presidents may be re-elected after an intervening term, while legislators may be re-elected immediately. Suffrage is universal and obligatory for literate citizens 18–65 years of age and optional for other eligible voters; active duty military personnel may not vote.

The principle of "legislative co-participation" allows the president to share in the development of laws as well as in their execution and application. The executive branch includes fifteen ministries. Provincial governors and councilors, like mayors and aldermen and parish boards, are directly elected. Every two years, legislators are elected from the majority parties. The Unicameral National Congress (123 seats; 20 members are popularly elected at-large nationally, 103 members are elected by province) meets throughout the year, except for recess in July and December. Justices of the Supreme Court are appointed by the Congress for indefinite terms. The Constitution prescribes the independence of the Judiciary and prohibits any other function of the State to interfere in the exercise of judicial tribunals and judges.

## POLITICAL CONDITIONS

Ecuador's political parties have historically been small, loose organizations that depended more on populist, often charismatic, leaders to retain support than on programs or ideology. Frequent internal splits have produced extreme factionalism. Persistent regional rivalries between Quito and Guayaquil (Sierra and Costa) also contributed to contentious political debates. However, a pattern has emerged in which administrations from the center-left alternate with those from the center-right.

Although Ecuador's political elite is highly factionalized along regional, ideological and personal lines, a strong desire for consensus on major issues often leads to compromise. Opposition forces in Congress are loosely organized, but historically they often unite to block the administration's initiatives and to remove cabinet ministers.

Constitutional changes enacted by a specially elected National Constitutional Assembly in 1998 took effect on August 10, 1998. The new constitution strengthens the executive branch by eliminating mid-term congressional elections and by circumscribing Congress's power to challenge cabinet ministers. Party discipline is traditionally weak, and many deputies routinely switch allegiance during each Congress. However, after the new constitution took effect, Congress passed a code of ethics that imposes penalties on members who defy their party leadership on key votes.

Beginning with the 1996 election, the indigenous population abandoned its traditional policy of shunning the official political system and participated actively. The indigenous population has established itself as a significant force in Ecuadorian politics, as shown by the selection of indigenous representatives in Congress. One who led the indigenous political party, Pachakutic, was second vice president of the 1988 Congress. The present minister for social welfare and several mayors also belong to the indigenous population.

Perhaps the most consistent element of Ecuador's republican history has been its political instability. In just over 170 years, there have been no fewer than 88 changes of government, making for an average of 1.95 years in power for each regime. The long periods of civilian constitutional rule were from 1912 to 1925, from 1948 to 1961, and the longest, from 1979 to 1997.

## FOREIGN RELATIONS

Ecuador always has placed great emphasis on multilateral approaches to international problems. Ecuador is a charter member of the United Nations (and most of its specialized agencies) and the Organization of American States and also is a member of the Nonaligned Movement, the Group of 77 and many regional groups, including the Rio Group, the Latin American Economic System, the Latin American Energy Organization, the Latin American Integration Association and the Andean Pact.

Ecuador's border dispute with Peru, festering since the independence era, has been the nation's principal foreign policy issue. For more than fifty years, Ecuador maintained that the 1942 Rio Protocol of Peace, Friendship and Boundaries left several issues unresolved. For example, it asserted that geographical features in the area of the Cenepa River valley did not match topographical descriptions in the Protocol, thus making demarcation of the boundary there "in-executable."

The long-running border dispute occasionally erupted into armed hostilities along the undemarcated sections. For example, on January 28, 1981, a serious incident broke out in the Condor Mountain range, which runs along the border between the Amazon Basin and Ecuador. However, the most serious conflict since the 1941 war occurred in January–February 1995, when thousands of soldiers from both sides fought an intense but localized war in the disputed territory in the upper Cenepa valley.

A peace agreement brokered by the four guarantors of the Rio Protocol (Argentina, Brazil, Chile and the United States) in February 1995 led to the cessation of hostilities and the establishment of the Military Observers Mission to Ecuador-Peru (MOMEP) to monitor the zone. In 1996, Ecuador and Peru began a series of meetings intended to set the stage for substantive negotiations to resolve the dispute.

Those talks were successful. In January 1988, Ecuador and Peru initiated a historic agreement in Brasilia, Brazil, which provided a framework to resolve the major outstanding issues between the two countries through four commissions. The commissions were to prepare a Treaty of Trade and Navigation and a Comprehensive Agreement on Border Integration, to set the common land boundary and to establish a Binational Commission on Mutual Confidence Measures and Security. The commissions began work in February 1988, with the intention of reaching a definitive agreement by May 30, 1998.

The commissions on border integration and mutual confidence measures successfully concluded their work, and the commission working on a treaty for trade and navigation produced a draft treaty text, but the commission on border demarcation failed to produce an agreement by the May 30, 1998, deadline. A flare-up in military tensions in the disputed region in August 1998 led to the creation of a temporary second MOMEP-patrolled demilitarized zone just south of the first demilitarized zone.

Presidents Mahuad (Ecuador) and Fujimori (Peru) established direct communication by meetings and phone calls in an effort to overcome the two countries' remaining differences. In October 1998, after asking for and receiving a boundary determination from the guarantors, the two presidents reached agreement. On October 26, 1998, at a ceremony in Brasilia, the presidents of Ecuador and Peru and their foreign ministers signed a comprehensive settlement.

According to this agreement, Peru recognized as Ecuadorian two sites at the far limits of the Amazon River where centers to facilitate Ecuadorian navigation and trade were to be established. Peru also ceded to Ecuador, as a private property, a parcel of land of one square kilometer in the Cenepa Valley known as "Tiwinza."

## CONTROL OF ILLEGAL DRUGS AND RELATED OFFENSES

Ecuador shares the international concern over increasing drug trafficking. Ecuador is not a drug producer but is a significant transit country for cocaine and derivatives of coca originating in Colombia and Peru. There is increasing activity on the northern frontier of Ecuador by trafficking groups and Colombian insurgents. The government has maintained Ecuador virtually free of coca production since the mid-1980s and is working to combat money laundering and the transshipment of drugs and chemicals essential to the processing of cocaine. In this context, Ecuador is fully cooperating with international organizations and other countries to combat drug trafficking.

According to the National Plan 1999–2003, the number of persons detained on the grounds of drugs trafficking and the amounts of drugs captured have increased. Cocaine seized in 1994 was 1,789 kg, and in 1998 was 3,854 kg. Money seized in relations with these operations in 1994 was US$31,659 and in 1998 was US$272,767.

The objective of the Plan is to maintain an ongoing control to avoid the country becoming a drug producer, to strengthen the mechanisms of control and dismantling of drug traffic organizations and to implement a strategy of border controls. However, as a result of the implementation of the Colombia Plan, the northern Ecuadorian frontier is a vulnerable territory where Colombian traffickers have found refuge and assistance. This section of the Ecuadorian territory is economically depressed.

As a member of the Andean Community, Ecuador is a party to Decision 505 of the Andean Cooperation Plan for the Control of Illegal Drugs. There are three main chapters of the Program of Action adopted by that Decision: (1) reinforcement of national strategies, (2) reinforcement of bi-national strategies, and (3) community strategy.

Ecuador and the United States agreed in 1999 to a 10-year arrangement whereby U.S. military surveillance aircraft could use the airbase at Manta, Ecuador, as a location to detect drug trafficking flights through the region.

In March 2002, during the meeting held in Lima, Peru, between members of the Andean Pact and U.S. President Bush, Ecuador insisted that the drug-consuming countries had to adopt strict measures aimed at the control, distribution and consumption of drugs. In the same meeting, Ecuador called attention to the urgency of renovation and expansion of the Andean Trade Preferences Act, considered to be an efficient mechanism to help combat drug trafficking. According to press information, President Bush in April 2002 requested that the Senate extend the application of this Act.

## COMBATING TERRORISM

Ecuador has always taken measures to combat terrorism both internally and internationally and has energetically condemned terrorist activities, whether directed against government officials or private citizens. Ecuador is a party to most of the international conventions on these matters.

As a consequence of the terrorist attacks of September 11, Ecuador has reinforced measures in the administrative, police and military spheres to control any vestiges of terrorist activities, especially at its land, maritime and aerial frontiers. It has increased its cooperation with other governments and international organizations (in particular the UN Security Council and the Organization of American States) to exchange information to combat terrorism or prepare new instruments for that purpose. Ecuador has established a permanent inter-institutional working group in charge of monitoring the application of these measures and suggesting new actions.

## ECONOMY

The Ecuadorian economy is based on petroleum production and export of bananas, shrimp, coffee, cocoa, cut flowers, fish commodities and other primary agricultural products. Exports of petroleum from 1970 to the present represent 46 percent of total exports.

Substantial economic growth occurred in the 1970s following the discovery of new petroleum fields in Oriente and international price increases for petroleum. Increased external debt, lower petroleum prices, devastation from floods and earthquakes and economic mismanagement combined to produce serious economic problems during the 1980s. GDP declined by 5.2 percent in 1987, increased by 8 percent in 1988 and grew by only 1 percent in 1989.

Exports are worth US$4.59 billion (f.o.b., 2001). Imports are worth US$4.98 billion (f.o.b., 2001). Export partners (in millions US$, 2000) are United States, 653; Colombia,

259; Italy, 160; Germany, 123; Russia, 120; Venezuela, 100; Japan, 94; Argentina, 84; Netherlands, 82; Chile, 75; and others, 630. Import partners (in millions US$, Jan–Nov. 2000) are United States, 797.7; Andean Community, 770.8; Latin America Association, 1,255.3; Central America Common Market, 13.6; other American countries, 182.9; Europe, 477.1; Asia, 329.9; and Africa, 41.5. Other important suppliers of imports are Germany and Brazil. External debt is US$15.3 billion (1999).

Fluctuations in world market prices can have a substantial domestic impact. Industry is largely oriented to servicing the domestic market. Deteriorating economic performance in 1997–1998 culminated in a severe economic and financial crisis in 1999. The crisis was precipitated by a number of external shocks, including the El Niño weather phenomenon in 1997, a sharp drop in global oil prices in 1997–1998 and international emerging market instability in those years. The beginning of 1999 saw the banking sector collapse, which precipitated an unprecedented default on external loans later that year.

These factors highlighted the government of Ecuador's unsustainable economic policy mix of large fiscal deficits and expansionary money policy and resulted in a 7.3 percent contraction of GDP, annual year-on-year inflation of 52.2 percent and 65 percent devaluation of the national currency in 1999. With the purpose of coping with this situation, the government ordered the freezing of all banking deposits. Many banks were closed.

On January 9, 2000, the administration of President Jamil Mahuad announced its intention to adopt the U.S. dollar as the official currency of Ecuador to address the ongoing economic crisis. Subsequent protest led to the removal of Mahuad from office and the elevation of Vice President Gustavo Noboa to the presidency.

The Noboa government confirmed its commitment to dollarize as the centerpiece of its economic recovery strategy. On March 20, 2000, the Central Bank of Ecuador started to exchange sucres—the recognized and traditional Ecuadorian currency—for U.S. dollars at a fixed rate of 25,000 sucres per U.S. dollar; since April 30, 2000, all transactions are denominated in U.S. dollars. The government also entered into negotiations with the International Monetary Fund (IMF), culminating in the negotiation of a 12-month stand-by arrangement with the Fund.

Additional policy initiatives include efforts to reduce the government's fiscal deficit, implement structural reforms to strengthen the banking system and regain access to private capital markets. Buoyed by high oil prices, the Ecuadorian economy experienced a modest recovery in 2000, with GDP rising 1.9 percent. However, 70 percent of the population lives below the poverty line, more than double the rate of five years ago. Inflation in 2000 remained at 95.1 percent, but the rate of inflation continued to fall. By February 2001, monthly inflation was 2.9 percent. With great difficulty, the government has undertaken the task of repaying bank depositors. This situation is aggravated by the heavy burden of the external debt.

One of the main objectives of the government is to promote exports and to attract foreign investment for developing and strengthening productive nontraditional sectors like mining, agro-industry, fishing, tourism and services. Guarantees for foreign investment are contained in the Constitution and the Law on Promotion and Guarantee of Investment.

During 2001, there were some signs of economic recovery. Exports amounted to $4,594,000 and imports to $4,981,000. The inflation rate (consumer prices) was reduced to 22.5 percent. The unemployment rate of 12 percent (November 1998 estimate) was also reduced to 10 percent. Even though the balance of trade fell by 14.2 percent in 2000, it produced a surplus of more than US$1,300 million in 2001.

The Ecuadorian government, in its memorandum of understanding addressed to the International Monetary Fund on May 14, 2001, announced these signs of recovery. It indicated that real GDP was estimated to have increased by 2.5 percent in 2000, and that real growth would be boosted by investment associated with the construction of a new oil pipeline that was begun in March 2001. In the banking sector, total deposits grew at a fairly steady rate, increasing by 25 percent in 2000 and 26 percent (year-on-year) in March 2001. A presidential decree was issued in February 2001 to tighten control over public expenditure. Priority was given to addressing the needs of the poorest segments of the population; this will continue to be one of the main aspects of public expenditure.

## EFFORTS OF INTEGRATION: THE ANDEAN COMMUNITY

Ecuador has been participating in all efforts at regional and subregional integration. Among others, it was a party to the Treaty of Latin American Association for Free Trade (ALALC), Montevideo, 1960; and, later, of the Treaty of Montevideo, 1980, establishing the Latin American Association of Integration (ALADI), which replaced the 1960 treaty. It is also a party to the Treaty of Panama, 1975, establishing the Latin American Economic System (SELA), and to the Treaty of Amazonian Cooperation (Brasilia, 1978). In the subregional sphere, Ecuador is a party to the Agreement of Cartagena (Andean Pact, Bogotá, 1969). It has also participated in and subscribed to the various declarations and other instruments promoting integration, among them the Free Trade Area of the Americas.

The Andean Community supports an integration process with a highly developed institutional framework. Its main purpose is to "promote a balanced and harmonious development" of the States' parties through an "equitable distribution of the benefits derived from integration." The principle of solidarity is based on the preferential treatment for the relatively less developed economies (Bolivia and Ecuador). Founding members are Bolivia, Colombia, Ecuador and Peru. Venezuela joined in 1973 and charter member Chile withdrew in 1976. During its thirty-two years of existence, the Andean Community has had periods of expansion and others of stagnation.

In the present world, in which globalization is unavoidable, systems of open regional integration like the Andean Pact afford an economic and political space for countries to adapt to globalization and emphasize its positive aspects while reducing the negative effects.

In the last decade a considerable expansion of inter-community trade has occurred. In 1997, imports to and exports from Ecuador to the Andean subregion were the equivalent of 8 percent of its GDP and 15 percent of its trade with the rest of the world. This development was the result of the new unilateral openness of the economy. Two community mechanisms began to function: the free trade zone starting in 1992–1993 and, since 1995, the Common External Tariff (applied by Ecuador, Colombia and Venezuela). During the 1969–1998 period, the economy of Ecuador was the most open among all the Andean partners. This liberalization of trade in the subregion has produced a large trade deficit in Ecuador.

The importance of the Andean Community for Ecuador in the year 2000 was reflected in its external trade in the subregional process: 14 percent of its exports and 24 percent of its imports, much higher than the 6 and 7 percent, respectively, in 1992. But the most significant element of this development was that the inter-community exports of Ecuador, which go mainly to Colombia and Venezuela, were principally of manufactured goods with a high aggregate value. In this sense, the core of Ecuadorian exports to the subregion is substantially different from the core of its exports to the rest of the world, where nonrefined products (petroleum, bananas, shrimp, flowers) represent almost 90 percent of the total.

During 2001 (January to October), exports from Ecuador to its Andean Community partners increased. Peru was the main recipient of these exports, which increased by 8 percent to US$281.4 million. This sum exceeded exports to Colombia, which reached US$246.9 million. Imports from Peru were US$83.6 million, or US$24 million more than in 2000, and imports from Venezuela were US$235.5 million. The trade of Ecuador with members of the Andean Pact (exports and imports) during 1999 and 2000, as well 2001 (January to September), produced a negative balance (130.6, 177,02 and 231.4, in thousands of US$, respectively).

Ecuador declared in November 2001 that in the near future it would have to revise its participation in the Andean Pact, not only to correct the negative tendencies in its trade balance with its community partners but also to give more balance to its industry to face the challenges of dollarization. Ecuador maintained that the Common External Tariff (CET) had to be adopted by all members of the Andean Community no later than May 2002. In November 2001, Ecuador announced that it had to consider its possible suspension as a member of the Andean Pact if the members of the group did not put into effect the customs union for the first semester of 2002.

In the Declaration of Santa Cruz de la Sierra (January 30, 2002), the presidents of the five member nations of the Andean Pact established that the agreement to consolidate and improve the subregional free trade zone would be ready no later than June 1, 2002. They also declared that, no later than December 31, 2003, the five countries would apply a Common External Tariff at four levels: 0, 5, 10 and 20 percent.

In the March 2002 meeting held in Lima, Peru, between members of the Andean Pact and the U.S. president, Ecuador expressed its concern about a 38-percent reduction in funds originally allocated to Ecuador within the framework of the Andean Regional Initiative. This reduction also affects the already promised funds by the U.S. government to support the Northern Development Unit (UDENOR), charged with implementing measures aimed at social reactivation of this part of the country, now affected by problems arising from the armed confrontation in Colombia.

The preferential treatment established in favor of Ecuador has been present in all the spheres of the regional integration process, especially in trade (flexibility in the application of the common external tariff) and the financial cooperation through the Andean Development Corporation (ADC) and the Latin American Fund of Reserves (FLAR), institutions that help integrate the Andean Community.

The financing by the ADC has been of special significance for Ecuador (US$800 million in disbursements in 1998–2000), to the point that it is more indebted to the ADC than to the World Bank. At the same line, FLAR approved in October 2001 a credit to Ecuador of US$411 million when the International Monetary Fund(IMF) was opposed to granting it a stand-by credit line for a lesser amount.

## THE FTAA AND ECUADOR

The project of creating a free trade zone from Alaska all the way down to Tierra del Fuego was agreed upon in the Partnership for Development and Prosperity in the Americas, approved by the Summit of the Americas in December 1994 in Miami. The Free Trade Area of the Americas (FTAA) was one of 23 issues dealt with in the Plan of Action of the Partnership. Since then, the creation of the Free Trade Area of the Americas has become a comprehensive process of negotiations. Once established, the FTAA will be the world's largest regional trade area, with more than 800 million inhabitants. It will be the expression of a new cycle of relations in the hemisphere, not limited only to trade, since it aims to go beyond the mere search for new markets and investments.

In order to carry out these complex negotiations, the countries involved decided to establish a coordination system. The coordinating country (the "Chair") monitors the activities of all official FTAA groups and guides all other countries in their efforts to accomplish their mandate. Nine negotiation groups have been established. To provide an adequate Plan of Action as a follow-up, it was decided to hold regular Ministerial Meetings, the first of which took place in Denver in June 1995. As a result, it was agreed to develop a working plan for the initiation of negotiations. It was considered indispensable that the entrepreneurial sector have an active and clear participation in it. The fifth Ministerial Meeting was held in Toronto in November 1999.

The FTAA negotiations are being carried out according to a framework agreed upon through 2004. This framework is flexible, since it assures an ample geographical representation of the participating countries by rotation of the process's Chair, the location of negotiations and the responsibilities of the negotiating groups. The Chair rotates every 18 months or after concluding a Ministerial Meeting.

Ecuador was entrusted with the responsibility of chairing the process between May 1, 2001, and October 31, 2002. This is one of the most significant responsibilities the country has had to assume at the international level. Ecuador participates in this negotiation process jointly with its partners in the Andean Community who, from the very beginning, have maintained a common position. Their efforts are directed toward the opening of their national economies and the achievement of new economic relations, based on international integration and competitiveness.

It was Ecuador's turn to preside over the FTAA at a moment when the negotiation groups had already reached final agreement. The results of these negotiations are obviously also subject to Ecuador's progress in matters of economic stabilization and the creation of an investment friendly climate.

## ECUADOR AND BANANA NEGOTIATIONS

For seven years the European Community (EC) has maintained an import, sale and distribution regime for bananas outside their obligation to the GATT and the WTO, thus illegally discriminating against Ecuador and seriously affecting the trade of its main export commodity. During this time, the GATT and the WTO determined, on seven occasions, that the EC maintains a banana import regime that violates several of GATT's provisions.

Ecuador became a member of the World Trade Organization (WTO) in 1996. During the following four years, Ecuador made significant efforts, insisting that the European Community comply with its obligations and commitments and discontinue discrimination against the banana exports from Ecuador. The Ecuadorian position in the controversy with the European Union has been fundamentally the same: remove access restrictions and promote liberalization of the EC market in order to import the greatest amount of fruit. In this sense, Ecuador has favored a transitory tariff system consistent with the regulations of the WTO, which takes into account the interests of the fruit producers and distributors.

Ecuador sought concessions corresponding to the value of damage it suffered, which has been estimated at $450 million per year. As was foreseeable, the EC questioned this amount and, at a meeting held by the Difference Solution Organization (OSD), resorted to arbitration in order to establish the amount of concessions to be paid. The EC recognized the existence of a prejudice against Ecuador and stated that it would respect the arbitration findings.

On March 17, 2000, the OSD, in an historic sentence, authorized Ecuador to impose sanctions on the European Union for a yearly amount of US$201.6 million in retaliation for the restrictions imposed by the Community on the Ecuadorian banana imports. In this way, Ecuador has become the first developing country to invoke the regulations of the Examination of Difference Solutions (ESD) on the imposition of sanctions.

## THE MIGRATION PROCESS

Reflecting the economic crisis, unemployment in 1999 was at one of the highest levels ever in the country: 15.1 percent. Due to the acute banking crisis, many people lost their jobs. The rate of unemployed men increased from 7 percent in 1997 to 11 percent, while that of unemployed women increased from 13 to 20 percent. In 1999, poverty was 1.6 times higher than in 1995. The number of persons living below the poverty line increased from 34 percent in 1995 to 46 percent in 1998 and to 56 percent in 1999. Extreme poverty also increased; from 1995 to 1999, it increased from 12 to 21 percent. Poverty was more acute in the countryside than in the cities. The coastal region was most affected by this situation: its poverty level increased from 29 percent in 1995 to 56 percent in 1999.

The consequence of this situation was a massive migration of Ecuadorians, either legally or illegally. The United States is undoubtedly the principal country of attraction. It has been estimated that approximately one million Ecuadorians are now residing in the United States, half of them in New York and others in New Jersey, Los Angeles, Chicago, Miami, Houston, San Francisco and Washington, D.C. According to the 2000 U.S. census, 260,559 Ecuadorians are registered in the country. One may conclude that the rest are present under illegal conditions. The countries of Central America are used by migrants as a bridge to reach the "American dream." Most of them have to withstand very difficult conditions before being repatriated. The Ecuadorian government has as one of its purposes the initiating of a process of negotiation with the U.S. government in order to legalize the situation of Ecuadorian migrants in that country.

Migrants, especially those of low educational level, are often victims of traffickers who exploit them not only in Ecuador but also in other transit countries. Ecuadorian migration to Colombia is mostly illegal. In the streets of the main Colombian cities—Bogotá, Medellin and Cali—migrant Ecuadorians, adults and children, are seen asking for work and living from public assistance.

Spain has been a new attraction for Ecuadorians. At present, between 150,000 and 200,000 Ecuadorians reside in that country, especially in Madrid, Murcia and Valencia. The illegal migration to Spain led governments of both countries to conclude an agreement on May 29, 2001, to regularize the Ecuadorian migration movement. As a consequence of this agreement approximately 25,000 Ecuadorians residing illegally in Spain were legalized. The main purpose of the agreement is to select Ecuadorians to work legally in Spain and in this way to regularize the migration movement from Ecuador, so Ecuadorian workers can enjoy the same rights as Spanish workers.

Ecuadorian migration to Italy has also increased. At present, it is estimated that around 80,000 Ecuadorians, mostly illegal, are residing in Italy. The Ecuadorian government is trying to negotiate an agreement to normalize this situation.

To confront the problem created by migration, the Ecuadorian government has established a special administrative organ in the Foreign Ministry in charge of giving advice and assistance to prospective migrants, monitoring the compliance with international agreements on migratory problems and combating the illegal traffic in migrants. The government has initiated the preparation of a National Plan for Ecuadorians Abroad, the main purpose of which is to protect migrants residing abroad and to assist their families in Ecuador.

Conscious of violations of human rights against Ecuadorians abroad, the government has undertaken a process of information on the human rights of migrant people in order that all Ecuadorians are duly informed of their rights in the country and abroad. The Commission on Human Rights of the United Nations adopted a proposal submitted by Ecuador, Resolution 2001/56, on "Protection of Migrants and their Families."

## ECUADOR AND HUMAN RIGHTS

In 1980, the president of Ecuador, Jaime Roldos, proclaimed the doctrine that there is no opposition between the principles of nonintervention and that of defense of human rights, because fundamental rights inherent to the human being are universal values that go beyond national borders. Therefore, actions taken by the international community to assure the protection of those rights are legitimate. This doctrine was later incorporated into the Charter of Riobamba (Ecuador), signed in 1980 by the presidents of the Andean region.

The 1998 Constitution prescribes that the highest duty of the State is to respect and enforce human rights. The State guarantees all inhabitants the free exercise and enjoyment of human rights established in the Constitution, as well as in the declarations, pacts, covenants and other international instruments in force. Those rights and guarantees are directly and immediately applicable by judges, tribunals or other authorities.

The Constitution determines which are the civil and political rights, as well as the economic, social and cultural rights to be protected, and recognizes the collective rights of indigenous, black and Afro-Ecuadorian peoples. Among the guarantees for the respect and exercise of these rights, the Constitution establishes the judicial recourses of habeas corpus, habeas data, protection and ombudsmen.

On June 18, 1998, the government of Ecuador adopted by law the National Human Rights Program, a program that resulted from a consensus among state entities and numerous nongovernmental organizations devoted to the protection and respect of human rights in the country. This program is the only such plan in the region, prepared collectively and by consensus, and recognizes "all human rights contained in international declarations and treaties, in the Constitution and even those being created, processed and regulated by international law or our internal legislation."

The general objective of the Program is to "guarantee and develop actions and services aimed at complying with all economic, social and cultural rights, with special emphasis on socially and economically excluded sectors. Furthermore, the State will work on the establishment of a sustainable, sovereign and participatory development model that ensures work, food, housing, health, education and a pollution-free environment for all."

The Program identifies the principal sectors of Ecuadorian reality demanding particular attention from the State and civil society. It contains 26 operational plans in favor of women, children, family, disadvantaged and vulnerable groups, elderly persons, aliens, indigenous peoples and Afro-Ecuadorians.

According to the Program, the "Ecuadorian State recognizes the jurisdictional exclusivity of the Judiciary and therefore is committed to prevent any interference by the Executive on the judiciary, in order to ensure an effective separation of State powers." A national commission of evaluation and follow-up, with representatives of governmental organizations and the civil society, has been established to monitor the application of the Program, which has been widely diffused among Ecuadorians, in the principal languages spoken in the country.

Ecuador has ratified the main international agreements, either on the sphere of the United Nations or the Inter American system. Ecuadorian citizens have served, most of them in personal capacity, as members of human rights treaty organizations of the United Nations, like the Committee for Human Rights; the Committee on the Elimination of Racial Discrimination; the Committee on Economic, Social and Cultural Rights; the Committee on the Elimination of Discrimination against Women; the Sub-Commission for the Promotion and Protection of Human Rights; as well as, within the regional sphere, the Inter American Commission of Human Rights.

## BIBLIOGRAPHY

Cámara de Comercio de Quito. (2002) *Información Económica Boletín*: 50(Marzo).

Cámara de Comercio de Quito. *www.ccq.org.ec/*.

Comercio Exterior, *www.sica.gov.ec/comext*.

(2000) "Evolución del Proceso de Integración, 1969–1999." *Comunidad Andina* 28 de Enero.

(2002) "Revista Mensual de la Cámara de Comercio de Quito." *Criterios* 44 (Abril).

Diplomacia para el Desarrollo, Ministerio de Relaciones Exteriores # 3. *www.consecuador-quebec.org*

Ecuador. Comportamiento del Comercio Exterior en el año 2000 *www.mmrree.gov.ec*

Embassy of Ecuador, Washington DC. *www.ecuador.org*

Evaluación de la Participación de Ecuador en el Proceso de Integración Andina.

Comunidad Andina, Lima, 15 de diciembre del 2000.

Free trade zone in the Americas. *www.mmrree.gov.ec*

Geographia. Ecuador. *www.geographia.com/ecuador/*

González Suárez, Federico: Historia General de la República del Ecuador (3 vols.) Quito. Casa de la Cultura Ecuatoriana, 1970.

Hurtado, Osvaldo: Political Power in Ecuador (2nd ed) (Trans., NickD. Mills, Jr.) Boulder, Colorado. Westview Press, 1985.

International Monetary Fund. *www.imf.org/external/countryECU/index.hml*

Luis Valencia, R.: "Visión del Ecuador," Imprenta del Ministerio de Relaciones Exteriores, 1982.

Mejía, Leonardo, and others: Ecuador: Pasado y Presente. Quito: Editorial Alberto Crespo Encalada, 1983.

Ministerio de Industrias, Comercio, Integración y Pesca—Ecuador. *www.micip.gov.ec*

Ministerio de Relaciones Exteriores. (2001) *El Fenomeno Migratorio en el Ecuador*. Quito.

_____. (2002) *Ecuador, un País en Imágenes*. Quito.

_____. (2000) *Plan Nacional de Derechos Humanos del Ecuador*. 2d ed. Quito.

Pareja Diezcanseco, A. (1979) *Ecuador: La República, de 1830 a Nuestros Días*. Quito: Editorial Universitaria.

Reyes, O. E. (1978) *Breve Historia General del Ecuador*. 11th ed. Quito.

Salgado Pesantes, H. (1987) *Instituciones Políticas y Constitución del Ecuador*. Quito: Instituto Latinoamericano de Investigaciones Sociales.

Stornaiolo, U. (1989) *Anatomía de un País Latinoamericano: El Ecuador*. Quito: Ediciones Culturales BSM..

U.S. CIA. *www.cia.gov/cia/publications/factbook/geos/ec. html.*

U.S. Department of State. *www.state.gov*.

U.S. Library of Congress. *www.memory.loc.gov*.

Villacrés Moscoso, J. W. (1978) *Historia Diplomática de la República del Ecuador*. Guayaquil: Universidad de Guayaquil.

World Bank. *www.worldbank.org*

# CHAPTER 8
# PERU

FATHER JUAN JULIO WICHT

In Latin America, Peru stands out for its millenary history, its incredibly rich and varied geography, its economic and political evolution during the last fifty years and its future prospects as it begins the twenty-first century. All these aspects make Peru a country that captures the attention of historians and scientists, politicians and businessmen alike.

Over the last twenty years, Peru has lived through a crisis that many analysts consider the worst and most violent in the Western Hemisphere. After the hard adjustment in 1990 came economic recovery, with the highest growth and stability rates on the continent, political breakdown and recent recovery of democracy, and an economy that has reaffirmed itself in a free, competitive market system open to the world.

This chapter will follow the Peruvian people as the thread leading from the past to the present. The people themselves, with their geographic setting and their cultural features, are advancing firmly toward the future, full of challenges and hope. Throughout its history, many ethnic and social groups have coexisted in Peru. Will they be able to integrate in a common effort to achieve and to share their economic development?

## THE PERUVIAN POPULATION

Peru is its people. Everything else—the beautiful scenery; the foreign impacts on the economic, cultural and political situation; and the changes in the country's development models throughout history—can be understood only insofar as they have been carried out and lived by the Peruvian people. At the same time, these cultural and economic influences have changed and affected the people. Such is the case in any country, but much more so in Peru, with its geography and history so full of contrasts, but with a population that gives it continuity, courage and permanence. Although heterogeneous, its population is a crucible of races, conflicts and hopes.

## THE GEOGRAPHICAL SCENE

For more than 4,000 years there have been people living in the present territory of Peru, a vast expanse of 1,285,000 square kilometers (approximately 495,000 square miles), composed of three north-south regions: the Coast, a long, dry strip on the Pacific Ocean; the Sierra, with its imposing Andes range and perpetual snowy peaks; and the extensive wet tropical Amazon jungle, reaching into Colombia, Brazil and Bolivia.

**FIGURE 8-1** Map of Peru

Very few countries in the world have the diversity of geography, climate and natural biological species of Peru.[1] The sea off Peru is relatively cold due to the Humboldt current which comes up from the South Pacific. The Humboldt impedes the necessary condensation to form rain on the coast, despite its proximity to the equator. But it does make the climate on the Peruvian coast very pleasant and provides Peru with a great wealth of fish (placing the country among the first in the world in fishing volume).

---

[1]See "The Environment in Peru, 2001," various authors, published by the Instituto Cuanto and the National Environmental Council (CONAM), Lima, 2002.

The rugged mountain chains in the Sierra have a dry climate, with fertile valleys, large and varied mineral deposits underground (gold, silver, copper, lead, zinc) and great hydroelectric potential. The jungle is flat, hot and very humid. In Peru, the great Maranon and Ucayali rivers converge, and at less than 400 feet above sea level the tremendous Amazon River is born, slowly flowing 1,500 miles across northern Brazil to empty into the Atlantic Ocean. The Peruvian jungle has extraordinary biodiversity and considerable deposits of petroleum and natural gas.

## FROM THE ANCIENT PAST TO 1940

Little is known of their origins, but archaeological remains show that the first Peruvians established themselves on the Coast and in the Sierra valleys, high in the Andes. However, they never managed to penetrate the Amazon jungle very deeply. On the Coast, they developed important civilizations such as those of Moche, Chimu, Nazca and Paracas and produced superb textiles, handicrafts and medicines. They learned how to overcome the arid desert with ingenious irrigation works and to meet the challenge of the high mountain ranges in Chavin and Tiahuanaco, with stone-step walled terraces to grow their crops.

Political and cultural unity came with the Inca Empire in the fourteenth century, which extended from southern Colombia to the north of Argentina, with Cuzco as its capital. Thus, the Sierra was the predominant region when the Spaniards arrived. The natives had not learned to write, had no form of money and did not yet know the wheel (due to absence of draft animals). Nonetheless they were developing an advanced agricultural civilization admirably adapted to the diverse climes and altitudes of their territory.

With Spanish conquest in the sixteenth century and subsequent colonization, new and essential elements of Peruvianism appeared on the scene. Western culture superimposed itself on the native base, as did the Catholic Church, the Spanish language, the raising of cattle and new agricultural products, money and commerce. The center of political and economic power passed from Cuzco to recently founded Lima, on the coast, which was subordinated to Spain in a rigidly stratified society. In addition to agriculture, mining and overseas trade assumed growing importance. To the subject native population, the sixteenth century meant not only destruction of their culture but also a drastic reduction in their numbers which, due to wars, ill-treatment and, above all, epidemics, fell from nearly five million inhabitants to under two million.

The country's later demographic recovery was very slow, as was normal for almost all peoples at that time, with birth and death rates being almost balanced, and both very high. With the moderate flow of immigrants from Spain, and even more moderate ones from African populations, the total population of Peru at the time of independence in 1821 was scarcely two million inhabitants, and Lima with its 100,000 inhabitants was the largest city in all of South America and the center of Spanish power. The Republic opened up the country's doors to immigrants from other places, especially from the south of Europe. But unlike other Latin American countries, such as Brazil and those of the Southern Cone and the Caribbean, the number of Europeans who came to Peru was very small.

To offset the lack of laborers on plantations on the Coast, the country successfully attracted several thousand Chinese and Japanese immigrants. In the first national census of 1876, the population amounted to 2,699,000 inhabitants. It took fifty more years, during Leguia's last government, for the population of Peru to recover the number of inhabitants that Peru had held during the reign of Atahualpa, the last Inca, four centuries before, when Pizarro and his companions arrived.

The population's recovery was slow for four hundred years, due not only to the low number of immigrants from abroad, but also because real economic and social progress was almost nil. Under the Inca, the viceroy or the president, the majority of native Peruvians had a precarious state of health and of life, close to the bare subsistence level. Most of the people lived in Sierra valleys. The 1940 national census gives an image of a rural Peru, backward and poor, in which Lima clearly stands out as the aristocratic capital. Peru was weighed down by its difficult and varied geography, its uneven ethnological and social composition and by its ancient and colonial history.

Life expectancy at birth was only 35.7 years (with notable regional and social class differences). Eight-nine percent of the population failed to complete primary school; 57.5 percent of adults over 15 years old were illiterate. More than one-third of all Peruvians (34 percent) did not speak or understand Spanish. There was an oligarchy of land owners—of old Spanish origin and limited business sense—and some new fortunes in mining, industry and banking, with foreign capital and management panels of recent European immigrants, especially Italians. But the distribution of income throughout the country was uneven and unfair. The Indian, compared to the half-caste and white man, the peasant compared to the city dweller and women compared to men were the most disfavored groups in this poor, heterogeneous and inarticulate Peruvian society.

In the first decades of the twentieth century, two personalities of both Peruvian and Latin American fame arose in the social and political milieu: Jose Carlos Mariategui and Victor Raul Haya de la Torre. The first founded the Communist Party in Peru and the second the American Popular Revolutionary Alliance (APRA), but the conservative forces in the country, backed by the army and the police, repressed any movement toward change. Women and illiterate men were not allowed to vote in the elections. Only a small proportion of the Peruvian people had any real access to democratic participation in the life of the country.

## THE ECONOMIC, SOCIAL AND DEMOGRAPHIC EXPLOSION

From the middle of the 1940s to 1965 the country underwent an extraordinary change in its economic, social and demographic structures. Peru entered fully into what is called "development growth" and managed to almost double the annual growth rate of its national product. The growth was driven by a surge in primary exports (cotton, sugar, iron, copper and fish). During this period Latin American economic growth rates were slightly above the world average, and those of the Peruvian economy, which started at a lower level, were even higher (averaging 6 percent annually).

Abundant foreign exchange and fiscal reserves translated into economic growth indices in electrification, road work, urban infrastructure and creation of industries, while social indices showed an accelerated expansion in education and health services. The national average "standard of living," while still very low, was approaching the modest but increasing Latin American average. At the same time, however, and in the midst of this general progress, the relative internal differences among geographical regions and social classes were even further accentuated.

In these socioeconomic circumstances and during this time period arose the most crucial, although virtually unperceived phenomenon in the history of Peru: the beginning of its demographic explosion. Improvements in roadways, education and health services pushed the annual growth rate of the population to 3 percent in the mid-1960s. The demographic structure changed, expanding the base of the pyramid (infant mortality diminished, while a high birthrate was maintained). An internal demographic drive was created that immediately began to manifest itself in absolute annual growth increases,[2] catapulting the total numbers of the 1940 population, which scarcely reached seven million, to a level six or seven times higher some decades later in the twenty-first century.

Peru's demographic explosion, closely related to its geography and lack of arable land and economic, social and political factors, can be defined as an internal migratory explosion, from rural to urban areas, from the Sierra to the Coast and from the interior of the country to the capital. The rural population did not diminish. It was over four million in 1940 and is over seven million today. But the urban area has undergone explosive growth from scarcely two million in 1940 to nineteen million today, eight million of whom are in Lima (a population greater than the entire country population less than three generations ago).[3]

Andean people, relegated for centuries to the mountains, now form a massive part of the urban population on the Coast, especially in the capital. They set up their huts on the sand dunes around the city in order to seek work and schooling for their children within one kilometer of home. In the beginning they lacked everything: water, electricity, etc., but they have shown a remarkable capacity for sacrifice and assimilation into the urban world. Peru, as indicated by Matos Mar, has a "new face."

The population explosion and its new distribution across the country has meant an explosion in unsuspected potential for development, as well as concrete, urgent demands that politicians can no longer ignore. For hundreds of years in Peru, power, knowledge and wealth have been in the hands of the minority. In the last fifty years, the population has tripled. However, the number of literate adult Peruvians has risen more than nine times from 1.6 to 15 million (close to 89 percent of the present population over 15 years of age). The number of university students has multiplied by more than twenty to half a million young Peruvians seeking higher education.

Two-thirds of the economy's labor force in 1940 was in the rural areas. Rural workers have increased by more than 27 percent, but today they account for only one-seventh

---

[2]At the beginning of the 1960s, when Peru had ten million people, it was growing at 3 percent per annum, that is, 300,000 persons a year. Now the rate has moderated to 1.7 percent, but with 26,530,000 inhabitants, the absolute annual increase is 430,000.

[3]Geographical mobility is one of the characteristics of the labor force in the United States. But more than one American expert in development has pointed out that internal migrations in Peru have been larger and different. In 1940, two-thirds of the Peruvian population lived in the Sierra, only 28 percent on the Coast, and a scattered 5 percent in the Amazon region. Today 57 percent live on the Coast, and less than one-third in the Sierra. For those millions of migrant peasants, it meant a move with no return to a world that had a climate, an economy, a language and a culture completely different from theirs.

of the national total of 12,400,000 workers. The economy has become urban. The number of men and women who are working or looking for a job in the cities has increased more than 1,100 percent.

From October 1968 to 1980 Peru had a sui generis military government. General Juan Velasco Alvarado overthrew democratically elected President Fernando Belaunde Terry and imposed the Revolutionary Government of the Armed Forces, with its nationalist and leftist authoritarian policies.

After the early 1960s, the political mentality in Latin America shifted to the left, following the example and propaganda of the Cuban revolution. In Peru, without shedding a drop of blood, the military government adopted revolutionary policies in response to the popular demands manifested in isolated guerrilla outbreaks in the Andes during previous governments. It changed the economic and political power structure of the landowner oligarchy and urban business groups.[4] From then on, the State was a present protagonist in designing policies and economic activity, through expropriation of foreign companies, public investment, control of foreign currency, the handling of domestic credit, etc. The military mistrusted foreign capital and the ideas of leftist Peruvian intellectuals, with a simplistic authoritarianism, summarized in the phrase "neither capitalism nor communism."

Although it launched a series of social reforms, the military government finally succumbed to two serious weaknesses: its economic errors (excessive growth of state institutions, rigid, inefficient control of the internal market and carelessness on the external front) and its lack of popular support for its trampling of democratic institutions (unions, political parties, the press, etc.). At the end of the Second Phase, General Francisco Morales Bermudez convened a Constituent Assembly in 1979 and democratic elections were held in 1980. The latter were a tight struggle against the Aprista party. President Belaunde and his Acción Popular party, overthrown by force twelve years before, were re-elected.

The general global result of the military government is rather modest: 4 percent of annual GDP growth (5 percent in 1968–1975 and 2.7 percent from 1975 to 1980), but with growing fiscal and external pressure and ever-increasing internal social pressures. The agrarian reform in 1969 eliminated the large rural estates, but did not solve the problems of lack of lands and low productivity. The growing Andean population was still transferring massively from the sunny valleys of the Sierra to the cloudy sand dunes surrounding coastal cities, in search of jobs and basic social services.

Only one in three workers could find a job in the organized or formal sectors of the economy. There have been budding "informal" activities, especially in handicrafts and street vendors, with low levels of productivity and income, but which have demonstrated an enormous amount of creativity and effort by the immigrants—a phenomenon that very few development experts would have dared to predict fifty years ago.

---

[4]Since the end of the nineteenth century, the Peruvian economy had been dominated by private business interests based on agricultural property and livestock. Especially in the time of Leguia (1919–1930), foreign investments in mining and later on family business groups in industry, urban construction, banking and fishing were added. See "Power Strategies: Economic Groups in Peru" by Enrique Vasquez Huaman, Research Center of the Universidad del Pacifico, Lima, 2000.

## THE CRISIS (1975–1990)

The growth model of the Peruvian economy could not continue much longer based on primary exports and the growing State role of protecting industry for import substitution. Peru applied, a bit late but with great intensity, the ideas that had been implanted by ECLA in the 1950s. The scheme for controlling imports and replacing them with domestic production of doubtful quality at higher prices has the initial advantage of boosting domestic industry, but it soon reveals a serious disadvantage: imports are not final goods but mostly inputs and capital goods. By making these imports more expensive and scarcer, domestic production is slowed, inflationary pressures arise and exports of final goods become impossible. This model brought the Peruvian economy to crisis in 1975 in an international context and the crisis was aggravated in the second half of the 1980s by the fiscal and foreign trade imbalances and the increasing weight of foreign debt.

The decade of the 1980s in Latin America has been called "the lost decade." In Peru it was much worse than that. While from 1980 to 1990 the Peruvian population increased by more than four million inhabitants, the GDP in real terms fell 28 percent. President Belaunde's second government (1980–1985), with its moderate populist and protectionist policies to meet the growing demands of business and urban labor unions, could not prevent the economic decline. At the same time, the terrorist violence of the Shining Path broke out in the interior of the country. The economic disaster and social chaos were accentuated during the government of Alan Garcia (1985–1990) when the APRA rose to power for the first time with this new leader, a young and brilliant orator who raised many hopes.

Garcia began his government with a brief idyll with the business sector.[5] But soon there was a change: public spending increased, inefficient controls and subsidies were established, and banks were nationalized by the government, leading most public businesses to bankruptcy and imposing severe difficulties on all sectors of the economy. In 1986–1987 Peru had a short period of high growth based on expansion in domestic demand, but the fiscal breach began to widen as did the external trade imbalance. Then came the debacle. During the sixty months of Garcia's government, accumulated inflation reached the astronomical figure of 2,178,482 percent, the real value of salaries diminished by 53 percent, the proportion of Lima families below the poverty line rose from 17 to 44 percent, tax collections dropped from 14 to 4 percent of the GDP and, due to Garcia's defiant failure to comply with international financial agencies, Peru was declared ineligible to receive foreign credit.

Because of its price structure distorted by controls and subsidies, and the fall in production and income, the Peruvian economy in 1990 was at its lowest level in recent memory. The timid, belated "readjustment" policies that Alan Garcia's government approved

---

[5]The military government had tried to complement and control, but not to destroy, the strong national private business groups. These had survived with some readjustments and expansion (by acquiring assets from foreign investors who preferred to withdraw from the country) and after negotiating their lines of action with the government. At the beginning of his period of government, Alan Garcia sought a new rapprochement and convened the twelve most powerful businessmen (called the "12 Apostles" by the press) with the urgent objective of increasing investment in the country. But the businessmen's distrust of the president's demagogic language delayed and finally impeded reaching any positive agreement. (See the historical analyses by Francisco Durand, especially "Adios to the 12 Apostles," in the newspaper *La Republica*, September 1, 2002.)

only accentuated inflation, product scarcity and unemployment. The national product per capita fell to the level it had held fifteen years before, while terrorist violence advanced.

The national crisis that the country underwent could be defined as a crisis of the Peruvian people—a people that grew in number, in educational level, in capacity to work and in their hopes, but could not escape poverty. There were no real political parties that were well organized with a coherent program and a large allegiance. People lacked representative, honest political leadership and a proper economic model to enable them to progress toward development with efficiency and equity. The crisis was not only of an economic nature; it was so deep it affected the total economic, social and political reality of the country.

In summary, in the past the absence of development kept most of the population in a state of poverty, isolation and backwardness. From the end of the 1940s there was partial and unbalanced "developments" (which was really underdevelopment, since it was not accompanied by any parallel social progress, raising of the status of women nor a greater public awareness). This did help lower the mortality rate but hardly affected the birthrate, thus sparking the demographic explosion. From the mid-1970s on, while rural areas were at a standstill and cities were expanding with generations of young people seeking work, all stops were pulled out and the economy opened up to all kinds of imbalances (foreign trade and balance of payments, fiscal budget, savings and investments). The reforms of the military government of 1968–1980 were authoritarian but made some social sense.

The 1980s began with a constitutional government, but the formal frameworks of democratic institutions appeared to be inadequate to channel the overflow of people's demands. The inflation rate rose, reducing the purchasing power of salaries. At the same time the recession became even more acute, as did unemployment and poverty, which was no longer only rural but also increasingly urban.

## THE 1990 ELECTIONS AND THE ADJUSTMENT

In the midst of the chaos and the frustration of the final years of the 1980s, new ideas and proposals arose in Peru. Proposing them was the author Mario Vargas Llosa, who burst on the political scene and founded the Libertad Movement. His message was clear: democracy and free markets. He promoted a democracy that would free itself from the abusive and corrupt weight of the State, an economic model that promoted freedom for all producers and consumers to make their own decisions without any interference from the government, respect for private initiative and human rights and opening up Peru to the rest of the world. It was a totally new message that tuned in to the ideas and advances made in the international context, one responding to long-standing repressed desires of all Peruvians.

This development was totally contrary to what Peru had previously known, especially during the authoritarian military government and the chaotic Aprista government. It evoked an enthusiastic response throughout the country, but since Vargas Llosa had no structured political party, he decided to call on and unite himself with two respectable leaders, Fernando Belaunde Terry (Accion Popular) and Luis Bedoya Reyes (Partido Popular Cristiano), in a wide democratic front (FREDEMO). Four months before the elections, public opinion surveys gave the FREDEMO candidate an ample victory, although he openly insisted that drastic political changes and severe economic readjustments would have to be made.

Two months before the elections, a deceptive political maneuver became evident. The APRA and various leftist groups withdrew their candidates and decided to support an unknown, who was then in fifth or sixth place in the surveys. They undertook an aggressive campaign to discredit the leaders of FREDEMO (whom they called bourgeois traditionalists) and frightened the population with the price adjustments and unemployment that FREDEMO intended to apply. Surprisingly, in the second round of voting, this unknown candidate won. He was Alberto Fujimori. But the surprises had only just begun.

It is not surprising that the Peruvian people elected Fujimori. The initial enthusiasm for Vargas Llosa and his message was, to a large degree, an expression of rejection of the disorderly, controlling and inefficient policies of Alan Garcia. But when the actual moment for electing a new government arrived, the popular distrust of the ruling classes that were supporting FREDEMO reappeared. There was a great fear of losing the existing subsidies on food, education, fuel, etc. through the announced adjustments in a hyper-inflationary and recessive situation.

The greatest surprise of all was the personality of Fujimori himself. He had no experience in governing, no political party of his own, no government plan and no majority in Congress. Thus it was assumed that Fujimori would have to govern by submitting to the pressures of the old political parties and groups in power.

However, before assuming the presidency, Fujimori traveled to the United States and Japan and became convinced of the need to undertake drastic change in the Peruvian economy. And he did, with clear ideas and after ensuring the support of the armed forces. The severe economic adjustment was terrible. This adjustment included a several hundred percent devaluation, a free floating rate of exchange, an unrestricted goods and services market, the elimination of subsidies, the raising of income taxes and severe fiscal discipline, free trade abroad and a major reduction in customs duties, plus a commitment to renew payment of the foreign debt. This economic earthquake was accepted calmly and quietly by the people.

Various factors make it easier to understand how the country could withstand this drastic change in direction. The public had been informed of and warned by Vargas Llosa of the need for adjustments in order to rise above the chaos. FREDEMO businessmen and experts, themselves surprised, gave their open support to the new economic policy. Political parties were discredited and weak, and threats of subversive terrorism made the need for change in the country urgent. Fujimori's personality made his tough program acceptable in the eyes of the people.

In a country marked by long-term, generalized racism, the "chino" Fujimori was accepted by the masses as one of them, far from the monied classes and the social apparatus as well (although he had been Professor of Mathematics and rector of a state university). Moreover, Fujimori not only showed strong character, but was charismatic when approaching people in the capital and the interior of the country in an approach he called "direct democracy."

## PACIFICATION AND ECONOMIC GROWTH (1992–1997)

Both houses of Congress, elected in 1990, were resistant to approving the laws he needed in order to apply his new free market policies and to energetically repress the terrorism that was devastating the country. On April 5, 1992, Fujimori, in authoritarian manner, dissolved Congress. His "auto coup" surprised the Organization of American States and international public opinion since it broke with the norms of democracy. However, he received astonishing popular approval throughout the country. Some months later, he convened a new Constituent Congress in which he obtained a clear majority. The armed forces made decisive, sometimes brutal, advances in repressing terrorism, and the principal leaders of the Shining Path and the MRTA subversive movements were put in prison.

The reordering of the previous fiscal chaos and the new liberalization policies were carried out at the cost of great sacrifice, which the population accepted with admirable stoicism. They soon began to see signs of macroeconomic recovery. The annual inflation rate, which had been 7,000 percent in 1990, was reduced to 10 percent in 1995. Investment increased from 16 percent of GDP in 1990 to 24 percent in 1995. There was a large savings effect from privatizing old public companies. From 1992 to 1997 the real growth in GDP of the Peruvian economy increased 7 percent per year.

On December 17, 1996, a tragic episode occurred in Lima that took the country and the world by surprise. During the celebrations of the Day of the Emperor in the Japanese Embassy, a small, heavily armed MRTA group broke into the Embassy and took 400 guests hostage. Among them were more than thirty ambassadors; many high functionaries of international organizations; several ministers; and congressmen, businessmen and Peruvian academic personages.

The terrorists demanded the liberation of their leaders and companions who were in prison. Fujimori firmly refused, pretending to arrange negotiations but actually preparing a military rescue operation that was to be carried out by the marines four months later. However, this ending, violent but inevitable due to the stubbornness of the terrorists, was sullied by the personal political use Fujimori made of it after the tragedy.

On the nation's agenda for public and economic life in 1998, several outstanding tasks and challenges remained. These included modernizing the public administration, making progress in privatizing state companies, rendering the stagnating agricultural sector more dynamic, raising the level of public education, closing the gap in foreign trade (imports had doubled since 1990, thanks to the entry of capital, but exports had not increased at the same pace, despite a notable increase in mining), promoting the domestic market and fostering employment in cities.

Once these adjustments were made at the beginning of the 1990s, the national macroeconomy was re-ordered and stabilized. Now it was necessary to launch a second generation of reforms to consolidate socioeconomic development. Fujimori, however, ignored these challenges and focused his efforts at staying in power by seeking re-election for the third consecutive time in 2000. For this, and with the help of his personal advisor, Vladimiro Montesinos, he did not hesitate to override all legal forms and ethical principles.

## CORRUPTION, SCANDALS AND POLITICAL DEBACLE (1998–2000)

The abuses of Fujimori's authoritarian power in handling institutions and people, widely demonstrated since 1992, became increasingly more obvious. The president's skill, with the assistance of his advisor, Montesinos, was in maintaining an appearance of orderly and efficient democracy. He barely succeeded in being re-elected in 2000. But the country soon discovered the abyss of corruption that existed in all state institutions. Congress, the Judiciary Power, the leaders of the Armed Forces and the National Police, owners of the communications media and many important businessmen had all been seriously compromised and were the recipients of millions of dollars in bribes. The surprising discovery was made of hundreds of videos that Montesinos himself had taped, showing him bribing congressmen, judges and businessmen. All of this forced Fujimori to resign and flee the country for Japan in 2000. Montesinos also escaped but was captured and extradited to Peru. He is today imprisoned in Lima, for the multitude of crimes and killings he caused.

The Peruvian people, profoundly shaken by the discovery of the Fujimori regime's corruption and without an executive power since all the ministers resigned, reacted calmly and maturely. Congress, under the Constitution, elected a transitional president to call general elections in 2001 to restore democracy to the country. Valentin Paniagua was named and fulfilled his mission extremely well. He named a new Cabinet with outstanding people, presided over by Javier Pérez de Cuellar.

Elections were held after a hard fought but clean campaign, under the supervision of the OAS (Organization of American States). There were three very strong candidates: Lourdes Flores, democratic leader of the United National Front; Alan Garcia of the APRA, who had returned to the country after eight years abroad awaiting the expiration of the serious economic and political accusations made against him; and Alejandro Toledo, the fiery new leader of Peru Posible, who had already nearly won the election against Fujimori in 2000. On July 28, 2001, Toledo was sworn in as president, the first person of Indian ancestry to hold this office. He emphasized his origins with pride, together with his higher education at Stanford University, California. After the years of *fuji-montesinoist* authoritarianism and corruption, the Peruvian people could see with relief and great expectations the recovery of democracy in Peru.

## THE PRESENT ECONOMIC AND POLITICAL PANORAMA

During his campaign, Toledo announced, and has been firmly carrying out, a responsible economic policy, including fiscal and monetary balances and the opening of the country to world trade. The Peruvian people still remember the economic chaos and the social cost of populist policies applied by APRA at the end of the 1980s. The problem is that the adjustment and the macroeconomic reordering applied by Fujimori has not brought well-being to the majority of Peruvian families, many of whom continue to live in abject poverty.

Toledo made many promises during his campaign, and after being elected promised above all that there would be work for all. [The letter *T* for Toledo and Trabajo ("work" in Spanish) is the emblem of his "Peru Posible" party.] However, the unemployment rate (8.3 percent) and underemployment (nearly 50 percent) remained. Surveys showed that his margins of credibility and approval have risen somewhat, but they scarcely reach 28 percent.

This situation is the result of three causes. The first is the unfavorable international situation. The tragedy in New York on September 11 occurred only six weeks after his election and changed the world outlook, especially insofar as foreign investment is concerned. The uncertain situation in South America, especially in Argentina, Brazil, Colombia and Venezuela, casts a shadow over the whole continent. Nonetheless, Peru is now the Latin American country with the greatest stability and strongest growth indices, including Chile and Mexico.

The second factor is Toledo's personality. His inexperience in governing and excessive tendency to make promises, combined with the weakness of his "Peru Posible" party, which is more of an electoral alliance than a party—incoherent and without any defined government plan—make him a frail president.

Third, the very difficulty of the problems themselves means they cannot be resolved with the speed that the public demands. The poverty level in 1997, after five years of strong economic growth, was 42.7 percent (10,406,000 inhabitants), of which 18.2 percent (4,436,000 inhabitants) lived in abject poverty.

Then came the climatological phenomenon of El Niño in 1998, which, in addition to the adverse foreign economic impact and domestic electoral uncertainties, produced a recession in the Peruvian economy from 1998 to 2001. The poverty index increased to 49.8 percent (12,993,000 inhabitants), and that of extreme or abject poverty to 19.5 percent (5,088,000 inhabitants). There was no fall in the GDP, but rather a minor growth rate of 1 percent per annum. However, in the four years from 1998–2001, the total number of poor in absolute figures increased by two and a half million, and those in abject poverty by 650,000.[6]

The present Peruvian labor force has some 12,400,000 workers, including people working or those seeking jobs. Every year this figure increases by 380,000 workers. Each year it is necessary to create more than 350,000 productive jobs for the unemployment and underemployment percentages to begin to decrease.

## BUSINESSMEN'S THINKING AND ORGANIZATIONS

The Peruvian business world is as varied as Peru itself. There are businessmen who lead large companies and others who manage medium-sized companies, but there are also small companies and a multitude of microbusinesses (those with less than ten workers each). Thus it is difficult to talk of any particular attitude, mentality or tendency. There are, of course, clear differences by sector of activity, be it the financial sector, the commercial sector or the industrial or the mining sector. The greatest concentration of large companies and foreign direct investment is in banking, mining and telecommunications.

The greatest variety is found in trade and manufacturing, which has some large and medium-sized companies and half a million microbusinesses. Most of the latter are in the "informal" sector. They are not legally registered, do not pay taxes and have

---

[6]The high percentages for 2001 are due, in part, to having utilized a very demanding measurement method, extended throughout the whole country. See "La Pobreza en el Peru 2001" (Poverty in Peru, 2001), INEI, National Institute of Statistics and Information, Lima, June 2002.

very low productivity, but give work and income to millions of workers living in poverty. Following the pacification of the country, a new category has been added to this framework: the tourism sector. Peru boasts modern four and five star hotels in the cities and inns in the interior of the country, as well as access roads and tourist services. The farming and livestock sector after the agrarian reform, which was badly designed and implemented by the military government and scarcely improved by any successive government, is the most backward sector and is fragmented into small productive units. However, here too new dynamism is afoot, with new investment and an export mentality.

Until the 1980s, a closed, protectionist mind-set prevailed as indicated by the growing influence of state companies. It was believed, erroneously, that the foreign currency needed by the country could be obtained through primary exports from mining and fisheries. Private industrial businessmen and producers of other goods and services (in agriculture, trade, transport, etc.) not only did not think of exporting but made no effort whatsoever to improve their business to make them more competitive. Nearly all their time and effort was spent in lobbying state functionaries to obtain exoneration from government controls. The fiscal gap and foreign trade imbalance, together with hyperinflation and hyper-recession, led to readjustment and change in 1990.

The State retreated. In the context of a globalized economy, businessmen understood that to survive and prosper they had to adopt a competitive free market attitude. This change in the economy, adopted by Chile years previously and accompanied by strong political and social conflict, was made surprisingly rapidly and calmly in Peru. Most of the population now feel that "subsidy" is a dirty word and that it is necessary to compete. They feel it is for the private sector to seize the initiative and take responsibility for advancing the economy.

People still retain a few myths today because they are deeply rooted in the Peruvian way of thinking. Myths are dangerous, because they are partly true and partly false. The most common of these is that "Peru is a rich country" thanks to the great abundance and variety of its natural resources. Manco Capac, according to legend, founded the Inca Empire by burying a bar of gold in Cuzco. Influenced by such legends, Pizarro encouraged his companions to leave Panama and conquer Peru, believing it was an emporium of riches. The liberator, San Martin, placed in the national emblem the three kingdoms of nature and the cornucopia of abundance. Humboldt, the scientist, forged the famous phrase "Peru is a beggar seated on a bench of gold," and even the French added to their language the expression "Ça vaut un Perou" (worth a Peru) to describe something of great wealth. In fact, Peru is privileged by geography with a variety of climes and riches underground and in the sea, but only hard work and good management can generate economic wealth.

Another idea that still remains, even after the changes in 1990, is that the people expect a lot from the State. The deepest roots of this expectation can be found in colonial times, when the Spanish monarchy imposed their authority and established a semi-feudal, exploitative and paternalistic economic system. During the Republic and modern times, a double, reciprocal motivation was established between the impoverished people and their political leaders. The people had to ask and the politicians had to promise in order to win elections and take power. After much frustration, the people are gradually learning. They now demand clarity, honesty and public service from their government. The people are learning that political democracy goes hand in hand with an efficient and dynamic economy in which everyone participates in the work and in the fruits thereof.

The great variety of companies in Peru has led to the establishment of diverse business organizations. Microbusinesses have their associations, which are widespread throughout the country and in the districts of the capital. Large and numerous medium-sized companies are grouped into associations by economic activity, such as the National Society of Industry; National Society of Mining, Petroleum and Energy; Peruvian Chamber of Construction; National Fishery Society; Chamber of Commerce; National Exporters Association; etc. These associations have united to form the powerful CONFIEP (Confederation of Private Business Institutions in Peru). Despite frequent opposing interests, they have managed to maintain a certain unity and coherence in defense of business activity and the free market. Their political influence is obvious. According to the institutional statutes, CONFIEP may not unite nor affiliate with any political party. This independence contributes to its increasing influence, as well as its attitude toward dialogue with workers' unions. In past decades, unions were very strong. Fujimori dismantled antiquated labor legislation that stipulated job security for all workers and other excessive social benefits. It is now necessary to review the situation.

This is being done by the National Labor Council, in which labor and management representatives and the Ministry of Labor discuss and propose measures. As in many countries, only a very small part (less than 15 percent) of all workers are organized into unions. Six of every seven workers in Peru are independent, informal or work in small microbusinesses. Many of them fall within the general category of underemployed.

Another important change in the thinking and attitude of Peruvian workers and businessmen is the open door policy. Peru is convinced of the need to increase international trade and foreign investment. All political leaders now include this open door policy in their platforms and government plans. The only exception is a small leftist minority, which does not question the open door but rather how it should be implemented in order to obtain greater advantages for the country.

It is necessary to distinguish between the regional processes that involve trade negotiations (such as ALCA, CAN and Mercosur) from those that are economic and political cooperation processes (such as APEC). With respect to the former, Peruvian government authorities have clearly given a high priority to both ALCA (and to an eventual Free Trade Agreement with the United States) and to CAN and are projected to do the same for Mercosur.

These priorities are not contradictory per se, since most trade is within the ALCA area, but the composition of trade varies with each group. There is greater manufacturing content in trade for Peru with CAN and with Mercosur as compared to that with NAFTA. The benefits that Peru can receive from each option are different and complementary, insofar as the type of investments to be attracted are concerned. Everyone admits that the greatest benefit that can be expected from commercial agreements is their potential to attract more and better investment with greater industrial and technological content.

With respect to the second type of regional process (economic and political cooperation), APEC is undoubtedly the highest priority. Peruvian participation in this forum is very active. A current emphasis of great importance is creating a better connection between Peru and the dynamic centers of trade and investment in the Pacific Basin. These are the purposes of the Hub Peru Group that is working on formulating basic infrastructure projects (transport, communications, energy and integrated logistics centers). As they become firmer, these projects will permit Peru to take full advantage of its unique location on the South American coast of the Pacific Ocean, as well as of its still underexploited position as a neighbor of Brazil.

The business groups are increasing their active participation in all regional processes mentioned earlier. The government is increasingly requesting their opinion, which is a positive sign. However, compared to what is happening in some of the more advanced Latin American countries, the dynamism of Peruvian businessmen is still at an embryonic stage. It is necessary to have professionals with more training in order to confront the complex challenges of globalization and contemporary regional issues. Business unions and some universities, among them the Universidad del Pacifico, are undertaking to reduce these deficiencies.

## ECONOMIC STRENGTH AND POLITICAL WEAKNESS

On the threshold of the twenty-first century, Peru presents a contrast: a healthy, stable economy, with a solid financial system, strong international reserves and GDP growth rates that, although modest, were in 2002 the highest on the continent,[7] while at the same time the country is living through a stage of domestic political weakness and uncertainty.

Within international circles, Peru's political image is respected and admired because it recovered democracy in a peaceful manner after the serious crimes and excesses of the Fujimori government. The brief transitional government of Valentin Paniagua initiated urgently needed reforms in the public administration and convened orderly and free elections. These took place in July 2001 and brought Alejandro Toledo to the presidency as well as a new Congress. On September 10 of the same year in Lima, the 28th Extraordinary General Assembly of the Organization of American States (OAS) approved and signed the Inter-American Democratic Letter. Peru participated decisively in the preparation of this Letter, a fundamental document in the democratic history of the hemisphere.

On the domestic front, however, the population's social expectations, weak government institutions (including the Judiciary Power) that had been undermined by the authoritarianism and corruption of the Fujimori and Montesinos regime, as well as the incoherence and broken promises of the Executive Branch, have led to a low approval index for President Toledo. Expected State reform has been paralyzed. The regionalizing of the country after the elections of November 17, 2002, opened up a wide range of uncertainties for the population.

---

[7]See "Peru, Economic and Social Indices, 2002," Proinversion, Lima, 2002. Numerous statistical charts can be seen at www.proinversion.com.

## NATIONAL CONSENSUS

At the beginning of his administration, President Toledo had the inspiration to convene all the political parties and institutions of civilian society (labor and business unions, nongovernmental organizations, associations, churches, etc.) to meet to draw up a National Agreement. This agreement is a composite of long-term State policies that mark the fundamental path to be followed for successive governments until the year 2021.

This was an extraordinary idea that might have remained just a good will gesture. But, to the surprise of everyone, it actually happened. Unprecedented in Peruvian political history, or indeed in the hemisphere itself, as the Secretary General of the OAS pointed out, all the leaders of Peru's political parties and representatives of civilian organizations met in long sessions to dialogue in the offices of the Prime Minister. Despite the normal diversions in a democracy, these leaders agreed by consensus to 29 State policies, aimed at achieving four great objectives:

- Democracy and a state of law
- Equity and social justice
- National competitiveness
- An efficient, transparent and decentralized State

The complete, detailed announcement of these 29 State policies is contained in a 25-page document signed by all the members of the National Agreement on March 5, 2002. It is not a governmental plan; this is the task and responsibility of each democratically elected government in successive periods. The agreement is a coherent guide to the basic long-term lines that Peru has approved to achieve human development and national solidarity "to the execution of which we commit ourselves as from today," as the signers state at the beginning of the document.

## A FUTURE WITH STRONG EXPECTATIONS

The crisis consisted of an enormous imbalance between the available resources and their effective access for national development in an integrated society. The critical element in this misalignment was the human being, who is called upon to be the subject and the object of the development. The population is both actor and recipient as it creates wealth through its work and benefits from the increased standard of living. In both dimensions, as joint creators of their own destiny and as beneficiaries of the advances achieved, Peruvians have been found doubly displaced.

The crisis must be seen from both aspects: as a socioeconomic disorder that omitted human resources in their capacity and right to produce, and as a serious reduction of consumption of essential goods by most of the population at basic levels. All this accentuated the domestic contrast between races, regions and social classes, in a way that diminished the collective hopes for the future of the country and actually furthered the fanatic terrorism of some extremist groups, weakening institutional stability and respect for human rights.

The difficulties are not due only to high demographic growth. This growth arose specifically as a result of the imbalance between economic development and true social and human development. But high demographic growth has become a serious obstacle to achieving development goals, both on the national level as well as the family level. As always, the most poverty-stricken social sectors with the fewest economic opportunities are those with the largest families.

There have been grave errors and injustices in economic, social and political planning by diverse governments and groups in power. At the same time there was a demographic reality that the leaders preferred to ignore, despite the fact that it arose from these same social circumstances and aggravated them considerably. There is an urgent need to change these socioeconomic structures, to increase production and to correct the uneven income distribution. There is also a need to respect the freedoms and rights of every family to have only the number of children they want and are able to educate.

The human situation of the population is critical. The first step to finding solutions is to recognize this reality and to take the necessary steps to overcome poverty. Peru needs an efficient and just development policy "that puts the economy at the service of man," as the Constitution states, and follows the State policies approved in the National Agreement. One goal must be to diminish the differences that exist among regions and social classes. Moreover, based on moral and realistic criteria, the population policy approved in 1985 must also be applied to promote the family and the rights and duties of individuals.

Economically, with obvious social and political consequences, the key problem is employment. From 1975 to 2002, Peru's labor force (people who work or seek work) has almost tripled, increasing by 7,600,000 workers. In the mid-1970s there was already a serious employment deficit, with more than 40 percent of workers underemployed and unemployed. The millions of workers added to the labor force by 2002 did not increase the number of "adequately employed" workers.

On the contrary, the underemployed increased by more than 5,200,000 and the openly unemployed increased by almost a million. The employment problem is worldwide at the beginning of the twenty-first century; it requires great investment and higher qualification of workers, together with new technologies in a globalized, competitive world. Peru will have to multiply its efforts in order to increase savings and investment, both domestic and foreign, and to raise the level of education in the country. The reordering and reactivating of the Peruvian economy are urgently needed, because by 2015 the labor force will have greatly exceeded the figure of 16 million workers (63 percent of the working age population), will have an average educational level higher than at present, will have greater participation by women and will have 85 percent of the workers in urban areas.

Together with solid economic progress, Peruvians need greater social progress and greater national integration. The Peruvian people have clearly manifested their rejection of violence and their love for democracy and peace. In spite of the fact that the majority of the poor in Peru have Indian roots, they have never organized a native political party that is opposed to the other cultural sectors of the population. They feel themselves united to the whole country, and look to the future.

The human situation in the country is certainly critical, but there is hope: the Peruvian population itself is varied but laborious and strong. They must be able to forge their own destiny in Peru's economic, social and political life. The origin of the crisis is the strongest reason for hope: the Peruvian people themselves.

## ACRONYMS

| | |
|---|---|
| ALCA | Área de Libre Comercio de las Américas |
| | *Free Trade Area of the Americas* |
| APEC | *Asia Pacific Economic Cooperation* |
| | Foro de Cooperación Económica del Asia Pacífico |
| APRA | Alianza Popular Revolucionaria Americana |
| | *American Popular Revolutionary Alliance* |
| CAN | Comunidad Andina de Naciones |
| | *Andean Community (of Nations)* |
| CONAM | Consejo Nacional del Medio Ambiente |
| | *National Environmental Council* |
| CONFIEP | Confederación Nacional de Instituciones Empresariales Privadas |
| | *National Confederation of Private Business Institutions* |
| ECLA | *Economic Commission for Latin America (U.N.)* |
| | Comisión Económica para América Latina |
| FREDEMO | Frente Democrático |
| | *Democratic Front* |
| INEI | Instituto Nacional de Estadística e Informática |
| | *National Institute of Statistics and Electronic Information* |
| Mercorsur | Mercado Común del Sur |
| | *Southern Common Market* |
| NAFTA | *North American Free Trade Agreement* |
| | Tratado de Libre Comercio de América del Norte |

## BIBLIOGRAPHY

Contreras, C. and M. Cueto. (1999) *Historia del Perú Contemporáneo.* Lima: Red para el Desarrollo de las Ciencias Sociales en el Perú.

Cortez, R. ed., (2002) *Salud, Equidad y Pobreza en el Perú: Teoría y Nuevas Evidencias.* Lima: Universidad del Pacífico.

Cotler, J. (1994) *Política y Sociedad en el Perú: Cambios y Continuidades.* Lima: Instituto de Estudios Peruanos.

Dancourt, O. (1997) *Reformas Estructurales y Política Macroeconómica en el Perú: 1990–1996.* Lima: PUCP.

Dornbush, R. and S. Edwards. (1992) *Macroeconomía del Populismo en América Latina.* México: Fondo de Cultura Económica.

Durand, F. (1997). *Incertidumbre y Soledad. Reflexiones Sobre los Grandes Empresarios de América Latina.* Lima: Fundación Friedrich Ebert.

Figueroa, A., T. Altamirano, and D. Sulmont. (1996) *Social Exclusion and Inequality in Peru.* Geneva: International Institute for Labour Studies.

Gonzáles de Olarte, E., and L. Samamé. (1991) *El Péndulo Peruano: Política Económica, Gobernabilidad y Subdesarrollo.* Lima: Instituto de Estudios Peruanos.

Hunt, S. (1995) *Crecimiento Económico a Largo Plazo: Perú y América Latina en el Contexto Mundial.* Lima: Instituto de Estudios Peruanos.

Jochamowitz, L. (1994) *Ciudadano Fujimori: La Construcción de un Político.* 2d. ed. Lima: PEISA.

Matos Mar, J. (1984) *Desborde Popular y Crisis del Estado.* Lima: Instituto de Estudios Peruanos.

Pacheco Vélez, C., ed. (1988) *Perú Promesa.* Lima: Universidad del Pacífico.

Parodi, C. (2002) *Perú 1960–2000: Políticas Económicas y Sociales en Entornos Cambiantes.* Lima: Universidad del Pacífico.

Portocarrero F. S., ed., (2002): *Políticas sociales en el Perú: nuevos aportes.* Lima: Universidad del Pacifico.

Quincot, C. A. (1994) *La Modernización Autoritaria.* Lima: Fundación Friedrich Ebert.

Sagasti, F. (1994) *Democracia y Buen Gobierno: Informe Final del Proyecto Agenda Perú.* Lima: Apoyo S.A.

Schydlowsky, D. and J. J. Wicht. (1979) *Perú 1968–1978: Anatomía de un Fracaso Económico.* Lima: Universidad del Pacífico.

Sheahan, J. (1997) *Effects of Liberalization Programs on Poverty and Inequality: Chile, México and Peru.* in Latin American Research Review, vol.32.

Tanaka, M. (1998) *Los Espejismos de la Democracia: El Colapso del Sistema de Partidos en el Perú, 1980–1995, en Perspectiva Comparada.* Lima: Instituto de Estudios Peruanos.

Tapia, C. (1997) *Las Fuerzas Armadas y Sendero Luminoso: Dos Estrategias y un Final.* Lima: Instituto de Estudios Peruanos.

Thomas, J. and J. Crabtree, eds. (1998) *Fujimori's Peru: The Political Economy.* London:

University of London Institute for Latin American Studies.

Thorp, R. and G. Bertram. (1985) *Peru 1890–1977: Crecimiento y Políticas en una Economía Abierta.* Lima: Mosca Azul.

Tuesta Soldevilla, F., ed. (1996) *Los Enigmas del Poder: Fujimori 1990–1996.* Lima: Fundación Friedrich Ebert.

_____. (1999) *El Juego Político: Fujimori, la Oposición y las Reglas.* Lima: Fundación Friedrich Ebert.

Vargas Llosa, M. (1994) *The Fish in the Water. A Memoir.* New York: Farrar, Straus and Giroux.

Vásquez, E. (2002) *Estrategias del Poder: Grupos Económicos en el Perú.* Lima: Universidad del Pacífico.

_____. ed. (2002) *Impacto de la Inversión Social en el Perú.* Lima: Universidad del Pacífico.

Webb, R. (1977) *Government Policy and the Distribution of Income in Peru.* Cambridge: Harvard University Press.

Wicht, J. J. (1985) *Realidad Demográfica y Crisis de la Sociedad Peruana,* in *Problemas Poblacionales Peruanos,* Roger Guerra García, ed., Lima: AMIDEP.

Zuzunaga, C. (1992) *Vargas Llosa: El Arte de Perder una Elección.* Lima: PEISA.

# CHAPTER 9
# MEXICO

Dr. Bobby James Calder

## INTRODUCTION

One thing is certain about Mexico—it has never been predictable. The history of modern Mexico begins with the small army of conquistadors that conquered the flourishing Aztec Empire. They succeeded in part because the Aztec emperor Moctezuma (Montezuma) mistook the Spanish leader Cortes for the returning Aztec god Quetzalcoatl. During the colonial period of the next three hundred years the economy was based on the exploitation of the labor of the Indians.

A revolution that began in 1810 resulted in independence from Spain in 1821 under the Emperor Agustin de Iturbide. The post-colonial period pitted the colonial economic model against a variety of new sources of political power. During this turmoil, symbolized by the multiple presidencies and military campaigns of Antonio de Santa Anna, Mexico lost much of its territory, including Texas and California.

In 1858 another revolution, La Reforma, yielded some economic as well as political change. Benito Juarez expelled the French under Maximiliano (Maximilian). The economy was, however, still not organized around business firms. The three-decade-long dictatorship of Porfirio Diaz finally resulted in economic progress, but was followed by more political upheaval. Eventually a period of relative political stability emerged with the one-party rule of the Partido Revolucionario Institucional (PRI) in 1929.

We now turn to the Mexico of today. Mexico is a country with a promising but, as ever, uncertain future.

## RESOURCES

Today Mexico covers 1.95 million square kilometers, ranking as the fourteenth largest country in the world. Mexico and the United States share a 3,118-kilometer common border, one of the largest in the world: it spans from the Pacific Ocean to the Gulf of Mexico, from San Diego-Tijuana to Brownsville-Matamoros. Mexico is bordered to the south by Guatemala (943 km) and Belize (249 km), to the west by the Pacific coast (7,360 km) and to the east by the Gulf of Mexico and the Caribbean coast (2,780 km).

Much of the country is dry and water is unevenly distributed. Due to the topography and climate, only 21 percent of the country is suitable for arable farming; a further 57 percent is suitable for pasture. Forest and woodland cover around 17 percent of the land. Mexico also has abundant mineral resources, ranking as the largest producer of silver in the world (with mines mainly based in the states of Chihuahua and Zacatecas).

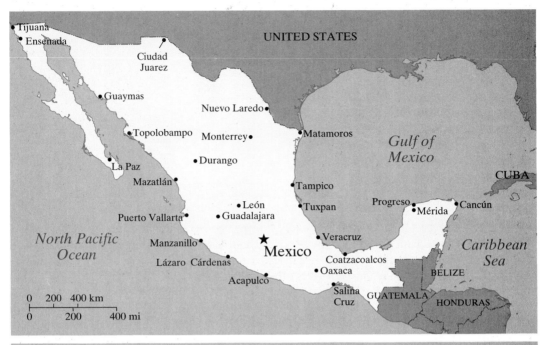

**FIGURE 9-1** Map of Mexico

The country is a world leader in the production of many other minerals, including fluorite, celestite, sodium sulphate, arsenic, sulphur and copper. In addition, Mexico ranked as the fifth largest oil producer in 2000. Although Mexico enjoys a great abundance of natural resources, it has not yet taken full and sustainable advantage of them.

While blessed with natural resources, Mexico has been slow to enact environmental standards. The General Law of Ecological Balance and Environmental Protection was not enacted until 1988. As a consequence, the country suffers severe air and water pollution, and the depletion of natural resources is a serious concern. With the North American Free Trade Agreement (NAFTA), Mexico has had to enforce stringent environmental regulations. Although the concept that polluters should pay was enacted into law in 1996, enforcement is very low. Nevertheless, the government has taken some cleanup measures, especially in Mexico City. This has been necessary to save the lives of thousands of people. Heavy industries have been moved outside the city and power plants switched to natural gas. Car standards for vehicles have been tighter since 1997. Even so, in addition to severe traffic congestion, approximately two-thirds of the city's vehicles are old and lack proper pollution controls.

## HUMAN RESOURCES

The population of Mexico reached 97.4 million people in 2000 (the 11th most populous country in the world). The rate of population growth has decreased significantly in the last three decades, from more than 3 percent per year in the early 1970s to 1.5 percent in the late 1990s. Owing to the increase in the potential workforce, the population dependence index [computed as the ratio of the dependent population (15 years old or under and over age 65) to the potential workforce (population between 15 and 63 years old)] has decreased by almost 10 percent during the last decade (Plan Nacional de Desarrollo, 2001–2006).

The economically active population is expected to further increase from 49 million to 69 million by 2030. This factor, together with the decrease in population growth, will significantly reduce the dependence index. Thereafter, there will be a rapid increase in the population of the elderly. Over the next three decades, the challenge is to create millions of jobs and generate enough savings to improve the retirement contribution system.

The population distribution in Mexico is polarized. Twenty-five percent of Mexicans live in localities with 2,500 inhabitants or less, and more than 26 percent live in localities with more than 500,000 inhabitants (Instituto Nacional de Estadística, Geografía e Informática: INEGI). The average population density of 50 inhabitants/km$^2$ is not representative. While entities such as Distrito Federal and Morelos have a density of 5,643,611 and 313 inhabitants/km$^2$, respectively, Chihuahua, Sonora, Campeche and Durango each have a density of 12 inhabitants/km$^2$.

The heavily populated industrial cities of Mexico City, Guadalajara (Jalisco) and Monterrey (Nuevo León) reflect the important internal migration from rural to urban areas experienced during the twentieth century, one that has accelerated since the 1970s. According to the 2000 census, urban population accounts for 75 percent of the total population. Following the present trend, it is expected that over 80 percent of the population growth in the coming 25 years will be concentrated in the cities. The Mexican states with a higher migration rate (more than 30 percent of the state's total population in 1995) are the northern states—Baja California and Baja California Sur, the central states—Mexico, Morelos, Colima and Distrito Federal, and the southern states—Quintana Roo and Campeche (Economist Intelligence Unit: EIU).

The percentage of urban population falls to less than 59 percent for those living in the nine southern states. The states with the lowest proportion of urban population are Chiapas (46 percent), Hidalgo (about 50 percent) and Oaxaca (45 percent). Rural areas show the highest levels of population dispersion, and 7 out of 10 villages suffer from extreme poverty. The pure Indian population (around 6 percent of the total population) is concentrated in rural areas. The Indian groups differ greatly in customs and languages, but they all have suffered from marginalization and poverty. A rebellion in 1994 increased the awareness of the poverty and problems of the Mexican indigenous population.

Education is crucial for the innovative capacity of any nation. The weakness of its education system is one of Mexico's biggest challenges. In 2000, 9.5 percent of the population of 15 years or over was illiterate, and less than one-half had completed secondary school or completed studies at a technical school. One explanatory factor is that basic and primary education has suffered continuous budget cuts during crises.

If we want a complete picture of the Mexican population, we need to study the composition of the people of Mexican origin in the United States.

Many Mexicans started seeking work in the United States half a century ago, and by 1990 there were about 13.5 million Mexicans (EIU) living in the United States, increasing to around 21.7 million residents (66.1 percent of the total United States Hispanic population) in the year 2000 (U.S. Census Bureau).

The education level of the U.S. Mexican population is lower than for other Hispanic groups and non-Hispanic whites. For example, in 2000 the estimated percentage of the population age 25 and older with at least a high school education was 51 percent, as compared to 57 percent for the total Hispanic population and 88.4 percent for non-Hispanic whites. However, this low percentage is clearly above the level of education of Mexico's population. In addition, the poverty level of the Mexican community in the United States is higher than the average for the total Hispanic population, and almost 24 percent of the population was living below the poverty level in 1999.

## ECONOMIC OVERVIEW

### STRUCTURE OF THE ECONOMY

The GDP distribution across sectors is a good indicator of the key competitive activities of a country (the GDP data refers to the year 1999). The main generator of GDP and employment in Mexico was the service sector, accounting for around two-thirds of the GDP during the last two decades. Commerce, restaurants and hotels as well as financial services, insurance and real estate accounted for almost one-third of the GDP generated by the service sector.

The service sector employed approximately 53 percent of the working population in 2000, but it is composed of many informal activities, especially in commerce and restaurant services. Mexico's total informal sector, excluding illegal activities, is very high, adding up to more than 12 percent of the GDP by 2000. The large size of the shadow economy is both the result of and a factor behind the recurrent economic crises. The job losses suffered during crises have pushed people to the "more steady" informal activities, in particular street vending.

Tourist services are a key source of government revenue and foreign reserves. Mexico captures 3 to 4 percent per year of tourism worldwide, and around 80 to 85 percent of tourists come from the United States every year. In 1993–1998, tourism represented 8.3 percent of GDP and employed 6 percent of the total working population. These figures are relatively small given Mexico's abundance of tourist destinations (two very long coasts, archaeological resources, forests, etc.).

The industrial sector is the main source of growth in the Mexican economy. It generates about 29 percent of the GDP and absorbs almost the same percentage of the working population, offering higher wages than many activities in the service sector (a salary of 2 to 3 times the minimum is accepted in many industries). The main productive sectors are manufacturing (more than 20 percent of the GDP and over 83 percent of total exports) and construction services. Although Mexico has abundant mineral resources, mining activities accounted for just over 1 percent of the GDP; but the state-run oil sector alone accounts for more than one-third of total government revenue. Finally, electricity, water and gas-related industries generate less than 2 percent of the total GDP.

Because manufacturing accounts for most of external trade, it is clear that Mexico has a competitive advantage in this sector. This reflects the fact that Mexico enjoys privileged access to the United States and Canadian markets guaranteed by NAFTA (the main implications of this trade agreement are discussed in more detail later).

The main manufacturing sectors in terms of output are (in ranked order) metal products, machinery and equipment; food, beverages and tobacco; and chemical, petroleum products, rubber and plastic. A high proportion of manufacturing activities take place in the *maquiladora* (in-bond assembly plants for re-export) sector, mainly the assembly of vehicles and electronics goods, and the production of textiles and furniture. The manufacturing sector is concentrated in high-tech clusters strategically located on the northern border with the United States, especially in the western city of Guadalajara (which touts itself as "Mexico's Silicon Valley") and in the Southern Yucatán, which is a short distance from the United States by sea.

The primary sector (agriculture, fishing and forestry) generated around 6 percent of the GDP (more than 4 percent is agricultural output), but it employed around 16 percent of the labor force. These natural resource–intensive activities have underperformed. Lack of investment to modernize the production process explains this poor output. An additional problem in the agricultural sector is land reform. Also, excessive exploitation and fires are other factors explaining the poor performance of forestry. At the end of 2000 the Federal Office for Environment Protection (Procuraduría Federal de Protección al Ambiente) reported that forestry areas in 23 states were in severe danger. As a result, the new administration has founded a national forestry commission (EIU).

So far we have examined the GDP generated by the different economic sectors. In order to better understand the performance of Mexico's economy, we must look at the GDP distribution across states (Figure 9-2).

The main finding is that the distribution is extremely uneven. The leading industrial states—Distrito Federal and Jalisco y Nuevo León—generate the highest level, contributing more than 46 percent of the total GDP in 1999. Other states (especially in the south) seem isolated from the great growth experienced by the manufacturing sector. For example, southern states such as Chiapas, Guerrero and Oaxaca and the central state Hidalgo suffer from extreme poverty, generating around 6 percent of the GDP in 1999, although they account for around 13 percent of the population. The lack of proper infrastructure helps to explain the disintegration of the economy.

**FIGURE 9-2** Mexico's 1999 gross domestic product per capita

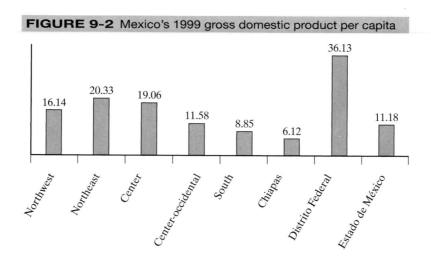

In the agricultural sector, it is remarkable that the northern parts of Mexico, which are very dry and suffer from drought, have become the most productive areas. Two important assets explain this fact: (1) these areas benefit the most from public irrigation infrastructures, and (2) farms here specialize in the nearby U.S. market. There is potential for farms in the center and south, which have suffered from a long and confusing land distribution that partitioned land into small, inefficient units and left many families without land property rights.

In 1992, the Salinas administration (1988–1994) initiated a new land ownership reform intended to provide ownership titles to around 2.8 million families. The arbitration process has created many disputes among villages, especially in Chiapas where the Zapatistas invaded disputed lands. The current Fox administration faces many pending cases. Farmers with ownership titles could sell their lands and join the urban population, concentrating land in fewer hands and improving the efficiency of the agricultural exploitations. However, this process has barely taken place.

## INFRASTRUCTURE

The isolated sources of growth reflect the weakness of crucial linkage variables—that is, those that measure the interaction between a firm's strategies and government policies and institutions (Porter and Stern, 2001). It is a challenge to provide adequate education, health, transport and communications services in a nation with 97 million people that ranks as the fourteenth largest country in the world and has a low GDP per capita.

The Mexican population is poorly educated. Better education services require not only higher education spending (which is around 5 percent of GDP, compared with 7 percent in the United States and Canada), but also addressing child malnutrition and other health problems. These are an even more serious concern in rural areas.

The main health care providers are the Instituto Mexicano del Seguro Social (IMSS, the social security institute) and the Instituto de Seguridad y Servicios Sociales de los Trabajadores del Estado (ISSSTE, the social security institute for public sector workers). Both organizations are funded by employer and employee contributions, returns on investments and, in the case of the ISSSTE, transfers from the federal government.

In 2000, about 47 million people were covered by the IMSS, with only an estimated 15.4 million affiliates paying contributions, while the ISSSTE, with 2.4 million affiliated state workers, offered services to more than 10 million people. In addition, about 4 percent of the population has private medical coverage. The population that does not contribute to the national social security system and private plans can obtain free healthcare from the Ministry of Health or the IMSS-Solidaridad (EIU).

The lack of proper transport and communication infrastructures has also impeded more balanced growth. In the last decade, the process of privatization and liberalization of many infrastructures, including ports, railways, airports and communications, has facilitated better management and development of these facilities. The new administration has to improve the liberalization and privatization strategy to attract additional private and foreign investment. Although transportation and communication infrastructures could rely heavily on private and foreign investment, education and health services and the provision of loss-making infrastructures require government funds. Thus, the government has to define adequate fiscal reform to generate enough funds.

## EXTERNAL SECTOR AND COMMERCIAL INDICATORS

Mexico's external sector is shaped by its relationship with the United States. The famous saying about Mexico and the United States has been attributed to Porfirio Díaz, the dictator who ruled Mexico from 1877 to 1910: "Poor Mexico so far from God and so close to the United States!" (Fuentes, 1996).

The integration of Mexico and North America was consolidated with the North American Free Trade Agreement (NAFTA) that went into effect January 1, 1994. It created the largest free trade area in the world, including Canada, the United States and Mexico. Some tariffs and tariff barriers were eliminated immediately; others are phased out gradually through 2008 (like corn, sugar, beans, etc). In response to environmental concerns in the United States, several agreements were added to enforce environmental law in Mexico.

The benefits from NAFTA are obvious when all member nations grow. During NAFTA's infancy, Mexico was plunged into a severe recession, accompanied by the peso devaluation of late 1994. NAFTA helped Mexico recover from the 1994 recession sooner than in the previous external debt crisis (1982–1983). Mexico is especially sensitive to shocks from the United States, since export sectors and foreign direct investment are the main generators of employment. In addition, transfers from the large Mexican population working in the United States are important sources of income and investment for Mexico.

Other concerns for Mexico are the possible extension of NAFTA-type benefits to other Latin American countries, such as Chile, and better implementation of the World Trade Organization. Both could reduce the share of its exports to the United States. Although NAFTA helps sustain real Mexican stability and growth, commercial integration is not enough. There are other crucial innovative capacity factors that we will discuss later.

### INTEGRATION WITH SOUTH AMERICA

The Fox administration has expressed interest in reaching agreements with the Mercado Común del Sur (Mercosur), although similar intentions have failed in the past due to trade conflicts with Brazil. On the other hand, there is a proposal by the president to increase integration between southern Mexico, which has scarcely benefited from NAFTA, and Central America. The proposal is known as the Puebla-to-Panama Plan, and would link nine states in southern Mexico to the isthmus with new roads and electrical and telecommunication links. However, this proposal is still vague, and we must not forget that Central America has been trying to develop in this way for over 160 years without much success.

### INTEGRATION WITH THE REST OF THE WORLD

Mexico joined what is now known as the World Trade Organization in 1986. Thus it faces intense competition from other countries. For example, China and Japan are two main trading partners. In addition, the country was admitted to the Asia-Pacific Economic Co-operation forum in 1993 and to the Organization for Economic Cooperation and Development (OECD) in 1994. The Fox administration favors an activist foreign policy, entering into free trade agreements with Israel and the European Union (2000), and starting negotiations with Singapore and Japan.

## COMMERCIAL INDICATORS

Mexico's exports are led by manufactured goods (over 87 percent of total exports in 2000–2003 in comparison with 68 percent in 1990), including clothing and textile products, electric and electronic parts and materials, and construction and assembly of transport equipment. By contrast, the share of crude oil and minerals fell from 25 to 10 percent in 1990–2000. Apart from the United States, which accounts for roughly 89 percent of Mexican exports, other main export partners are Latin America and the Caribbean (Venezuela), the European Union (Spain, Germany and the United Kingdom), Canada and Japan.

Intermediate goods are the main imports (approximately 75 percent of the total imports), mainly because Mexican in-bond assembly plants rely heavily on imported inputs (accounting for over 45 percent of the total intermediate goods imported). Imports come mainly from the United States (almost one-third), followed by the European Union (Germany and Italy), Japan, Latin America and the Caribbean, Canada, South Korea and China.

The trade balance has become increasingly negative since 1998, a result of strong internal consumption, trade liberalization and the strong peso. Despite a large tourism sector, service deficits have been increasing, primarily because of interest payments. Transfer payments have been increasingly important—some $6 billion—made up mainly of remittances from migrant workers. Adding the balance of trade, services and transfers, we get the current account balance, whose deficit has been growing very fast in the last decade. The current account deficit has been balanced in the main by foreign direct investment (FDI) followed by portfolio investments. The distribution of FDI across sectors is analyzed in the following section.

## OTHER ECONOMIC INDICATORS

Other key economic indicators for Mexico's economic performance include the inflation rate, interest rates, external debt and unemployment rates (see Table 9-1 for a comparative analysis).

Although economic policies have been very successful in decreasing the inflation rate—which averaged 19.4 percent during 1996–2000 and fell to 9.5 percent in 2000—it still is relatively high in comparison to developed countries. Thus, over 55 percent of entrepreneurs consider inflation an obstacle to business growth (Latin America Competitiveness Report 2001–2002, LACR). High inflation leads to high interest rates, increasing the investment costs for the private sector. The cost of funds was almost 20 percent in 1999 (EIU).

The debt-service ratio is relatively low (23 percent) in comparison with other major Latin American countries, such as Brazil (almost 65 percent) and Argentina (over 75 percent). The public sector accounted for over one-half of the total external debt, followed by the non-bank private sector whose participation has increased significantly recently, adding more than one-third to the total external debt. The main factor behind the increased foreign borrowing by the private sector is that domestic credit has been severely rationed, as reflected in the high interest rates.

**TABLE 9-1:** Comparative economic indicators, 2000 (US$bn unless otherwise stated)

|  | Mexico | US | Canada | Argentina | Brazil | Chile | Venezuela |
|---|---|---|---|---|---|---|---|
| GDP | 561.2 | 9966.0 | 711.1 | 281.7 | 622.4 | 70.2 | 103.8 |
| GDP per head (US$) | 5,763 | 36,165 | 23,125 | 7,605 | 3,751 | 4,613 | 4,293 |
| Consumer price inflation (av:%) | 9.5 | 3.4 | 2.7 | –0.9 | 7 | 4.5 | 16.2 |
| Current account balance | –18.2 | –437.6 | 18.1 | –11.2 | –25.5 | –1 | 12.9 |
| % of GDP | –3.2 | –4.4 | 2.5 | –4 | –4.1 | –1.4 | 12.5 |
| External debt | 171.5 | N.A. | N.A. | 153.1 | 235.5 | 36.8 | 34.1 |
| Debt-service ratio, paid (%) | 23.1 | N.A. | N.A. | 75.6 | 64.8 | 23.8 | 17.4 |
| FDI inflows | 12.4 | 316.53 | 63.3 | 11.1 | 23.9[b] | 3.7 | 4.1 |
| Unemployment rate | 2.2 | 4[a] | 6.8 | 14.7 | 7.1[b] | 8.3[c] | 14 |

[a]Unemployment rate is computed as a percentage of the civilian labor force.
[b]Data for 1999.
[c]Fourth quarter.

*Sources:* EIU, Country Profiles 2001, and INEGI.

    All the factors analyzed in this section combine to affect Mexico's ability to provide jobs for its growing economically active population. In urban areas, the open unemployment rate (the economically active population that does not work) was 2.2 percent in 2000. This result is too optimistic, and the percentage goes up to about 19 percent if we consider the proportion unemployed plus those employed for less than 35 hours per week (underemployed), and to over 10 percent for the unemployed and employed earning less than the minimum wage (insufficient income).

    The distribution of jobs across gender is uneven. The rate of employed women to the working population was about 35 percent in 1999. The main factor behind this is the low proportion of women in the economically active population. For example, in urban areas, about 39 percent of the total number of women 12 years old and over belonged to the economically active population in the year 2000, versus 75 percent for men (INEGI).

## CRISES AND ECONOMIC POLICY

Since the end of the 1920s, the economy of Mexico has been shaped by the Partido Revolucionario Institucional (PRI), defeated in the 2000 elections by the Partido Accion Nacional's (PAN) candidate, Vicente Fox Quesada. For many years sustained economic growth ensured strong popular support to the corporatist system developed by the PRI. Deterioration in the 1970s precipitated an external debt crisis in 1982. The administration of President Miguel de Madrid (1982–1988), forced by the external debt crisis, embarked on a major structural economic reform, including the liberalization of the economy (EIU).

The structural reform was enhanced during the presidency of Carlos Salinas de Gortari (1988–1994). The economy was opened to market forces and the role of the state was reduced considerably. The liberalization process was consolidated with free-trade pacts, most notably NAFTA, and more attractive investment rules.

During this period, the inflation rate decreased from 52 percent in 1988 to 7 percent in 1994, based on the use of a pegged exchange rate. At the same time, lower inflation led to lower interest rates, which helped to lower the cost of domestic debt. The government also took advantage of the corporatist structure of the PRI to enforce important austerity measures, wage restraint among them.

The reduction in the interest rate was spurred by the liberalization of the financial sector. The government privatized its commercial banks in 1991–1992, allowing the creation of new domestic banks in 1993 and the establishment of some foreign banks in 1994. The Banco de Mexico (the central bank) became independent in 1994, but the government retained control of the exchange rate policy.

Despite the fact that overvaluation, trade liberalization and economic growth produced increasing trade and current account deficits, the government kept its exchange rate control policy. The administration justified its policy on the wrong belief that the current account deficit only reflected the dynamism in the private sector, and that if capital were to cease to flow in the economy, the current account deficit would disappear.

In 1994, the current account deficit was unmanageable, and the government had to issue US$29.2 billion of *Tesobonos* (United States dollar-dominated bonds) to deal with domestic debt and stop the loss of reserves provoked by speculative attacks.

In 1994, the uprising of the Ejército Zapatista de Liberación Nacional (EZLN) weakened investor confidence, reducing international reserves dramatically. The incoming government of Ernesto Zedillo Ponce de León (1994–2000) was unable to sustain the exchange rate band system and devalued the peso. Without reserves to control the volatility of the peso in the new floating exchange rate regime, the peso collapsed at the end of 1994. In addition, the increase in interest rates to keep the capital in the country damaged the solvency of the banking system, which faced huge external debt servicing costs along with the bad debts resulting from improper credit management.

In January 1995, the government agreed to an emergency plan as it lacked the funds to pay the $29.2 billion of *Tesobonos*, due that year. The plan included the devaluation of the peso together with credible austerity measures and a bank bailout to avoid the collapse of the banking system. It secured the support of the United States, which contributed US$20 billion, the Bank for International Settlements (US$10 billion) and the IMF (US$17.8 billion). By the end of 1995, the trade account had a surplus of US$7.1 billion. Over time, confidence and reserves were restored, and the peso remained relatively stable.

In 1998, lower oil prices pushed the deficit further, and Mexico was also impacted by the general loss of confidence in emerging markets in response to the crisis in Southeast Asia. Depreciation of the peso helped exports, and with the recovery in oil prices the government was able to keep the public debt under control. As a result, 1999 ended with a stable peso, a successful 12.3 percent inflation rate and economic growth of 3.8 percent. During the year 2000, the strength of the U.S. economy and the strong growth in domestic demand, government consumption and gross fixed investment increased the GDP growth rate to its highest level of the 1990s (almost 7 percent).

## MEXICO'S ECONOMY IN THE TWENTY-FIRST CENTURY

In December 2000, the political system changed after the defeat of the long-ruling PRI by Vicente Fox, candidate of the coalition formed by the PAN and the green party Partido Verde Ecologista de México (PVEM). Mexico's congress is now divided among different political forces. For the first time, no political party holds a working majority. However, the transition to an open democracy will be slow, as Mexico lacks the proper institutions. The country is still under the system inherited from the PRI. Therefore, negotiations are crucial to implement the necessary social and economic reforms. Tax reform is the first test for the president's agenda.

The Fox administration faces an important socioeconomic task. First, it needs to face the deep-rooted conflicts over land, religion and politics, which most affect the poorest southern states of Mexico, and which provoked the uprising by the Zapatistas in 1994. The government so far has been unable to negotiate a peaceful end to the rebel conflicts in Chiapas.

To support the middle class and reduce social inequalities, the president plans to continue with the reform of social institutions (education, health and infrastructures) begun by his predecessor. The government has initiated a fiscal reform to generate enough funds. In addition, private and foreign investment and transfers will continue to play a crucial role as a source of funds. The next announced step is to open the state-run energy sector to private investment, helping to develop the electricity and natural gas sector. The telecom and petrochemical sectors are two other crucial sectors for increasing domestic and foreign competition.

Mexico's tax base is very narrow. It has one of the lowest tax collection rates in Latin America. A challenge for fiscal reform is to improve tax collection without worsening the very low income of many Mexicans. This has been the main argument used for the opposition against high tax increases. The main problem with tax reform is not raising more money to pay for better infrastructure and past debts, but to improve the efficiency of tax collection and enforcement. For example, a major problem is that informal activity (black market) is very important and concentrated in sectors that are crucial for government revenues, such as tourism.

In addition, high-tech sectors have lobbied hard to get fiscal incentives and avoid high value-added taxes (VAT) that could damage domestic demand. The telecom sector has been successful in convincing the senate to lower the increase in the telecommunications tax. Telmex (Mexico's largest telecom firm) played an important role in this. Finally, tax legislation has been approved to increase VAT and other taxes, but government negotiations did not succeed in the goal of a single VAT rate across all industries.

Since 2001 Mexico's economy has faced a major turndown. Could a recession such as the one in 1994 take place again? Does the present recession differ from the facts of the 1994 crisis? Both questions underscore the need for structural reforms to increase the competitiveness of Mexico's market. One important difference now is that, after NAFTA and other trade agreements, the Mexican market is open to a level of foreign competition much higher than in 1994. At the same time, the biggest threat for the Mexican economy is a prolonged recession in the United States.

As an indicator of improved debt management, in February 2002 the top credit-rating agencies (Standard & Poor's among them) lifted their ratings for Mexico's long-term foreign debt to investment grade (BBB-minus). The decision is the result of the observed behavior of the country's fiscal and monetary policies. Now Mexico should benefit from lower borrowing costs, entry of new investors and consolidation as a place for safe investment in South America.

Another special feature of the present recession is that it is accompanied by a strong currency. From December 2000 to February 2002, the peso appreciated substantially. This situation earned the free-floating Mexican currency the nickname of "super-peso." Although the strong currency is the result of a successful monetary policy accompanied by increasing investment, export-oriented companies complain of a strong real cost rise and are surprised at the ongoing strength of the Mexican peso.

The strong peso has kept inflation and interest rates relatively low, helping the recovery of the Mexican economy. However, if imports keep growing faster than exports, along with a strong currency and domestic demand, the current account deficit could become unmanageable, as happened in 1994. There are many uncertainties about whether the peso will collapse or will depreciate smoothly, but the negative shock would not be as bad as in previous crises.

Another factor that threatens the macroeconomic environment is that since 1999 Mexico has suffered a significant slowdown in productivity growth in the manufacturing sector. Mexico's cost competitiveness is decreasing because wages in U.S. dollars increased more than the gains in productivity and prices. This is a clear threat for the competitiveness of Mexico's economy.

The main reason for the productivity growth decline may have been that the labor force is not sufficiently educated to take advantage of the technological changes that took place during the 1990s. Also, the effort that Mexico has placed on improving its macroeconomic management is still incomplete. While high inflation and major fiscal deficits have been reduced, the high cost of access to internal and external financing for the private sector is still a major problem.

In the rest of the chapter we pay closer attention to the Mexican consumer market. First, we analyze the potential of the internal market. Then, we focus on the competitiveness of the Mexican market—contending that the potential of the consumer markets is contingent on the competitiveness of the Mexican economy. We will close the chapter with the analysis of alternative marketing strategies.

## EMERGENT CONSUMER MARKET

We now turn to the great potential of the Mexican consumer market, which must provide goods and services to more than 97 million people. The potential of the market is driven by private consumption, which relies on job creation and real earnings. In terms of GDP per capita in 1999, Mexico ranked 39th among the 75 countries included in the Latin American Competitiveness Report (LACR), below Costa Rica (35th) and Chile (36th), but above other Latin American economies including Brazil (43rd) and Venezuela (52nd). Mexico's GDP per capita has experienced a positive change from 1996 to 2002, growing by 6 percent in the year 2000. As a result, private demand has experienced a high rate of growth, reaching approximately 10 percent in the year 2000.

While Mexico's economic accomplishments are indisputable, wealth inequalities among families are severe. Thus, the 10 percent of wealthiest families account for over 38 percent of total income, while the poorest families in the bottom decile account for less than 1.5 percent. The growth potential in the southern states is clearly hindered by severe poverty conditions, as they have not benefited from the foci of growth in northern and central Mexico. The integration of the market through improved education, health, transportation and communication infrastructures is a crucial factor to generate millions of jobs throughout Mexico. In a later section, we discuss in more detail the main weaknesses and strengths of Mexico's competitiveness.

Mexican society has experienced significant changes that have modified the structure and role of the family. One main factor behind these changes is the transition from rural to urban population. This process has accelerated since the 1970s. At that time women started to gradually participate in the labor force. They were mostly young and educated and worked for the administration and in private services, contributing to the emergence of the middle class. In the 1980s, economic crises boosted the incorporation of women into the labor supply. They were mostly poorly educated and they held low-wage jobs, but their role was crucial in increasing low family incomes.

Today, economically active women suffer significant wage discrimination—the average gap in wages is over 30 percent—and high unemployment rates. This is a limitation for the potential consumer market, especially as an increasing percentage of families are headed by single women (over 20 percent in 2000).

## ROLE OF THE MEXICAN POPULATION IN THE UNITED STATES

In addition to the increasing potential of the internal market, Mexico enjoys privileged access to the U.S. market, where approximately 21.7 million Mexicans live (U.S. Bureau of the Census). The Mexican population in the United States interacts with Mexico's internal demand in several important ways. First, transfers from Mexicans working in the United States are crucial assets for Mexico's economy. Total transfers recorded in the current account add up to approximately $6 billion. They are made up mostly from remittances of Mexicans working in the United States. This figure underestimates the total money that Mexican immigrants send to Mexico, which could account for over $9 billion yearly. This amount is equivalent to more than 75 percent of the total FDI that has been flowing into Mexico yearly. So far, most of the money sent is spent on private consumption, and little is invested in projects that generate jobs. The government and Mexican banks are trying to channel some of these transfers, offering special investment opportunities for immigrants in projects that could stimulate growth.

The Mexican government has also encouraged the formation of associations of Mexicans from the same town. There over 400 such groups in the United States. They raise money among themselves and finance public works projects and small businesses in Mexico. In addition, recently some banking institutions in the United States agreed to allow immigrants from Mexico, whether legal or not, to use identification cards received from Mexican consulates to open bank accounts. These accounts will allow them to send money transfers to Mexico easily.

Transportation and communication services between Mexico and the United States have improved significantly, mainly because of the development of the Mexican export sector, including tourism. This factor facilitates the interaction between Mexican internal demand and the Mexican community in the United States, which is mostly concentrated in the nearer western and southern United States—over 56 and 32 percent, respectively. The short distance from Mexico allows Mexican immigrants to visit their families and to provide them with more sophisticated manufactured goods. They are also able to run small businesses in Mexico while working in the United States. Others are working in Texas border cities while living in Mexico. This possibility is partially offset by the reallocation of some Texas border cities' manufacturing industries to Mexico to benefit from lower wages.

The great potential of the Mexican population in the United States is contingent on the U.S. market's ability to generate labor opportunities for its Hispanic population. On the other hand, immigration issues are a great concern today in the United States, where more than 3 million Mexican immigrants work illegally (Bean et al., 2001). The Mexican administration wants America to institute legalization programs for this group in return for policing Mexico's border with the United States more closely. So far no agreement has been reached.

## COMPETITIVENESS OF MEXICAN FIRMS

As an indicator of the prospects for growth and competition in the Mexican economy, we look at the distribution of foreign direct investment (FDI) across economic sectors (Figure 9-3).

The Foreign Investment Law enacted in 1993 stimulated FDI flows, which reached more than $12 billion by the year 2000. The United States dominates FDI—some 70 percent of the total in the first quarter of 2001—followed by Switzerland, Sweden and the Netherlands (23 percent of the total); Canada (2.5 percent); and Japan (1.4 percent).

Under the new government, foreign investment promotion is the task of Nafin (Mexico's development bank) and Bancomext (the foreign trade bank). The investment rules vary by sectors. For many activities, 100 percent foreign investment participation in the equity of Mexican firms is allowed. Other activities, including oil, hydrocarbons, basic petrochemicals, energy transmission and distribution, are reserved exclusively for the state. Still others, such as development banks, radio and television broadcasting other than cable television, and domestic cargo and passenger land transport are reserved for Mexican investment. Finally, foreign participation in other areas is limited to neutral investments—nonvoting equity. Examples are certain activities in finance, communications, transport and agriculture.

More than two-thirds of total FDI goes to the industrial sector. This reveals the increasing importance of this sector, which accounted for only about 30 percent of total FDI in 1990. Export-oriented manufacturing activities have experienced the highest rate of growth and account for the highest share of FDI. The export-oriented manufacturing sector relies heavily on imports of inputs and components, damaging many small Mexican firms oriented to the domestic market.

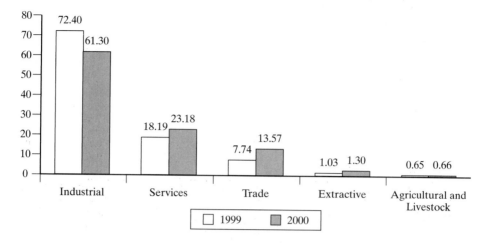

Source: *Secretaría de Economía. Dirección General de Inversión Extranjera.*

**FIGURE 9-3** Mexico's foreign direct investment (FDI) inflows: distribution by sector

On the other hand, product manufacturing for cement, glass, etc. is mostly dominated by large Mexican firms. The potential of the consumer market plays a crucial role in this sector, as the supply depends on housing demand and infrastructure development. The latter is a priority for the competitiveness of the Mexican economy.

Retail and wholesale commerce has also increased its participation in total FDI during the last decade, adding up to 14 percent in 2000. The retail market has faced major changes in the last decade. Large foreign companies have entered the market, such as Wal-Mart de México. The intense competition has pushed leading Mexican firms to modernize and increase cost controls and widen their areas of operation to the smaller provincial cities. Another major change in the retail sector has been the recent development of large shopping centers, but small family-run firms still account for more than half of retail sales (EIU).

The participation of foreign firms in the banking sector is significant, especially after the removal in 1998 of all limitations on the foreign ownership of banks. Acquisitions by foreign banks have created some of the country's largest financial institutions. Examples of such purchases are Banca Serfín (the third-largest bank in the country), which was sold to Spain's Banco Santander Central Hispano in May 2000, and Bancomer, which subsequently merged with Spain's Banco Bilbao Vizcaya Argentaria. Later that year, Bancomer absorbed Banca Promex. By 2000 there were more than 34 commercial banks, but the sector is still small in terms of credit opportunities. As a result, larger companies have found it cheaper to borrow from foreign banks and to raise money by issuing foreign bonds.

Another financial sector with potential is the stock market. The Bolsa Mexicana de Valores (BMV, Mexican Stock Exchange) opened to foreign traders just a decade ago. Foreign capitalization of the stock market has been increasing, but it seems that the

BMV is not able to attract more firms. One of the main factors behind the small size of the stock market is that big firms have access to the New York Stock Market through American Depositary Receipts (ADRs; for example, Telmex and Cemex, S.A.). Besides, meeting the requirements to access the BMV takes a long time, and many firms do not want to provide the detailed information required. Owing to the lack of dynamism in the stock market, domestic savings are mostly channeled through the banking system.

Firms that list on the stock market concentrate mainly in the manufacturing sector (approximately 39 percent). Food and beverage manufacturing firms add about 14 percent to the total number of firms. Financial services add over 12 percent, and retail and wholesale commerce adds 16 percent (Figure 9-4).

We could interpret this distribution as an imperfect signal of the more dynamic sectors in the Mexican economy. We cannot ignore that almost 90 percent of the total firms in Mexico are very small and obtain funds mainly through the banking system. Other larger firms prefer to generate funds through venture capital, mostly American.

The Telecom sector is dominated by the former state monopoly, Telmex. Competitors complain of the high interconnection fees charged by Telmex. Both domestic and foreign investors are awaiting the planned reform of the 1995 Mexico Federal Telecommunications Law. On the other hand, Internet-related firms have underperformed or gone bankrupt, due to low levels of personal computer penetration and Internet awareness. These firms could suffer in the short run from the approved increase in VAT. However, the potential of the consumer market will eventually benefit this sector.

FDI participation in primary sectors (including agriculture, forestry and fishing) has been relatively low. These sectors suffer from short-term investment and low productivity. However, given Mexico's abundance of natural resources and the great

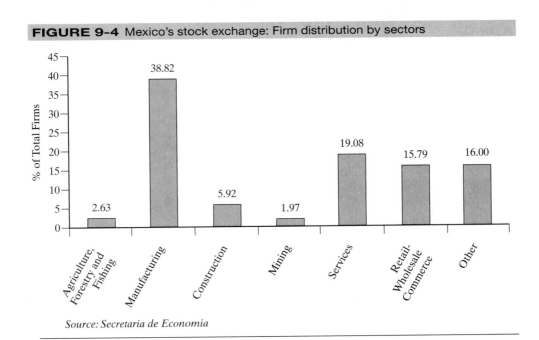

**FIGURE 9-4** Mexico's stock exchange: Firm distribution by sectors

*Source: Secretaria de Economia*

potential of both internal and external demand, they represent an important investment opportunity.

Another issue is the liberalization of the state-run energy sector. The energy sector is already on the agenda of the Fox administration, but any proposal of foreign involvement in the traditionally "nationalistic" energy sector, which includes one of the oldest Mexican labor unions, will be hard to negotiate. In order to meet the increasing demand the government needs to invest mostly in electricity and natural gas development. However, it lacks the funds to do so. FDI is required to take advantage of the full capacity in this sector.

In addition, new investments will increase employment, the biggest challenge of populous Mexico. However, reform will not be easy, as it must guarantee that the government not lose a crucial source of revenue and that Mexican firms be able to compete.

## THE GENERAL COMPETITIVE CLIMATE

After analyzing the investment opportunities and foreign competition faced by the different economic sectors, we will offer a more general picture of Mexico's competitiveness. Is the Mexican economy ready to take advantage of the growing domestic and international demand? We will answer this question by studying two competitiveness measures: the Innovative Capacity Index and the Competitiveness Index.

In developing countries, including Mexico, the challenges for competitiveness are lower costs and higher quality. However, in today's world the key factors for the future competitiveness must also come from the ability to innovate, that is, to create and commercialize new products and processes (Porter and Stern, 2001).

We analyze Mexico's innovative capacity based on the econometric analysis developed by Porter and Stern (2001). Using data and measures available from the Global Competitiveness Report 2001–2002 (GCR), they ranked 75 major countries, including 20 in Latin America, in terms of their national innovative capacity. They compute the Innovation Capacity Index as the sum of four subindexes: the Proportion of Scientists, Innovation Policy, Cluster Innovation Environment and Linkages.

In terms of its innovative capacity Mexico ranks fifty-third, far behind other major Latin American countries. This indicates that Mexico lacks proper innovative environments and, consequently, sustainable growth. One must analyze the innovation index's four components to get a better understanding of the major weaknesses of Mexico's innovation capacity.

Mexico ranks fiftieth for the proportion of scientists and engineers subindex. This reflects the poor performance of its education system. In terms of the innovation policy subindex, Mexico occupies forty-fifth place. This measure of cross-cutting investments and policies supporting innovations includes variables such as intellectual property protection, quality of education, attractiveness to retain scientists and engineers, and government R&D tax credits and subsidies. In order to improve the investment in R&D activities in Mexico, a crucial factor is to reduce the cost of and unstable access to internal and external financing for the private sector, along with further liberalization of the economy.

The cluster innovation environment subindex ranks Mexico Forty-sixth. This measure refers to the attributes of a cluster—a geographic concentration of interconnected companies and institutions in a particular field—that affect innovation. These attributes include buyer sophistication, local supplier quality, local availability of specialized research and training services and product and process collaboration. Although Mexico's manufacturing industry is highly concentrated in geographic areas, it lacks a favorable environment for innovation.

Finally, the linkages subindex summarizes the interaction between private-sector strategies and public-sector policies and institutions. It is the component with the worst performance, ranking Mexico sixty-third. Linkage variables include quality of scientific research institutions, university/industry research collaboration and venture capital availability. Thus the results are not surprising.

As we mentioned before, in developing countries the challenges for competitiveness rely significantly on their ability to efficiently produce to international standards of technology and quality, and consequently raise productivity and income. A measure of this ability is the Competitiveness Index, computed for the same 75 countries (Latin American Competitiveness Report 2001–2002, LACR). Mexico competitiveness ranking is forty-third, above Brazil but below Chile and China.

The three areas that comprise the Competitiveness Index are the Macroeconomic Environment, Technology and Public Institutions subindexes. The macroeconomic environment ranks Mexico thirty-fifth. In the technology index, the Latin American countries that occupy the best positions are Costa Rica (32nd) and Mexico (36th). Mexico's stronger relative performance in this index is related to the importance of FDI as a source of new technology and the technological content of the export basket (approximately 60 percent of its total exports are of high or medium technology content).

The worst Mexican indicator is the public institutions subindex that summarizes the opinion of the business community as to the rule of law and control of corruption. Mexico ranks fifty-sixth, close to Colombia, but far above the other main countries in Latin America. An important factor behind this result is the weak protection of creditors.

The interaction among the two competitiveness measures analyzed and the GDP gives additional information about a country's economic performance. Porter and Stern (2001) analyze the correlation of the Innovative Capacity Index with the GDP and the Competitiveness Index. Mexico's competitiveness reflects its innovative capacity and does not seem to rely on natural resources and low labor costs, factors that play an important role in other Latin American countries.

However, Mexico's standard of living (as measured by the GDP per capita) is higher than would be justified by its innovative capacity. This could be explained by its abundance of natural resources and favorable geographic location in comparison to other nations, in particular its close geographic and commercial relation with the rest of North America. In contrast, some Latin American countries have a GDP lower than expected according to their innovative capacity, indicating a huge effort to push the economy forward, for example, Chile and Brazil.

The great potential of the Mexican economy is contingent on overcoming the weaknesses revealed by the innovation and competitiveness indexes.

## MARKETING STRATEGIES

As we have seen, the growth of the Mexican consumer market is contingent on a number of economic and political factors. The fact remains, however, that there is the potential for the emergence of a strong middle-class consumer market. The prospects for this are bolstered when one considers the high probability that Mexican immigrants in the United States will continue to be not only a source of economic stimulation but also a model of consumer culture.

It is not difficult in this context to envisage an emerging consumer market that extends over at least the northern part of Mexico and is integrated with concentrations of Mexican immigrants in the United States. Such a market could resemble patterns of regional growth in the United States, such as the emergence of the Sunbelt.

Although this prospect of a stable and growing middle-class consumer market is far from certain, it represents a significant marketing opportunity. The question for businesses, both Mexican and international, is to decide on a strategy for approaching this market. Most firms will take a skim-and-wait strategy. Their approach will be to offer products and services to higher income consumers and to market these over time to new consumers as the income of these consumers rises. These firms will not target the very affluent consumer who is already well served and has established buying patterns. They will target consumers at the high end of the middle-income group. The strategy will be to get as much revenue from these consumers as currently possible but to count on growth coming from new consumers who reach this income level over time.

A bank with a skim-and-wait strategy might offer a prestige credit card that is coupled with personal services. With this card the consumer can contact a personal banker to discuss a variety of needs, a personal loan, for instance. Many consumers will not be qualified to receive this card; their income or credit worthiness will be too low. But the card would be marketed so that they become aware of it and aspire to it. When these consumers attain the necessary income level, they will essentially be presold on the card. The bank need only wait for newly minted target consumers to emerge.

The skim-and-wait marketing strategy has obvious merits. It certainly reduces risk and avoids the problem of offering quality products at lower price levels than the firm may be accustomed to. In our opinion, however, it should not be the only marketing strategy considered. The Mexican consumer of tomorrow with a higher income may not be the same as today's higher income consumer. Particularly because of the proximity to U.S. consumer culture, the Mexican consumer is likely to change over time in many ways.

## THE CHANGING MEXICAN CONSUMER

Consumers in an emerging market such as Mexico must be understood in terms of social change. At any given point in time consumers are oriented by established social values. By social values we do not refer to the monetary worth placed on products. Rather we refer to how the culture implies that people should live their lives. Social values provide direction and justification for how people live their lives. In Mexico there is, for instance, a strong value placed on the role of the mother. In particular, a very special sentimental value is associated with the mother-son relationship. This leads consumers to direct their lives in ways that emulate the household practices of the mother.

At any given time traditional values anchor the culture. But in the case of a society that is changing, such as Mexico, there are also new values that emerge from or are imported into the culture. These new values often conflict with the traditional values. People must resolve these conflicts in their daily lives. Out of this process comes social change. Conflict is resolved by adopting new behaviors that initially bridge the conflicting values until the conflict is resolved, usually with the new value becoming the traditional value.

A number of such value conflicts among Mexican consumers have been identified by Letelier, Spinosa and Calder (2000). One important value conflict is between the traditional importance of family and an emerging value of individual independence from the family. Others revolve around festive freedom (celebrating in the present with family and friends) versus planning and delaying gratification for future benefits. There is also the traditional value orientation to fate (things that happen in life are pre-determined and one should not try to control them) versus trying actively to control one's life. Another current value conflict surrounds seeking patronage from a higher status person versus learning new skills for advancement.

Value conflicts such as these represent significant marketing opportunities in Mexico. Consider an example from the work of Letelier, Spinosa and Calder (2000) on a new bank credit card product. A new card was designed that reflected the value conflict experienced by consumers around the traditional values of festive living and trusting fate versus a more planned, independent life. The new card was designed around a family money-market checking account that was shared by the husband, wife, children and often extended family.

The card was a family card, shared according to traditional values. Interest was based on all of the funds available. But it allowed each family member to have a sub-account in their name and to have control over the money in their account. Thus the wife could have a *guardadito* of her own. This would be valued according to the new value of independence but would still be aligned with traditional values of family unity. Subaccounts for extended family members have a similar appeal, especially for Mexican immigrants in the United States, in that they facilitate sharing with relatives and independence from them at the same time.

The new card was also designed to resolve the conflicts many Mexican consumers experience over credit and loans. These can violate the traditional values associated with fate and not planning for the future. The account was designed so that consumers would feel that credit or loans would be available only after the card had been used for some period of time. The bank would act as a patron giving credit as a reward for the past, not as an incentive for consumers to plan their futures in advance. The final step in this predetermined sequence would be access to investment services, again not as part of an active consumer planning process but as something determined by the consumer's status with the patron bank. In this way the new card is appealing precisely because it speaks to the value conflicts experienced by consumers.

## THE PENETRATE-AND-DEVELOP STRATEGY

The skim-and-wait marketing strategy is obviously applicable to the Mexican consumer market. We believe, however, that there is potentially even greater opportunity in Mexico for what we call a penetrate-and-develop marketing strategy. With this strategy a company does not assume that tomorrow's more affluent consumer will be the same as today's more affluent consumer. Mexico is undergoing social change, the result of traditional values conflicting with new values. There is an opportunity to address today's consumer in terms of this change. If we can provide products designed to fit today's consumer we can acquire consumers now rather than waiting for a future that may or may not arrive.

## CONCLUSION

Mexico has been, and will continue to be in the foreseeable future, an unpredictable economy. The growth of a middle-class consumer market that presents excellent marketing opportunities is a definite possibility. But, as we have seen, the size and level of affluence of this market is contingent on many factors, both political and economic.

This lack of predictability is another point in favor of the penetrate-and-develop marketing strategy we have described. If a company can design products to appeal to today's Mexican consumer because of their fit to the consumer's changing social situation, the company will not have to rely on higher priced offerings that can only be afforded by most consumers at some future point. A company that pursues this strategy, furthermore, will provide the kind of innovation needed by the economy and will participate in the realization of the potential of the Mexican economy.

## BIBLIOGRAPHY

Banco de México, www.banxico.org.mx.

Bean, F. D., R. Corona, R. Tuirán, K. Woodrow-Lafield, and J. Van Hook. (2001) "Circular, Invisible, and Ambiguous Migrants: Components of Differences in Estimates of the Number of Unauthorized Mexican Migrants in the United States." *Demography* 30:411–422.

Cooper, J. C. and K. Madigan. (November 19, 2001) "Mexico: Congress Faces a Taxing Time." *Business Week*.

*Economatica* (March 15, 2002), data and software for investment analysis.

Economist Intelligence Unit. (March 2002) "Country Commerce: Mexico." *The Economist*.

Economist Intelligence Unit. (2001) *EIU Country Profiles*.

Fuentes, C. (1996) *A New Time for Mexico*. New York: Farrar, Straus and Giroux.

Giugale, M. M., O. Lafourcade, and V. H. Nguyen, eds. (2001) *Mexico: A Comprehensive Development Agenda for the New Era*. World Bank.

Inweb18.worldbank.org/external/lac/lac.nsf/0/9364AB8A25BABD6085256A4C004B.

Gobierno Federal. *Plan Nacional de Desarrollo, 2001–2006*. www.pnd.presidencia.gob.mx.

Instituto Nacional de Estadística, Geografía e Informática (INEGI). www.inegi.gob.mx

Inter-American Development Bank. (2001) *Competitiveness: The Business of Growth. Economic and Social Progress in Latin America*. London: The Johns Hopkins University Press.

Letelier, M. F., C. Spinosa, and B. J. Calder. (2000) "Taking an Expanded View of Customers' Needs: Qualitative Research for Aiding Innovation." *Marketing Research* Winter:4–11.

Meyer, M. C. and W. H. Beezley. (2000) *The Oxford History of Mexico*. Oxford: Oxford University Press.

Pew Hispanic Center, USC Annenberg School for Communication, www.pewhispanic.org.

Porter, M. E. and S. Stern. (2001) "National Innovative Capacity," M. E. Porter and

J. Sachs (eds.), *Global Competitiveness Report 2001–2002*. New York: Oxford University Press.

Secretaría de Economía. www.economía.gob.mx.

Sistema de Información Empresarial Mexicano (SIEM). www.secofi-siem.gob.mx.

"A Survey of Mexico: After the Revolution." (October 28, 2000) *The Economist*.

Therrien, M. and R. R. Ramírez. (2000) "The Hispanic Population in the United States."

*Current Population Reports*. Census Bureau, Washington, D.C.: www.census.gov.

Thompson, G. (March 25, 2002) "Big Mexican Breadwinner: The Migrant Worker," *New York Times*.

World Economic Forum. (2002) *The Latin American Competitiveness Report 2001–2002*. New York: Oxford University Press.

# CHAPTER 10
# PANAMA

### DR. NICOLAS ARDITO BARLETA

## INTRODUCTION

Panama is an S-shaped isthmus located in the middle of the Western Hemisphere, linking North and South America. It is the narrowest landmass separating the Pacific and Atlantic oceans. At the turn of the twenty-first century, Panama consolidated its territory by receiving the Panama Canal and adjacent military bases from the United States. The country is now engaged in studying the canal expansion to serve the needs of world trade in this century, developing the emerging cluster of maritime and commercial activity at both entrances to the canal, strengthening its democratic and economic institutions and extending the benefits of development to all its population.

With a very small population base, the nation emerged in a strategic geographical location used through the centuries by world powers to enhance their international trade interests. The nation has been consolidated slowly as various technologies were applied to develop its potential as a key transit center for transportation and commercial activity. Today it looks toward a future of integration within Latin and North America serving the trade and transport needs of the world.

## THE LAND AND THE PEOPLE

Geography and climate have determined Panama's destiny. Because of its location, it became a crossroads for flora and fauna, for peoples, cultures, goods and services. The inhospitable tropical climate did not stimulate a large population settlement until the technologies of the twentieth century improved living conditions. Today standard health, sanitary and comfort practices make it an attractive country in which to live and do business.

As part of the ecological corridor of Mesoamerica, Panama has one of the richest biodiversities in the Western Hemisphere. Panama has a coastline of more than 2,000 kilometers on both oceans. It is a narrow strip of land between the oceans ranging in width between 50 and 165 kilometers, with a generally low mountain range. Thus nature has defined Panama as a crossroads.

The Panamanian people are a mixture of races and cultures. The majority are mestizos, combining European and indigenous ethnic groups, with an additional significant component of whites, blacks and Chinese. The early inhabitants, mostly Gnobe Bugles, Kuna and Emberá indigenous and ethnic groups, were partially replaced by the Spaniards during the colonial period. The Spaniards mixed with

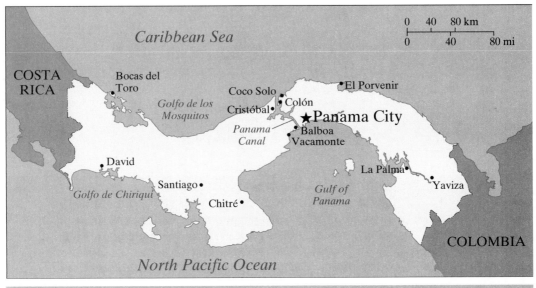

**FIGURE 10-1** Map of Panama

these groups, resulting in the mestizos. In the second half of the nineteenth century, significant groups of Europeans and Chinese came at the time of the trans-isthmian railroad construction and during the initial work to build the Panama Canal. At the beginning of the twentieth century Caribbean-African groups came as laborers for the canal construction. Together with the Afro-Panamanians of the colonial period, they make up over 18 percent of the population today. Small communities of Jewish, Arab and Hindustani peoples are members of the Panamanian ethnic and cultural mosaic.

Roman Catholicism is the faith of 85 percent of the population. Most of the rest participate in Protestant Christian churches, with significant minorities belonging to the Jewish, Muslim and Hindu religions.

Panama today is made up of three regions. Metropolitan Panama is located in the transit area where the Canal and Panama City and Colon are located. It hosts 80 percent of the nation's economic activity and 64 percent of the people. Interior Panama, on the Pacific coast to the border with Costa Rica, is typified by savanna and low hills, by agricultural and agribusiness activities in small towns and open country. This region has 17 percent of the country's economic activity and 27 percent of the population. Frontier Panama, on the Caribbean coast up to Darien, between the borders with Costa Rica and Colombia, has 3 percent of Panama's economic activity and 9 percent of the population, mostly indigenous ethnic groups. This region preserves the Mesoamerican biological corridor.

Geographically, Panama is part of Central America. Historically, it has been part of South America through the Andean nations. It received an influx of Caribbean culture at the time of the Canal construction. The Western, indigenous and Caribbean cultural traditions mix in this tropical land. U.S. traditions, present throughout the twentieth century, have likewise left an imprint.

**TABLE 10-1:** Panama geography

| Feature | Description |
| --- | --- |
| Location | Middle America, bordering both the Caribbean Sea and the North Pacific Ocean, between Colombia and Costa Rica |
| Geography note | Strategic location on eastern end of isthmus forming land bridge connecting North and South America; controls Panama Canal that links North Atlantic Ocean via Caribbean Sea with North Pacific Ocean |
| Area | Total: 78,200 sq km<br>Water: 2,210 sq km<br>Land: 75,990 sq km<br>Slightly smaller than South Carolina |
| Land boundaries | Total: 555 km<br>Border countries: Colombia, 225 km; Costa Rica, 330 km |
| Population | 3.1 million (UN 2003) |
| Capital | Lima |
| Life expectancy | 72 years men; 77 years women |
| Natural resources | Copper, mahogany forests, shrimp, hydropower |
| Land use | Arable land: 6.72%<br>Permanent crops: 2.08%<br>Other: 91.2% (1998 est.) |
| Main exports | Bananas, shrimp, sugar, coffee |
| Average annual income | US$3,260 |

## A BRIEF HISTORY

The Panamanian isthmus emerged some 3 million years ago, linking North and South America and separating the oceans. The resulting changes in ocean currents changed the European and African climates. Flora and fauna from the north and south met at the isthmus, creating a rich biodiversity. For over 10,000 years, people coming from the north came through the isthmus and settled, going through the stages of migratory peoples and then settling in sparse towns supported by agricultural practices. Population centers evolved with distant links to the Mayan and Incan cultures.

Bastidas and Columbus (on his last trip) explored the Caribbean coastline of Panama in 1501 and 1502. Several small Spanish towns were built. In 1513, Balboa crossed the isthmus and discovered for the Europeans the "Southern Sea" (Pacific Ocean). That event sealed the modern destiny of Panama. The Chagres River in the middle of the area going to the Caribbean was navigated in the 1520s. That led Charles V, Emperor of Spain and Austria, to order the study of a canal connecting the river to the Pacific Ocean. The project was not pursued.

Panama City on the Pacific Coast was founded in 1519 and, together with Nombre de Dios and Portobello on the Atlantic side 70 kilometers away, became the route for

South American treasures and goods going to Spain. Panama City was the point of departure for Pizarro to conquer Peru and Almagro, Chile. Nicaragua, Ecuador and other Pacific countries were colonized from Panama.

The transit of goods and treasures through Panama City, Camino de Cruces and the Chagres River to Nombre de Dios and Portobello led to the organization of the annual trade fairs in Nombre de Dios (1544–1596) and in Portobello (1597–1739), bringing the Spaniards and the colonies together to enhance commercial activity. British pirates made their presence felt from time to time, disturbing and blocking the trade and even sponsoring contraband routes near the main Spanish routes. Henry Morgan sacked Panama City in 1692. The city was then rebuilt in a nearby, safer place in 1693.

The evolution of Panama over the last 500 years has three basic stages:

1. The shock and clash between indigenous and European peoples and cultures between 1502 and 1600.
2. The colonial settlement period between 1600 and the middle nineteenth century.
3. The modern period when more urban and international links have been developed.

Transit through Panama has developed in stages according to available technologies. During the colonial period it was done with mules, barges and slaves. After 1855, the crossing was made via the first cross-continental railroad of the Americas—built by a U.S. corporation—and steamships. After 1914, transit was simplified thanks to the Panama Canal, also built by the United States, and modern ships. In the last fifty years, complementary trade has been enhanced by airline transportation.

Colonial trade declined after the Portobello fairs were discontinued in 1739. The activity moved to Cartagena. When transit activity declined, agricultural activities increased in the rest of Panama.

Panama declared its independence from Spain in 1821, following the Bolivarian independence movement in South America, and joined Great Colombia (with Ecuador and Venezuela) under Simón Bolívar, until it broke apart in 1830. Thereafter, a country with a very small population (150,000 inhabitants in 1840) remained attached to Colombia as a forgotten Federal State and then a province. However, it was always aware of its international transit potential. Meanwhile, in the 1850s, the United States, Great Britain and Colombia made agreements to guarantee safe transit through the isthmus.

The French Canal Company, under Ferdinand de Lesseps (builder of the Suez Canal), attempted to build a canal in the 1880s but failed due to disease, poor management and insufficient financing. The United States became interested in building the canal at the turn of the twentieth century and, after failing to reach agreement with Colombia, supported an independence movement initiated by Panamanians in 1903 and negotiated a treaty to build a canal through Panama with the new Republic.

The unequal partnership ("very favorable to the U.S. and not so favorable to Panama," said U.S. Secretary of State Hay) defined for Panama the long-term struggle to regain its ability to benefit from the Canal and to reincorporate the Canal Zone, which had been segregated from national jurisdiction "in perpetuity." Two amendments to the treaty (in 1936 and 1955) eliminated the protectorate status of Panama and increased the economic benefits to the country.

The treaties of 1977 abrogated previous agreements, eliminated the Canal Zone, increased Panamanian economic participation and benefits and defined procedures for the joint management of the Canal until 1999, when it was to be placed totally under Panamanian ownership and control. Since 2000, Panama has managed the Canal successfully through an autonomous public company, the Panama Canal Authority.

During most of the twentieth century, the Republic of Panama evolved with western-style democratic institutions. Democracy was interrupted by three coups that quickly returned to civilian democratic control, except during the 1968–1980 period. During that period, the National Guard controlled the government, which was managed by civilians. After the 1977 canal treaties, there was a commitment to return to fully democratic institutions with the 1984 elections. However, the new government was overthrown in 1985 and the military continued in control until 1989, when the United States intervened militarily to remove General Noriega and the defense forces from the scene. From 1990 to the present, governance has taken place through democratic institutions.

## THE ECONOMIC TRADITION

Panama has always had a small population. From 320,000 inhabitants in 1904, the population grew rapidly to 3.0 million in 2001. Nevertheless, Panama remains a small market economy.

As stated, the economic history of Panama evolved for 500 years with increasing international transit and trade as world commerce grew and new technologies were applied to the narrow geographic strategic location. Tropical agrarian activity complemented that evolution.

In the twentieth century the transit economy, with the Canal and U.S. presence, gradually became the main engine of growth.

Since 1904, Panama has defined a monetary system without a central bank, using the U.S. dollar as the medium of exchange—in effect a "dollarized" economy. Over the years, it has added legal definitions and administrative infrastructure to enhance the economic value of its transit economy. An example is the Corporation Law of 1927, based on the Delaware (U.S.) law. In the 1930s, the tax system was defined as "territorial," meaning that economic transactions of Panamanian firms made outside of the country need not pay taxes in Panama. In the 1940s, a legal framework was established to stimulate Panamanian registration of the international merchant marine, which led to the largest ship registration in the world. In 1948, a Free Trade Zone was created in Colón, the city at the Caribbean entrance to the Canal.

Today, it has an annual turnover of $10.0 billion, it is the largest in the Western Hemisphere. In 1970, a new, modern banking law was approved to set up the framework that led to the creation of an international banking center fully integrated with the international financial community. This is the largest such center in Latin America. In 1976, legislation was passed to sponsor the creation of a regional reinsurance center. In 1978, an agreement was signed with a U.S. company to build a trans-isthmian oil pipeline that for fifteen years transshipped Alaskan oil to the U.S. East Coast.

In the 1990s, the construction of private container transshipment ports and the privatization of the public ports of Balboa and Cristobal was carried out to complement the Canal operations, leading to dynamic growth in container transshipment. Since 1998, new submarine communication cables cross the isthmus alongside the Canal, broadening the communications potential of Panama.

All of the preceding legislation and activities have generated an international maritime and business cluster around the canal, which is now accelerating with the full integration of the former Canal Zone with Panama.

The long tradition of the Panamanian people of providing transportation and trade services was deepened and diversified in the twentieth century in the metropolitan transit region of Panama. The agrarian tradition of the country's other regions has evolved toward agribusiness. Manufacturing as a productive tradition grew after the 1940s.

From 1904 to the 1950s, the economy was heavily influenced by Canal activity. Two extensive booms (1904–1914 and 1939–1947) were led by canal construction and U.S. military activities to protect the canal during World War II. The Great Depression in the 1930s also led to an extended depression in Panama.

In the 1950s, the fashion of import substitution policies in Latin America led Panama to also initiate such a strategy, which led to inward-looking industrialization. The sector had high growth through 1975, when the narrowness of the local market and rigid new labor legislation reduced the profitability of the activity. Protection of agricultural production had similar results for the same time period. The heavy influence of trade did not allow tariff policies to become as protective in Panama as in other Latin American countries.

For the period 1955–1975, all the previous activity led Panama to have one of the highest economic growth rates in Latin America. The international trade sector was most active, representing 33 to 36 percent of gross domestic product (GDP).

The Panamanian economy is diversified, with a strong service sector that has grown to become 75 percent of total economic activity. Manufacturing reached 19 percent and then shrank to 11 percent of GDP. The primary sectors fell from 24 percent of GDP in 1950 to 9 percent by 1990.

Between 1970 and 1995 the export-oriented service sectors (the Canal, the Free Trade Zone, offshore banking, the oil pipeline, maritime registration services, tourism) were the most dynamic, as they were not hampered by social legislation and strong protective legislation. The primary and secondary sectors slowed and produced mainly for the local market and were affected by labor and social legislation.

In the 1980s, the Latin American external debt crisis and the Panamanian internal political crisis affected economic performance negatively. Panama accumulated high external debt between 1970 and 1984. The political crisis impeded the application of a sustainable stabilization and structural adjustment policy during the 1980s.

In the 1990s, Panama returned to governance through democratic institutions. As a result, economic stabilization and structural adjustment advanced. Panama joined the World Trade Organization (WTO) and regained an average GDP growth rate of 4.5 percent. The Free Trade Zone reached a gross volume of $10 billion, the largest in the Western Hemisphere. Banking recovered to reach $38.0 billion in assets. Maritime ship registration became the largest in the world and international legal and financial services continued to grow.

Tourism grew 9 percent per year. Container port transshipments grew to 1.5 million maritime volume units (twenty ft. equivalent unit, TEUs). Exports of fishery products and agribusiness, as well as industrial goods, picked up. Furthermore, the country prepared itself institutionally to receive both the Canal and the U.S. military bases located near the Canal, whose considerable infrastructure was worth over $3 billion.

A medium-term development strategy was prepared for the Interoceanic Region around the Canal with the clear objectives of protecting Canal operations and future expansion, consolidating an economic cluster of maritime and business activity, incorporating social development, guiding and providing for urban development in the former zone around Panama City and Colón and protecting the Canal watershed and the surrounding rich biodiversity with a combination of National Parks and reforestation projects. The plan has entailed the development of 100,000 hectares of land and 14,000 structures and buildings.

Today many of the initiatives in the Interoceanic Region have been launched: the modernization of the canal and preparation for its expansion; container transshipment ports on both sides linked by the railroad; tourism and communication infrastructure, including cruise ships; increased services to 13,000 ship transits, such as ship repair and maintenance and bunker fuel; and growing commercial and product processing activities. A "City of Knowledge," combining a research park and an academic center, has begun on a former military base; intermodal transportation logistic activities have started; and international submarine cable communications have been built.

A locally owned international airline has reestablished the Hemispheric air traffic hub that operated in the 1960s but which had disappeared with the North-South over flights.

Panama is positioned to build a cluster of transportation, maritime, commercial, tourism and manufacturing activities around the Canal. Indeed, as noted, many significant steps have already been taken in that direction.

For Panama to be successful, it needs to emphasize productivity and competitiveness. These goals are necessary not only at the corporate, labor and sector levels but also at the national level. Improvements in public administration services, institutional and legal security and transparency, infrastructure, technology, labor and professional training are indispensable to achieve this goal.

The dollar-based monetary system provides a stable foundation for local and international activity. The system works for Panama because it is a small economy whose exports are primarily geared to the United States. Service exports provide a steady stream of hard currency without wide fluctuations, and the international banking center integrated to the international financial system offers a stabilizing monetary support and cushion.

Such an economy needs to stimulate growth in real productivity and must avoid excessive external debt. As a result, Panama needs to emphasize policies in that direction. This policy emphasis will also be effective in continuing to improve an export-led economic growth performance. The potential to increase exports of maritime products, agribusiness and manufactured goods was proven in the 1990s. Development in these areas has contributed to generate much-needed employment.

Panama is among the top ten Latin American middle-income countries. Although 40 percent of the people are fully geared to modern employment, another 40 percent are poor. Such social disparities are clear in the regional contrasts of the country. Seventy percent of the poor are located in the agrarian border regions, which offer insufficient training, infrastructure and communications. Panama needs a sustained policy effort to maintain high export-led economic growth and human development with full participation of all members of the population.

## PANAMA IN THE WESTERN HEMISPHERE

In the 1970s Panama turned down the opportunity to join the Central American Common Market. Membership would have led to more trade deviation than trade creation, behind a high tariff wall, protecting a relatively small market—20 million people. Instead it negotiated bilateral free trade agreements with each of the five Central American countries. It also began to look southward to the Andean Common Market; however, negotiations have not advanced.

The Caribbean Basin Initiative (CBI), a unilateral policy of the U.S. government toward the region, opened up export opportunities to the U.S. market in 1982. Panama has not taken full advantage of the CBI. The Initiative favors U.S. imports of manufactured goods with 35 percent value added in the Caribbean Basin economies by tariff exemptions.

In the 1990s a new open trade policy took hold in most Latin American countries. Chile led the way by itself. The Latin American countries organized Mercosur, the Andean Pact and the Central American Common Market. Mexico joined NAFTA. The Caribbean countries improved their internal arrangements. These new integration schemes were predicated on low tariff walls in order to enhance trade and increase exports. Within that framework, the new regional integration schemes eliminated tariffs within each group of countries. By the late 1990s, most Latin American countries had adopted uniform tariff levels for imports from the rest of the world at levels between 10 and 15 percent. As a result, trade within each integration scheme increases as Latin American exports to the rest of the world grow.

The United States has proposed to create a Free Trade Association of the Americas (FTAA) by 2005, a proposal which was adopted by the region in a Heads of States meeting in 1994. Work has been advancing in that direction. Thereafter, the United States initiated negotiations with Chile and Central American countries for them to join the North American Free Trade Agreement (NAFTA). Conversations are ongoing to determine whether Panama will be invited to initiate similar negotiations with the United States.

After entering the WTO, Panama decided to improve the Free Trade Association agreements it had with the other Central American countries and to seek association with the Andean Group. The goal was to benefit from freer trade with the Andean countries and with Mercosur countries, once those two associations finished their internal negotiations. At the same time, Panama is actively participating in the FTAA negotiations.

Panama perceives the ongoing development of the transportation, trade and business cluster around the Canal as an important link with the Latin American integration movements. A large part of Latin American exports and imports go through the Canal. The new container transshipment facilities are processing cargo going from and coming to the region at lower cost. The Colón Free Trade Zone re-exports goods, primarily to Latin American countries. The development of an intermodal logistic transportation center in Panama will be inextricably linked to Latin American trade. The Latin American Export Bank (BLADEX), partially owned by Latin American central and commercial banks and located in Panama, has financed over $110 billion in Latin American trade in the last quarter of the twentieth century.

In this context the increased trade links resulting from new Free Trade Association agreements with Central American countries, with the Andean Group and with the whole Western Hemisphere under FTAA are important priorities for Panama. The country perceives that joining NAFTA and with the Central American countries is also a priority.

Most of Panama's international trade is with the United States, South and Central America and the Caribbean, in that order. The full development of the country's strategic geographical location with modern transportation and communication systems, maritime and trade facilities, merchandise processing centers, warehousing and manufacturing facilities, logistics and communication infrastructure is based on doing business between Latin America and the rest of the world.

The present Canal can only transship Panamax vessels, that is, ships of up to 75,000 tons. The increasing numbers of post-Panamax vessels of up to 150,000 tons has opened the opportunity to add new and wider locks to the present Canal in order to service such ships. The maritime transportation revolution using containers, land bridges and loading and unloading techniques from bigger to smaller ships is leading to the use of larger container ships, carrying some 7,000 containers, and to building ports with deeper draft.

Some experts consider that the expanded Panama Canal, with additional locks and deeper channels, will open the opportunity for the establishment of an "equatorial" route for post-Panamax container ships. The ships would load and unload large quantities of containers in some 12 key ports around the equatorial route in the world and smaller ships would carry them to and from their final destination. Panama would increasingly become one of such ports, servicing the Americas.

The Panama Canal Authority is finishing updated feasibility and engineering studies about Canal expansion in the next 10 years. Most studies foresee that the present Canal will have reached its traffic limit by 2013–2014 and that world maritime trade will require expansion of the Canal. If proven feasible, such a project will contribute to consolidating the development of the international transport, trade and business cluster around the canal. It should increase the trade links with all American countries.

The next twenty years may well witness the expansion of the Panama Canal to serve world maritime trade. The ongoing development of a cluster of complementary economic activities around an intermodal transportation center will continue and would certainly gather momentum if the Canal were expanded. The Panamanian people are aware that opportunities such as these are enhanced through greater integration with the Western Hemisphere.

## CONCLUSION

Panama is not only a crossroads for world trade in a strategic geographic location. The country is also at a crossroads in its national development. Strategic national priorities include full modernization of its democratic institutions, consolidation of the economic opportunities around the Canal servicing the region and the world economy, a more dynamic integration of the different regions of the country, greater social integration based on human development and greater opportunities for the poor and the creation of a more participative society, and the strengthening of the institutional base of the country so that both political democracy and a market economy may prosper.

Now in full possession of its national destiny, Panama needs to develop toward a fully interdependent world, more integrated within the Western Hemisphere and with closer economic ties to Central America and the Andean Group. A growing awareness of the opportunities and limitations of such realities is guiding the Panamanian people, sustained by their long tradition of being a crossroads for world trade.

## BIBLIOGRAPHY

Ardito–Barletta, N. ed. (2003) *Financial Panama*. Bogota: Ediciones Gamma.

Ardito–Barletta, N. (2004) "La Economía de Panamá en el Siglo XX." *Dimensiones de la Historia de Panama*. El Club Union de Panama, ed., Panama: Imprelibros, S.A.

Ardito–Barletta, N. (2003) "Panamas Economic, Transportation and Service Hub: Forecasts." *Financial Panama*. Bogota: Ediciones Gamma. 2003.

Castillero, A. C. (1984) *La Ruta Transistmica y las Comunicaciones Maritimas Hispanas Siglos XVI a XIX*. Panama: Editora Renovación, S.A.

CEPAL, ONU. (2004) *Balance Preliminar de las Economias de America Latina y el Caribe 2003*. Mexico.

CEPAL, ONU. (2003) *Panama: Evolucion Economica Durante 2002 y Perspectivas para 2003*. LC/Mex/L.563. Mexico.

Club Union de Panama, Ed. (2004) *Dimensiones de la Historia de Panama*. Panama: Imprelibros, S.A.

Cooke, R., (1978) *American Antiquity*. Vol. 43, No. 3, Washington.

Ediciones Balboa. (1999) *The Panama Canal*. Madrid: Ediciones San Marcos.

Instituto Geografico Tommy Guardia. (1998) *Atlas Nacional de la Republica de Panama*. Panama: Instituto Geografico.

Intracorp Estrategias Empresariales, S.A./Asesores Estrategicos, S.A. (2004) *Panama Canal Economic Impact on the Republic of Panama*. Study Prepared for the Panama Canal Authority, Panama.

Jaen, O. (1998) *La Población del Istmo de Panama*. Madrid: Ediciones de Cultura Hispanica.

Jaen, O. (1981) *Hombres y Ecologia de Panama*. Panama: Editorial Universitaria y. The Smithsonian Tropical Research Institute.

Jorden, W. (1984) *Panama Odyssey*. Austin: University of Texas Press.

Leigh, E.G. and C. Ziegler. (2002) *A Magic Web: The Forest of Barro Colorado*. Oxford: Oxford University Press.

Linares, O. (1977) *Ecology and the Arts in Ancient Panama*. Washington, DC: Harvard University, Domberton Oaks.

McCullough, D. (1977) *The Path Between the Seas*. New York: Simon and Schuster.

Ministerio de Economia y Finanzas. *La Economia Panameña: Situación y Perspectivas: Informes de Coyuntura Trimestrales*. 2000-04, Panama, www.mef.gob.pa.

Morales F. P. (1981) *Historia del Descubrimiento y Conquista de America*. España: Editorial Nacional.

Public Law. (1997) *The Organization of the Panama Canal Authority*. Panama: Asamblea Legislativa.

Public Law No. 61. (1997) *The General Plan for the Use, Conservation and Development of the Canal Area and the Regional Plan for the Development of the Interoceanic Region*. Panama: Asamblea Legislativa.

Revista Loteria. (1977) *Documentos de la Lucha Panameña y los Nuevos Tratados del Canal*. Agosto-Septiembre, Octubre, Panama.

U.N.D.P., ed. (2002) *Informe Nacional de Desarrollo Humano: Panama 2002*. Panama.

The World Bank. (2000) *Panama: Estudio sobre Pobreza*. Washington DC: W.B. Country Study Series.

# CHAPTER 11
# COSTA RICA

DR. RICARDO MONGE-GONZALEZ
JAVIER CHAVES

## INTRODUCTION

The Republic of Costa Rica is located in the Central American isthmus. With 51,000 square kilometers (19,652 square miles), the country has two immediate neighbors, Nicaragua in the north and Panama in the south. In addition, it has ports on both the Atlantic and Pacific Oceans. Costa Rica is a country characterized by a traditional, established democracy, especially since the army was abolished in 1949. With elections held every four years, Costa Rica has stable political and economic environments. The business environment and legal framework are also designed to favor foreign investment.

Costa Rica has a population of about 4.5 million. This number includes approximately 600,000 foreigners, of whom nearly 500,000 are from Nicaragua. The density of the population is 78.4 inhabitants per square kilometer (203.5 inhabitants per square mile). With a life expectancy of 76.1 years, a literacy rate of 95.1 percent and 98 percent of the population served with piped water, the standard of living indicators are the highest in Central America. The percentage of people living under the poverty line is close to 20 percent, less than half that of the rest of Central America. Comparing Costa Rica with the rest of the world, the indicators are also good. According to the United Nations Human Development Index (HDI) for 2001, Costa Rica held forty-first place and has one of the highest ratings for quality of human resources among the developing countries.

Some of the differences between Costa Rica and its neighbors have been present since colonial times. These differences have survived the years and have been important factors in the creation of the nation. Other differences are due to the long years of peace and democracy experienced during the last half of the twentieth century while the other countries were exhausted by domestic wars and fights with each other.

## HISTORICAL BACKGROUND

### PRE-COLUMBIAN ERA

When Spanish explorers arrived in what is now Costa Rica on September 18, 1502, they found a region populated by several poorly organized, autonomous tribes with around 20,000 indigenous people. Although human habitation can be traced back at least 10,000 years, the region had remained a sparsely populated backwater separating the two areas of high civilization: Mesoamerica and the Andes. High mountains and swampy lowlands had impeded the migration of the advanced cultures.

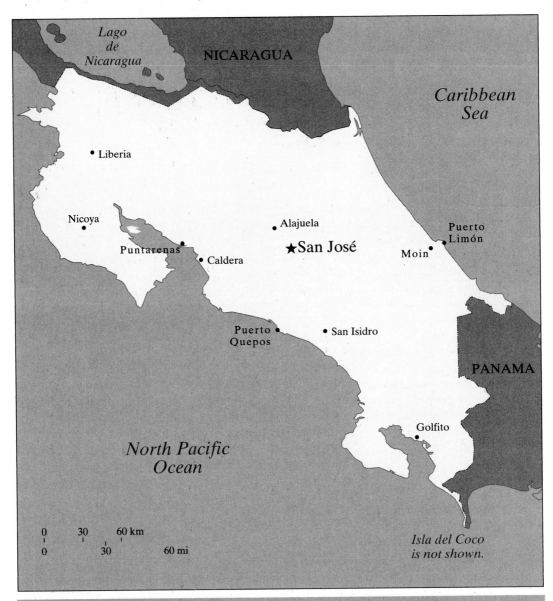

**FIGURE 11-1** Map of Costa Rica

The region was a potpourri of distinct cultures. In the east along the Caribbean seaboard and along the southern Pacific shores, the peoples shared distinctly South American cultural traits. In the highlands, the Corobicís tribe arrived from Mexico around two centuries before Columbus. Trade in pottery from the Nicoya Peninsula brought the northern area into the Mesoamerican cultural sphere. A culture also developed among the Chorotegas (the most numerous of the region's indigenous groups) that in many ways resembled the more advanced cultures farther north such as the Mayans and Aztecs.

## COLONIAL ERA

When Columbus arrived on the east cost of Costa Rica in the Bay of Cariari on his fourth voyage to the New World, he called the region La Huerta ("The Garden"). Starting in 1506, different expeditions tried to colonize the Atlantic coast of Veragua, but they failed. It was not until 1522 that an expedition under Gil Gonzalez Davila set off from Panama to settle the region. It was Davila's expedition, given quantities of gold, that nicknamed the land Costa Rica ("Rich Coast"). Davila's Catholic priests also apparently managed to convert many Indians to Christianity. For the next four decades Costa Rica was virtually left untouched. The conquest of Peru by Pizarro in 1532 and the first of the great silver strikes in Mexico in the 1540s turned all eyes away from southern Central America.

Guatemala became the administrative center for the Spanish in 1543, when the captaincy-general of Guatemala, answerable to the viceroy of New Spain (Mexico), was created with jurisdiction from the Isthmus of Tehuantepec to the empty lands of Costa Rica. By the 1560s, several Spanish cities had consolidated their position farther north.

Their representatives in Guatemala thought it was time to settle Costa Rica and Christianize the natives. It was late already since the epidemics of European diseases had already cut the Indian population. The survivors moved to the forests and eventually found refuge in the remote valleys of the Talamanca Mountains. Only in the Nicoya Peninsula did there remain any significant Indian population.

In 1562, Juan Vásquez de Coronado, the true conquistador of Costa Rica, arrived as governor. He treated the surviving Indians more humanely and moved the existing Spanish settlers into the Cartago Valley. Cartago was established as the national capital in 1563. The economic and social development of the Spanish provinces was traditionally the work of the soldiers, who were granted *encomiendas*, or land holdings, which allowed the use of indigenous serfs.

In the highlands, land was readily available, but there was no Indian labor to work it. Without native slave labor or the resources to import slaves, the colonists were forced to work the land themselves. Even Coronado had to work his own plot of land to survive. Without gold or export crops, trade with other colonies was infrequent at best. In fact, money became so scarce that the settlers eventually reverted to the Indian method of using cacao beans as currency. After the initial impetus given by its discovery, Costa Rica became the lowly Cinderella of the Spanish empire.

Intermixing with the native population was not a common practice. In other colonies, Spaniards married natives and a distinct class system arose, but mixed-bloods and mestizos represent a much smaller element in Costa Rica than they do elsewhere in the isthmus. Costa Rica became a traditional rural democracy with no oppressed mestizo class resentful of the maltreatment and scorn of the Creoles. Removed from the mainstream of Spanish culture, the Costa Ricans became individualistic and egalitarian.

## INDEPENDENCE

The independence of Central America from Spain on September 15, 1821, came on the coattails of Mexico's declaration earlier in the same year. Independence had little immediate effect, however, for Costa Rica had required only minimal government during the colonial era and had long since gone its own way. In fact, the country was so out of touch that the news that independence had been granted reached Costa Rica a full month after the event. A hastily convened provincial council voted for accession to Mexico.

In 1823, the other Central American nations proclaimed the United Provinces of Central America, with their capital in Guatemala City. After the declaration, effective power lay in the hands of the separate towns of the isthmus. It took several years for a stable pattern of political alignment to emerge. The local quarrels quickly developed into civic unrest and, in 1823, led to civil war. After a brief battle in the Ochomogo Hills between the republican forces of San José and the conservative forces of Cartago, the republicans were victorious. They rejected Mexico. Costa Rica joined the Central American Federation with full autonomy in its own affairs.

From this moment on, liberalism in Costa Rica had the upper hand. Elsewhere in Central America, conservative groups tied to the Church and the previous colonial bureaucracy spent generations at war with anticlerical and laissez-faire liberals, and a cycle of civil wars came to dominate the region. By contrast, in Costa Rica colonial institutions had been relatively weak and early modernization of the economy pushed the nation out of poverty and lay the foundations for democracy far earlier than elsewhere in the isthmus. While other countries turned to repression to deal with social tensions, Costa Rica turned toward reform.

After 1824, the Costa Rican government guided the country, establishing a stable judicial system and founding the nation's first newspaper and public education. It also encouraged coffee growing and gave free land grants to would-be coffee growers. The nation, however, was still driven by the rivalry between the two main parties. In 1838, Costa Rica withdrew from the Central American federation and proclaimed its complete independence. By 1849, a new elite emerged. The growing prosperity of the coffee growers, or *cafetaleros,* led to rivalries among the wealthiest family factions, who competed with each other for political dominance. Thus began a small but constant tension between the coffee growers and the military.

## DEMOCRACY

The shift to democracy came in 1889 through elections with popular participation. Women and blacks, however, were still excluded from voting. During the course of the next two generations, militarism gave way to peaceful transitions to power. On the other hand, several presidents attempted to amend the Constitution to continue their rule and even dismissed uncooperative legislatures. Throughout this time the country had been at peace. In 1917, democracy faced its first major challenge. At that time, Costa Ricans had come to accept liberty as their due. They were no longer prepared to accept oligarchic restrictions.

## REFORM AND CIVIL WAR

The decade of the 1940s and its climax, civil war, mark a turning point in Costa Rican history. From paternalistic government by traditional rural elites, Costa Rica turned to modernistic, urban-focused statecraft controlled by bureaucrats, professionals and small entrepreneurs. In a period when neighboring Central American nations were under the repression of tyrannical dictators, Costa Rica promulgated a series of social reforms such as land reform (the landless could gain title to unused land by cultivating it), establishment of a guaranteed minimum wage, paid vacations, unemployment compensation, progressive taxation and a series of constitutional amendments codifying workers' rights. The Catholic Church and the communists played important roles in these changes.

In 1948, after the association of different parties, the country was polarized and claims of fraud in the elections heightened the tension. This tension ended in revolution. The 40-day civil war claimed over 2,000 lives, most of them civilians. After the war, a Junta of the Second Republic of Costa Rica was constituted as a government. During this period, the government consolidated the social reform program and added its own landmark reforms, banning the press and the Communist Party, introducing suffrage for women and full citizenship for blacks, revising the Constitution to outlaw a standing army, establishing a presidential term limit and creating an independent Electoral Tribunal to oversee future elections.

## CONTEMPORARY SCENE

Social and economic progress since 1948 has helped return the country to stability, and though post–civil war politics have reflected the play of old loyalties and antagonisms, elections have been free and fair. With only two exceptions, the country has ritualistically alternated presidents between the two main parties, Liberacion Nacional (PLN) and Unidad Social Cristiana (PUSC).

By 1980, Costa Rica was mired in an economic crisis reflected in inflation; crippling currency devaluation; soaring oil bills and social welfare costs; plummeting coffee, banana and sugar prices; and the disruptions to trade caused by the Nicaraguan war. When large international loans came due, Costa Rica found itself burdened overnight with the world's greatest per capita debt. This situation required a great effort from all Costa Ricans to get the country out of that predicament.

In February 1986, Costa Ricans elected Oscar Arias as their president. Arias's electoral promise had been to work for peace in Central America. Immediately, he began working on resolving Central America's regional conflicts. He attempted to expel the Nicaraguan military forces located in the northern part of Costa Rica and enforced the nation's official proclamation of neutrality made in 1983. Arias's efforts were rewarded in 1987, when his Central American peace plan was signed by the five Central American presidents in Guatemala City, an achievement that earned the Costa Rican president the 1987 Nobel Peace Prize.

In the early twenty-first century, Costa Rica promoted the expansion of its exports and tourism. The promotion of the export-oriented manufactured goods has taken the form of special fiscal regimes, especially for electronics, under the free zone regime. Despite the efforts to generate linkages between export-oriented activities and the rest of domestic industry, spillovers have been limited. Apart from the special fiscal regimes, measures to promote industrial production have been focused on small and medium-sized enterprises.

Tourism remains a main attraction for foreign exchange and investment. Inefficiencies in some other service areas impose unnecessary costs on these activities. The State retains monopoly rights in insurance, telecommunications and energy distribution. State-owned banks still dominate the industry despite considerable growth in the private sector.

Costa Rica has been exploiting its two primary resources. These two resources are its biodiversity and its human capital. In the first case, the biodiversity has positioned Costa Rica as one of the top places to visit, attracting more and more people and investments every year. In the case of human capital, Costa Rica is characterized by a high level of knowledge not just in the technical fields but also in the knowledge of English as a second language, also attracting considerable investment to the country.

The main destination of Costa Rican exports is the United States. Its share of Costa Rican exports is around 50 percent. The European Union is the second destination for Costa Rican products, with close to 20 percent of all exports. It should be noted that the products traditionally exported to the European Union, coffee and bananas, have declined in relative importance compared to modular circuits and other non-traditional goods such as pineapples, ornamental plants and foliage and melons. The main sectors that attract the greatest volume of foreign investment are industry, tourism, services and agriculture. The main source of investment is the United States (64 percent) followed by Mexico (10 percent).

Costa Rica is now promoting a new development scheme. The new plan provides incentives to small and medium-sized enterprises, especially those that use high technology and those that focus on international markets. In this group are the companies that create new software and those dedicated to e-business.

## COSTA RICA AND ITS INTERNATIONAL TRADE POLICY

In the early twenty-first century, the government tried to encourage the participation of Costa Rica in international markets. The objectives of the government can be summarized in five main points:

1. Improve and secure access by Costa Rican products to foreign markets.
2. Promote domestic changes necessary to develop a more efficient production of exportable goods, including the use of new technology in the production process.
3. Defend Costa Rican trade interests against protectionist measures by other countries.
4. Fully involve all sectors of the country's economy in exporting.
5. Establish a legal framework for the proper management of trade relations.

These objectives are administered by the Ministry of Foreign Trade (COMEX) and are directly tied to the activities of two institutions: the Foreign Trade Promotion Body (Promotora de Comercio Exterior, PROCOMER), responsible for promoting exportable products abroad, especially those of small and medium-sized companies; and the Costa Rican Coalition for Development Initiatives (Coalición Costarricense de Iniciativas de Desarrollo, CINDE), a private organization whose object is to foster the conditions needed to attract domestic and foreign investment and at the same time establish investment programs.

Costa Rica has continued to step up the process of enlarging its trade, above all because the national economy is not large enough to provide the growth opportunities that the country needs. Therefore, a trade policy has been followed on a sustained basis over several years designed to achieve the fullest integration of Costa Rica into the global economy. The success of this policy can be seen in the growth of exports, the diversification of products and markets, the increase in foreign direct investment and the creation of employment.

The government has different instruments to achieve these objectives. Some of these instruments are participation in multilateral agreements, regional integration, negotiation of trade and investment agreements and unilateral liberalization initiatives.

## MULTILATERAL SYSTEM

### WORLD TRADE ORGANIZATION (WTO)

Costa Rica has always believed in the multilateral trading system and has supported all moves to buttress that system since the inception of the WTO. A strong multilateral system with clear and transparent rules is of enormous benefit to a small, international trade-dependent economy such as that of Costa Rica.

Costa Rica has adopted different commitments that are consistent with the country's policy, for example, the Agreement on Information Technology Products (ITA), which is consistent with Costa Rica's effort for development of the information technology industry. Costa Rica also welcomed the start of agricultural negotiations in the WTO. The nation's goal is the elimination and total abolition of agricultural export subsidies, which constitute the most unfair and trade-distorting mechanism in international trade. Costa Rica, with the Cairns Group, maintains that all forms of domestic aid that distort international agricultural trade should be eliminated.

### ANDEAN PACT

Although El Salvador, Guatemala and Honduras are negotiating with the countries of the Andean Pact an agreement about trade between the two blocs of countries, Costa Rica is not participating in the negotiations.

### CARICOM

The Central American countries have been talking, in the last decade, with CARICOM, the group of Caribbean nations, about different agreements. During this process topics such as technology, transport, the environment, tourism, development banks and natural emergencies have been the main interests. The possibility of a trade agreement has been mentioned in some informal meetings, but there is no agreement yet.

### MERCOSUR

In 1998, the presidents of the countries that form Mercosur and the presidents of the Central American Common Market (CACM) signed an agreement about investment and trade. The agreement is to increase the integration and trade between the two blocs. The main objectives of the agreement are:

- Tighten economic relations, especially trade, investment and the transfer of technology.
- Recognize the way and the specific actions that need to be taken in order to deepen the relationship among the parties.

- Give incentives to the free market economies and highlight the importance of the private sector in the economic development of the countries.
- Find the way to promote and protect the investments.

## REGIONAL INTEGRATION

### FREE TRADE AREA OF THE AMERICAS (FTAA)

As a result of its location in Central America, Costa Rica has not participated in the large trade agreements that have occurred in North America (NAFTA) or in South America (Mercosur and Andean Pact). For this reason Costa Rica has played an active and constructive role in the FTAA process since the launch of the initiative in December 1994.

The country has done so not only through its work throughout the process and its regular contribution of ideas to the negotiating groups, but also through its role in holding several important posts. Between May 1997 and 1998, Costa Rica chaired the FTAA process and played host to the fourth Ministerial Summit in San José. In addition, the country has chaired the Working Group on Investment, as well as the Negotiating Groups on Investment and Dispute Settlement.

The FTAA has special importance for Costa Rica, as the United States is the main market for Costa Rican exports. The FTAA would offset the advantage of Mexican products in the U.S. market. Costa Rica already has a free trade agreement with Mexico and it is in the last stages in negotiating one with Canada. The United States is the only country in NAFTA to which Costa Rican products do not have free access.

### CENTRAL AMERICA COMMON MARKET (CACM)

In 1963, Costa Rica became a signatory to the general Treaty on Central American Economic Integration, which established the CACM, which included El Salvador, Guatemala, Honduras and Nicaragua. Over the years, different efforts have been made toward the economic integration of the Central American countries. Despite the fact that in the past few years the trade flow between Costa Rica and the CACM region has grown more slowly than overall flows, Central America continues to be an important destination for Costa Rican exports.

The region has developed the legal framework necessary for the regulation of relations between the countries in the Central America Common Market. The regional trade rules are presently being aligned with the commitments of each Central American country in the WTO. By the end of 2000, nine new regulations had been approved in the following fields: origin of goods, unfair business practices, safeguard measures, standardization measures and metrology and authorization procedures, as well as sanitary and phyto-sanitary procedures. Approval of a regulation on disputes settlement is pending and negotiations are under way to conclude a treaty on services and investment. As of 2003, there were no initiatives concerning government procurement at the Central American level.

The region also has a common legal code for customs called Código Aduanero Común (CAUCA). Although Costa Rica has been using this legal code, it was not participating in the unification of customs until June 2002. The four other countries (Guatemala, Honduras, El Salvador and Nicaragua) have been implementing a plan that creates a common customs zone permitting the free movement of products regardless of origin. The result would be the elimination of customs among those countries. This is not the only initiative of integration in Central America in which Costa Rica has been cautious. Costa Rica has been wary of other integration initiations, especially the Central American Parliament. This discretion does not affect the desire of Costa Rica to integrate with the markets of the five countries or the initiative of the FTAA. The agreement of Costa Rica to join to the Central American common customs zone stems from the advantage of sticking together as a region in the negotiations with other countries and economic blocs.

## NEGOTIATION OF TRADE AND INVESTMENT AGREEMENTS

Bilateral free trade agreements and mutual investment promotion with other countries are the two main instruments used by the government in Costa Rica to achieve its objective in international trade: to become one of the pioneers in the region. These agreements make the rules clear to all economic agents involved in international trade. The improvement in access to new and larger markets is an important incentive in the attraction of new investment and the promotion of the export sector of the country. The eradication of the different barriers to imports generates greater competition within the country, forcing the improvement of the production process.

At the end of January 2001, Costa Rica had agreements on mutual investment promotion and protection with the following countries: Argentina, Canada, Chile, Chinese Taipei, Czech Republic, France, Germany, Netherlands, Paraguay, Spain, Switzerland, United Kingdom and Venezuela. Also, there are negotiations with at least nineteen additional countries. Foreign investment is promoted mainly through the Costa Rican Coalition for Development Initiatives (CINDE).

The investment arrangements in Costa Rica are supplemented by bilateral, regional and multilateral treaties providing guarantees and protection for foreign investment. Costa Rica has free trade agreements with Canada, Mexico, Panama, Chile and the Dominican Republic.

## FREE TRADE AGREEMENT WITH MEXICO

Since the entry into force of the Free Trade Agreement (FTA) between Costa Rica and Mexico in 1995, trade flows between the two countries have increased significantly. Costa Rica was the first country of Central America to have this kind of agreement with Mexico. During this time, the FTA has had a positive impact by reducing and even beginning to reverse in Costa Rica's favor the limitations that have typified the historical pattern of trade flows between Central American countries and Mexico. Costa Rican exports to Mexico have increased three times as fast as imports.

With respect to foreign direct investment flows, Mexican investment in Costa Rica has increased significantly since 1994. Mexico became the second most important country as a source of foreign direct investment in Costa Rica at the close of the twentieth century. Over half of Mexican investment in Costa Rica is concentrated in the food industry and mines and quarries. The latter is the result of the recent entry into the domestic market of the main cement manufacturer in Mexico (Cemex).

## FREE TRADE AGREEMENT WITH PANAMA

Since 1973, trade in goods between Costa Rica and Panama has been governed by the Free Trade and Preferential Trade Agreement. This agreement is rather more limited in scope than, for example, the agreement with Mexico. In 1998, Costa Rica, together with the other CACM countries, began negotiations with Panama with a view to establishing a new treaty that would not only cover a wider range of tariffs, but would also include provisions on rules of origin and customs procedures, investment, services, government procurement, anti-dumping measures, sanitary and phyto-sanitary measures and dispute settlement.

## FREE TRADE AGREEMENT WITH CHILE

In 1999, the countries of Central America and Chile signed a Free Trade Agreement. The CACM member countries and Chile agreed that market access would be negotiated bilaterally between each Central American country and Chile. Thus, Costa Rica and Chile bilaterally negotiated the entry of products into the Costa Rican and Chilean markets. In this agreement the majority of Costa Rican products entered Chile with zero tariff.

## OTHER AGREEMENTS

Apart from the integration programs negotiated, Costa Rica has enjoyed unilateral concessions granted by Canada, the United States and the European Union under the Generalized System of Preferences (GSP) and the United States' Caribbean Basin Initiative (CBI).

In May 2000, the United States passed the Trade and Development Act 2000, which extended the benefits of the CBI. With the passing of this Act, Costa Rica and the other countries in the region enjoy preferential access to the U.S. market for some products excluded in the past from the Initiative. This Act was the answer to the claims made after the introduction of NAFTA. NAFTA gave free entry to textile products from Mexico, while the same products from Central America and the Caribbean needed to pay an import tax. Given the importance of the textile sector in Costa Rican exports to the United States, the improvement of the CBI by the Act had a positive impact.

## UNILATERAL LIBERALIZATION INITIATIVES

This instrument is important since it increased competition in the local market and provided incentives for innovation and efficiency in companies that participate in international markets. A great deal has been done in the way of unilateral tariff roll-back measures. Between 1995 and 2001, Costa Rica's average tariff decreased from 11.7 percent for the entire tariff framework. In the same period, Costa Rica lowered 48.2 percent of its tariffs. But there is still work to do, especially in the farm production sector. This sector is still subject to higher tariffs than that for other products. On average, tariffs for the farm sector are 13.72 percent compared with 4.96 percent for the industrial sector.

## SOME CHARACTERISTICS OF THE COSTA RICAN ENTERPRISES

Companies in Costa Rica face an increasingly competitive environment. The international trade policy of the government attracts foreign companies and products that compete with the domestic products. Often, some sectors in the country are discontent with this policy. The production sector in particular often tries to maintain some protection. Businesses in Costa Rica have special characteristics. Some characteristics are similar to other businesses in Central America, but others are unique to Costa Rica.

In Costa Rica, most businesses are small or medium-sized enterprises. These businesses have fewer than 100 employees, less than US$500,000 in equipment and annual income less than US$1 million. These businesses represent 98 percent of industry and 62 percent of exporting companies. The majority of the small and medium-sized companies are micro-enterprises. These businesses have up to 10 employees (including the owner) and annual income less than US$150,000. Also, most Costa Rican businesses are family owned. Some other general characteristics of Costa Rican businesses are discussed in the following sections.

### SHORT-TERMISM

In general, Costa Rica enterprises do not have a specific strategy. The enterprises see strategy as an isolated event. They do not see strategy as a continuous process. Strategy in Costa Rican companies is not an important aspect. Any efforts to establish strategy are seen as a waste of time. Therefore, the strategy is not properly communicated to all parts of the company. In many Costa Rican companies, especially the small and medium-sized enterprises, communication is one of the major problems. There is no commitment to continuous improvement and important changes are always delayed. These changes are proposed until they become imperative. This situation creates isolated and discontinuous improvements. The lack of strategy and the desire for action showing immediate results often generate short-term thinking and goals in the companies.

### CULTURE AND VALUES

There are some cultural characteristics that represent a limitation for the performance of the companies. In general, Costa Rican companies do not dedicate enough time and resources to defining and implementing values to improve performance. Key values are rarely written or made explicit, in contrast to large international corporations for which values are defined by global headquarters. The necessity for prompt change does not allow for cultural and value changes in the companies, since these processes take time.

### STRUCTURE

As mentioned before, many companies in Costa Rica are family businesses or are owned by relatively few people. This characteristic creates companies that can decide their own futures, in contrast with the branches of an international corporation that must obey guidelines from headquarters. This structure also generates some degree of informality in the decision-making process. In large Costa Rican companies, the structure is complex, creating difficulties in relations and in the flow of information. The management, in general, acts only in crisis and concentrates decision-making power in the hands of the owner-manager, an attitude that may be perceived as autocratic. The owner-manager structure generates problems such as the lack of teamwork and a lack of management training stemming from the owner's fear of losing control. Given these structures, Costa Rican firms are still conservative, especially concerning decisions related to international markets.

### FINANCE, TECHNOLOGY AND INFRASTRUCTURE

The small and medium-sized enterprises have many problems of access to financial resources. The lack of capital produces delays in the adoption of technology even when the companies possess the human capital necessary to used the latest technology. This lack of capital combined with the lack of strategy generate unruly growth.

These characteristics give rise to some advantages and some disadvantages. Some of the disadvantages are that in many cases the companies lack the financial capital needed to make changes within the company. The management tends to be conservative and in some instances decisions are subordinated to factors not related to the market, particularly in family businesses. Some of the advantages are the flexibility of Costa Rican companies and the capacity to absorb changes in know-how and technology, given the high educational level of the Costa Rican workforce.

## PLANS FOR THE FUTURE

Costa Rica has an open economy in which foreign trade is of supreme importance. For this reason, the country will be pressing ahead with a foreign trade policy promoting greater and more secure access for Costa Rican products to international markets as a way of generating the growth and development opportunities that the country needs. Under this logic, Costa Rica wants to obtain the maximum benefits from the free trade agreements and it will continue to favor initiatives for more trade links with other countries and regions.

The country supports the proposal to strive to complete the negotiations of the Free Trade Area of the Americas in the shortest possible time. In Central America, Costa Rica will continue to support the regional integration scheme and its implementation of the dispute settlement system as soon as possible.

At the multilateral level, Costa Rica will continue to support the launching of a broad round of negotiations to serve the interests of all members and thereby further advance the trade liberalization process. From Costa Rica's point of view, in addition to the ongoing negotiations on agriculture and services, the new round of the WTO should also encompass negotiations pertaining to the creation of a multilateral framework for investments, rules on trade facilitation and commitments to electronic commerce.

Costa Rica will continue to support small and medium-sized enterprises. Currently, the government program in this sector is improving access to the financial markets through cooperation with two state banks. This program is intended to create links between the universities and the companies. In so doing, the government wants to encourage the flow of technology and managerial skills. Costa Rica's government also will encourage the commercialization of products and participation in different events. The plan also includes training for those companies that want to export their products.

## CONCLUSION

Costa Rica has its sight focused on international markets. It is convinced that in order to further economic development, the domestic market is not enough. The transfer of technology and knowledge is more likely to be possible with an open economy. Costa Rica is also conscious of the significance of its economic integration in the Central American region. This integration is the first step to deeper access to markets such as the United States and the European Union. With such integration, the Central American countries as a whole would have more bargaining power and would be more attractive to investors.

Costa Rica is also convinced that future development will be achieved through small and medium-sized enterprises. This scheme aims at cutting poverty levels and using all the human capital available in the country. Costa Rica is also placing a bet on technological development. The incentive given to the software sector, in addition to the development of an advanced Internet network and a national plan to improve English language instruction throughout the country, especially in the technical areas, would be a great impetus to the high-technology sector.

## BIBLIOGRAPHY

Arias, C. (1999) *Análisis de Estrategias Gerenciales de Compañías Multinacionales Establecidas en Costa Rica*. San José: Universidad de Costa Rica.

Cámara de Industrias de Costa Rica. (2002) *Guía Industrial 2002*. San José: Cámara de Industrias de Costa Rica.

Costa Rica Government. (2001) *Trade Policy Review Costa Rica*, Trade Policy Review Body, World Trade Organization. *www.comex.go.cr*

Jiménez, Ronulfo (2000). *Los Retos Políticos de la Reforma Económica en Costa Rica*. San José: Academia de Centroamérica.

Ministerio de Economía Industria y Comercio (2002). *Informe Final Programa Impulso*. San José: Ministerio de Economía Industria y Comercio.

WTO Secretariat. (2001) *Trade Policy Review Costa Rica*, Trade Policy Review Body, World Trade Organization. *www.comex.go.cr*

# CHAPTER 12
# THE DOMINICAN REPUBLIC

❧

AMBASSADOR ROBERTO SALADIN

Since 1492, the Dominican Republic, on the beautiful Caribbean island of Hispaniola in the West Indies, has been a bridge connecting Europe with North, Central and South America. It was from Santo Domingo that the New World was discovered. It has now become a crossroads of migrants of different origins and cultures. Dominicans are proud of their history, from their pre-Columbian archaeological inheritance to their Spanish cultural roots. The Dominican Republic is a multiracial country, where the merengue is the national dance and baseball the national sport. The country has a diversified, fast-growing economy with links to the United States, Europe, Latin America and the Caribbean region. The Dominican Republic is a country with a future.

## INTRODUCTION

The Dominican Republic, the second largest island in the Caribbean region, was discovered by Christopher Columbus in 1492. The explorer called the island "Hispaniola" on his arrival on December 5, 1492. Isabela was the first site of Spanish settlement in the New World. The capital city, Santo Domingo, was founded on August 4, 1496, by Bartolome Colon on the east side of the Ozama River; it was then moved in 1502 to the west side of the river.

## A BRIEF HISTORY

While ruled by Spain during the colonial period, the island was baptized the "Athens of the New World." It held the distinction in America of having the first cathedral, the first university, the first hospital, the first aqueduct, the first engraving and printing of money and so on.

The Dominican Republic was ceded to France in 1797 and regained by Spain in 1808. In 1821, Jose Nuñez de Cáceres declared what was later called the "Ephemeral Independence," as he sought to be part of Greater Colombia under the leadership of Simón Bolívar. From 1822 to 1844 the Dominican Republic was occupied by Haiti. The Dominican Republic became a sovereign state in 1844. In 1860, the Dominican Republic was annexed again by Spain. After the War of Restoration, the island again became an independent state in 1865 when Spain withdrew from the island, defeated. From 1930 to 1961 the Dominican Republic was ruled by the dictator Rafael L. Trujillo.

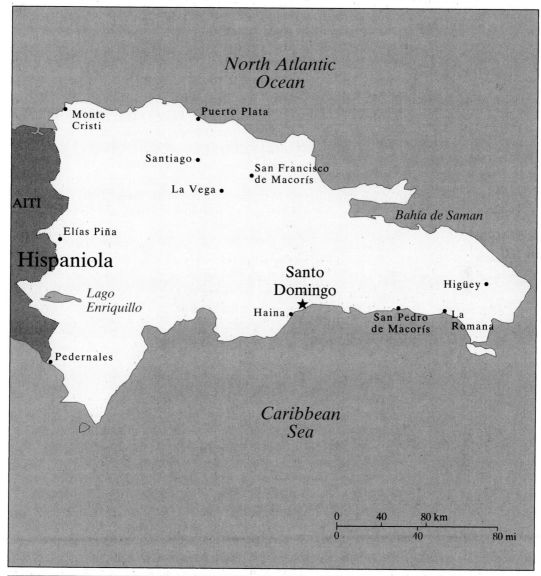

**FIGURE 12-1** Map of the Dominican Republic

In 1962 free elections were held for the first time in 38 years. Juan Bosch, who returned from exile, won the election but was overthrown in September 1963. As a consequence of the coup d'état, a civil war in 1965 opened the doors to intervention by the U.S. armed forces, later to be replaced by the Interamerican Peace Force, supported by the Organization of the American States (OAS). Since 1966, the country has had free elections every four years, thus being the strongest Spanish-speaking democracy in the Caribbean region to date.

## THE LAND, PEOPLE AND GOVERNMENT

The Dominican Republic has a surface area of 18,700 square miles and shares the island of Hispanolia with Haiti, which is 10,600 square miles. The island of Hispanolia is situated in the Caribbean between Cuba to the west and Puerto Rico to the east. The Cordillera Central mountains cross the center of the Dominican Republic, rising to over 10,000 feet, the highest altitude in the Caribbean. Peak Duarte, named to honor the father of National Independence, Juan Pablo Duarte, is found here. The country has thirty-one provinces and one National District, in which is located the national capital of Santo Domingo. The Dominican Republic has a population of 8,581,477 inhabitants. The population density is 460 persons per square mile. Among the principal cities of the country are Santiago de los Caballeros (second largest city), La Vega, Puerto Plata, Monte Cristi, San Cristóbal, Azúa, Barahona, San Pedro de Macorís, La Romana and Higuey y El Seibo, among others.

The Dominican Republic is a republic with separation of powers. The executive branch is headed by the president of the Republic, who is elected every four years. At present, the president is H.E. Hipólito Mejía Domínguez (2000–2004). The National Congress is divided into the Senate and the Chamber of Deputies, each having a president for the direction of each chamber. At the head of the judicial branch are the National Council of Magistrates and the Supreme Court of Justice. Judges for the latter are appointed and undergo examinations at public hearings.

## BRIEF INTRODUCTION TO THE ECONOMY

The Dominican Republic can be considered a "wirschafstwundert" (economic miracle) in the Caribbean region and indeed in Latin America in the last decade. The country has shown an extended period of economic growth, modest inflation and declining unemployment. The gross domestic product (GDP) reached US$19,711 million in 2000, and the per capita income US$2,304. The country has a manageable external position.

In 2001, real GDP grew at a rate of 2.7 percent, or five times the average of the rest of Latin America. The Dominican economy absorbed simultaneous external shocks such as a recession in the U.S. economy, the devaluation of the euro, oil price increases and the tragedies in New York on September 11th. According to projections of the Central Bank of the Dominican Republic, the GDP growth expected for 2002 is around 4 percent. (See Figure 12-2.)

Some of the key sectors of the Dominican economy that have accelerated the country's economic growth are tourism, telecommunications, trade, electrical power and construction. From 1995 to 2000, the economic growth of the Dominican Republic averaged 7.2 percent, more than twice the average growth rate of other Latin American and Caribbean countries, making the country one of the fastest growing economies in the region at the time. (See Figure 12-3.)

From 1995 to 2001, the per capita GDP increased at an annual average rate of 5.3 percent in real terms, and unemployment dropped 2 percentage points to 13.9 percent in 2000. The increase in the gross investment, as percentage of the GDP, increased from 19.5 to 23.7 percent in the period mentioned. (See Figure 12-4.)

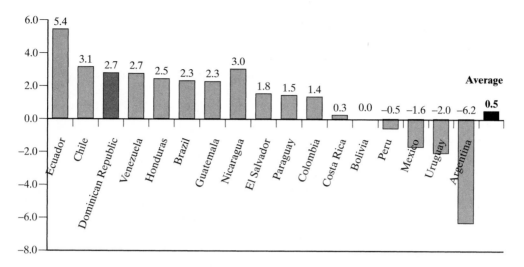

Source: Central Bank of the Dominican Republic

**FIGURE 12-2** Latin America real GDP growth for 2001

**FIGURE 12-3** Latin America's economic growth 1991–2000

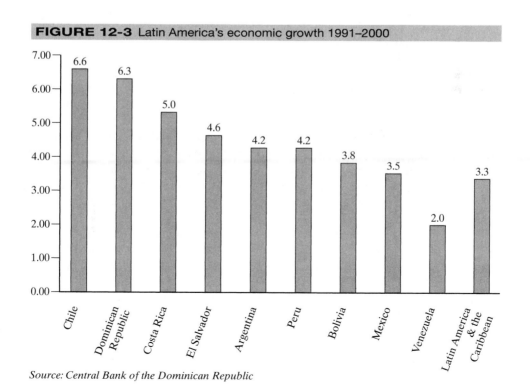

Source: Central Bank of the Dominican Republic

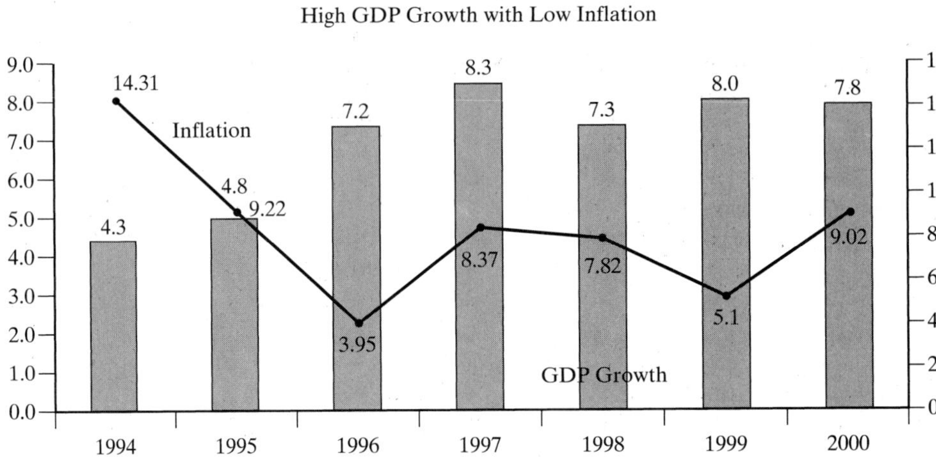

High GDP Growth with Low Inflation

Source: Central Bank of the Dominican Republic

**FIGURE 12-4** Recent developments

It should be pointed out that along with the strong economic growth, inflation has been controlled with an annual inflation average of 7.2 percent over the last six years, despite the harsh effects on prices of two external shocks: (1) Hurricane Georges (1998), which impacted production; and (2) the increase in oil prices, especially in 2000. (See Figure 12-5.)

Among the most important assets of the Dominican economy have been the growth, solvency and reliability of the financial sector; the renegotiation of the external debt; and the reduction in accumulated debt by around 20 percent between 1993 and 2000. Foreign public debt totaled US$3,765 million in the year 2000. On the other hand, at the end of 2001, international net reserves of the Central Bank reached US$962.3 million and gross reserves US$1,340.8 million. (See Figures 12-6 and 12-7.)

The Dominican Republic elected a new president and vice president on May 16, 2000: His Excellency Hipólito Mejía Domínguez and the Honorable Milagros Ortíz Bosch. On August 16, 2000, while the new authorities were taking office, the sudden increase in world oil prices struck, forcing the new government to increase the internal prices of oil and its by-products.

Immediately after assuming power, the new government implemented a full package of economic measures to maintain macroeconomic stability to attract foreign investment and to guarantee a positive investment climate in order to achieve sustained growth.

The government proceeded to readjust the economy. Increased oil prices led to (1) the adoption of laws allowing prices to fluctuate according to international markets, (2) a strict fiscal policy, and (3) tax reform to increase fiscal revenues, allowing the exchange rate to float. The last measure favorably impacted the international reserves.

To complete this general panorama of the Dominican economy, it should be pointed out that the current account deficit in the first seven years of the past decade

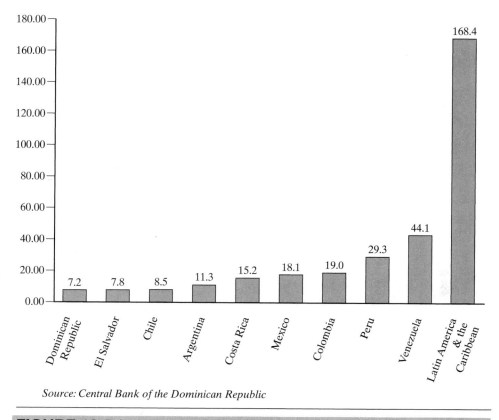

Source: Central Bank of the Dominican Republic

**FIGURE 12-5** Latin American inflation rate

was 1.4 percent of the GDP. Following Hurricane Georges, the deficit went up to 2 percent in 1998 and 1999. Due to the oil shock in 2000, it increased to 5.2 percent. On the other hand, the total foreign external debt/GDP ratio dropped from 47.0 percent to 18.6 percent. Also, the debt/export of goods and services ratio was reduced from 96.0 percent to 41.0 percent.

Twenty years ago, a new sector emerged in the Dominican economy, based on the export of services. The tourist sector today has 54,000 hotel rooms and is the largest tourist destination in the Caribbean region. It has become the largest source of foreign currency, generating a total of US$2,983 million in 2000. Remittances of Dominicans living in the United States and Puerto Rico became the second largest source of foreign exchange, reaching around US$1.8 billion per year. The industrial free zones ("Maquilas"), with 50 industrial parks and 500 enterprises in operation, became a powerful sector, thanks to the Caribbean Basin Initiative (CBI) of the United States, followed by the Caribbean Basin Trade Partnership Act (CBTPA). Twenty years ago, the Dominican economy's main source of foreign currency was the export of products such as sugar and its by-products, coffee, cocoa, tobacco, nickel and gold.

During the years 1995–2000, 85 percent of the exports of the country's goods were manufactured products. In 2000, exports of goods from the Dominican Republic

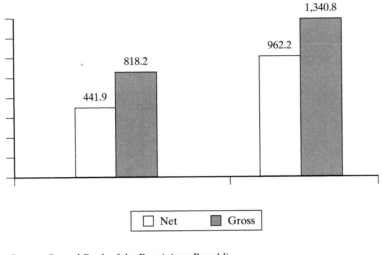

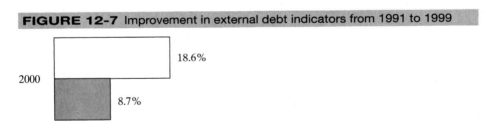

Source: Central Bank of the Dominican Republic

**FIGURE 12-6** International reserves of Central Bank

reached US$5,669 million versus US$9,488 million in imports, for a trade deficit of –US$3,819 million. Total exports to the United States from the Dominican Republic were US$4,383.3 million; total imports from the United States were US$4,472.8 million. The balance of trade with the United States was positive in 2000 and was US$89.5 million. (See Figure 12-8.)

**FIGURE 12-7** Improvement in external debt indicators from 1991 to 1999

External Debt/GDP
*Debt Amortization Service/Total Exports of Goods and Services*

Source: Central Bank of the Dominican Republic

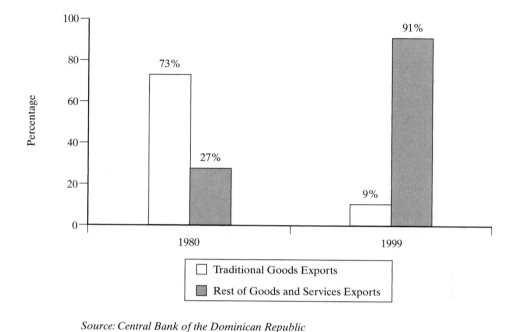

Source: Central Bank of the Dominican Republic

**FIGURE 12-8** Exports of traditional goods as % of the total exports of goods and services

## FOREIGN INVESTMENT CLIMATE

Since 1992, the Dominican Republic has strongly supported the creation of an attractive business climate for foreign investors through the implementation of its first generation of reforms based on its capacity to honor its financial commitments on time and a whole package of new laws in order to eliminate discrimination against foreign and U.S. investors. These reforms created equal treatment for national and foreign investors.

The government of President Hipólito Mejía Dominguez is implementing what has been called the "second generation of reforms," including tax reforms, a new customs tariff law and an increase in value-added tax (VAT) beyond the commitment of the Dominican Republic to the Free Trade of the Americas Agreement (FTAA) in 2005. The country signed and ratified two Free Trade Agreements with the Central American countries and the Caribbean Community (CARICOM) countries in the Caribbean. The Dominican Republic is also a member of the LOME IV Convention with the European Union and is a member of the Cotonou Agreement, being an Association of Caribbean and Pacific Countries (ACP) country having preferential access to the two major trade blocs, the United States and the European Union.

Another factor that attracts foreign investment into the Dominican Republic is the strong democracy. The Dominican Republic has had free elections for the last forty years, as well as democratic liberties, a respect for human rights and peace, all of which creates an excellent climate for business.

The factors just mentioned explain why in the period 1995–2000 foreign direct investment grew to an annual average rate of 18.1 percent, reaching a total of US$3,921.9 million. During the same period, the energy and sugar sectors, as well as other government-owned corporations, were opened for foreign investment for a total of US$664.9 million. Spain is the largest investor with 26.2 percent, followed by the United States with 21.2 percent and Canada with 19.7 percent, among others.

In the period of 1995–2000, foreign direct investment focused on electricity (25.4 percent), tourism (24.7 percent), trade (23.7 percent) and communications (16.1 percent), reaching a growth rate in those sectors of 10.6, 11.8, 17.5 and 17.4 percent, respectively. All of these rates were higher than the annual average growth of the economy of 7.7 percent, which explains the dynamism in those sectors of the Dominican economy. For the year 2001, foreign investment reached US$1,198.4 million.

As President Hipólito Mejía Dominguez pointed out in his speech in Aspen, Colorado, on June 23, 2001, to the American Apparel and Footwear Association, the entry of the Dominican Republic on U.S. markets "has been the product of a process of application of measures internally made by the Dominican Government and externally by the Government of the U.S., whose latest contribution has been the promulgation of the Caribbean Basin Trade Partnership Act (CBTPA)."

Some key elements to create a new environment for direct foreign investment in the Dominican Republic are:

Labor code (16-92)
Banking Supervision Reform (1993)
The new Foreign Investment Law 16-95
Public Enterprises Law (141-97)
The reform of the judicial system, which created the National Council of
    Magistrates, and a new Supreme Court of Justice. The new judges are chosen through open procedures without political influences (Laws 327-98
    and 75-97) by the Supreme Court
Telecommunications Law (153-98)
Capital Market Law (19-00)
Industrial Property Law (20-00)
Law for the Preservation of the Environment and Natural Resources (64-00)
Copyright Law (65-00)
Hydrocarbon Consumption Tax Reform (112-00)
A new Customs Tariff Law (146-00)
A new Tax Code (147-00)
Social Security Law (87-01)
Electricity Law (125-01)
Antidumping Law (01-02)
Monetary and Financial Code (Pending)
Market Competition Reform (Pending)

The new Foreign Investment Law (1995) eliminates any kind of discrimination against foreign direct investment, granting equal treatment to Dominican and foreign investors under national and international laws. Investors also have the right to repatriate up to 100 percent of the capital and profits should they decide to do so.

According to the Foreign Investment Law, every investor has the right to make his investment in any of the following forms: (1) converting foreign currency at the official rate of exchange through a local bank; (2) investing capital in the form of cash, goods or services; (3) using financial instruments approved by the Monetary Board; or (4) transferring technology by embracing technical licensing, technical assistance, "know-how," basic engineering, etc.

The Dominican Republic ratified the Multilateral Investment Guarantee Agreement (MIGA) of the World Bank for the resolution of differences among foreign investors.

## WHO IS INVESTING IN THE DOMINICAN REPUBLIC

For many years the Dominican Republic has been the choice for such U.S. investors as Verizon Communications; Citibank; Philip Morris International; Seaboard Corporation; Xerox; Texaco, Enron Corporation; Pan American Life Insurance Company; Exxon/Mobil Corporation; CEEP/Coastal Technology; AES Corporation; Maidenform Worldwide, Inc.; Tommy Hilfiger Corporation; Central Romana Corporation; Polo Ralph Lauren; Levi Strauss and Company; Liz Claiborne, Inc.; The Timberland Company; Baxter International; UPS; DHL; Federal Express; American Airlines; Wanaco; Fruit of the Loom; Bend & Stretch; Sarah Lee; Eddy Bauer; Oxford; Gap; Carter; Sebago; Johnson & Johnson and Abbott Laboratories; among others.

This is why in the year 2000, investment in the industrial tax free zones totaled US$60.0 million. The U.S. energy corporation AES invested US$330.0 million in a plant to generate electricity with natural gas. CSX World Terminal, in a joint-venture with Dominican entrepreneurs, is investing US$220 to build a megaport in Punta Caucedo. A tourist project named "Cape Cana" will invest US$1.0 billion in six hotels, golf courses and the largest marina in the Caribbean east of the Dominican Republic. A French group announced the construction of a 1,000 room hotel in Bayahibe, La Romana. Placer-Dome, a Canadian mining corporation, will invest over US$330.0 million to operate a government gold mine. A very large group of tourist promoters from Spain is planning an investment of some US$600.00 million in Bahia de las Aguilas, on the west cost of the country.

The Dominican Republic is the strongest Spanish-speaking democracy in the Caribbean region. The country has a cooperation program with the United States and is working closely with the Department of Justice, the DEA and the U.S. Coast Guard to reduce drug trafficking and fight money laundering. An extradition treaty between the Dominican Republic and the United States is enforced by Dominican authorities to avoid the Dominican Republic becoming a refuge for international criminals.

The first and second generation of reforms granted easier access for U.S. products than has been granted for the products of the European Union and other countries. The Caribbean region is the only one in the world in which the United States enjoys a surplus in its trade balance, exporting in 2001 US$22.0 billion to the countries benefiting from the CBI.

The Dominican Republic offers the fastest growing economy in the Caribbean and has an attractive package for offshore manufacturers, both large corporations as well as small and medium-sized companies. There is a new cyberpark in Andres. Boca Chica welcomes investors in the information technology sector. And the Technological Institute for the Americas offers IT training and specialization of the labor force.

## ENVIRONMENT

Like many developing countries, the Dominican Republic is deeply concerned about the environment as a consequence of its degradation of the natural resources and the strong link between these resources and sustainable development. It is for this reason, among others, that the authorities committed to the conditions of the UN Conference on Environment and Development (Conference of Rio, 1992). The Dominican Government promulgated Law 64-00 creating the Secretary of Natural Resources and the Environment as a Central Agency on August 18, 2000.

With its population of 8.5 million inhabitants plus the 2.8 million tourists that visit the Dominican Republic every year, there is a consensus among experts that the key challenges to preserving the nation's natural resources and environment are deforestation and soil erosion, not to mention the control of pollution. Sharing an island with Haiti, a country of 8.2 million inhabitants in 2001, the Dominican Republic has another growing concern. That concern is that policies stimulating improvements in environmental quality have a high priority for the quality of life on all of the 29,395 square miles of the island—both in Haiti and in the Dominican Republic.

The Dominican Republic is a country characterized by highlands and mountains, which make up 56 percent of the total area of the east part of the island. Here are to be found rich valleys and a great variety of ecosystems, segmenting the country into well-defined bio-regions. In fact, the Dominican Republic occupies second place for biodiversity richness in the Caribbean region.

According to regulatory and legal policies in the environmental domains, the total area of protected land in the Dominican Republic (1998) was 13,164.57 square kilometers, of which 7,914.6 square kilometers were land ecosystems and 5,250 square kilometers were maritime ecosystems. These areas are under administration in five categories: (1) national parks, (2) scientific reserves, (3) historical parks, (4) panoramic routes and (5) biospheric reserves with a total of forty units. On the other hand, the authorities have made a great effort to measure environmental purity based on international criteria such as level of pollutant particulates, $SO_2$ concentrations in urban areas and energy usage per unit of GDP.

Since 1967, the concern of the authorities to protect forest resources has initiated a period of technical studies on these matters, notably carried out by the OAS (1967), the Food and Agricultural Organization (UN) (FAO) (1981) and the Department of Inventory of Natural Resources (1998), known as DIRENA.

The country has 108 rivers distributed among its hydrographic regions. The total volume of surface water is estimated at 20,000 million cubic meters and the underground water is 1,500 million cubic meters. The total demand for water for the year 2000 was projected at 4,865 million cubic meters.

One of the most important programs in the Dominican Republic to combat the degradation of natural resources is the "National Plan Green Quisqueya" (Plan Nacional Quisqueya Verde), which involves in its implementation the General Directory of

Forestry, the National Technical Forestry Commission (CONATEF), the National Direction of Parks, the National Botanical Garden, the National Institute for Hydraulic Resources (INDHRI) and a large number of NGOs as well as the general population. The Plan covers 53 zones, with the participation of 8 official institutions and 10 non-governmental organizations, which have already reforested some 226,800 "tareas" of land. A pioneer effort in this field was the "Plan Sierra" (Sierra Plan), which set up in 1979 a rural program to face the deforestation and rural poverty around the rivers Mao, Amina and Bao, all effluents of the river Yaque del Norte.

Another important program implemented by the Dominican Republic is related to the creation of the Governmental Committee on Ozone (COGO). The country adopted a ruling on this matter on September 12, 1999, forbidding the import of refrigerators using freon 12. The goal of the program is to reduce the substances that deplete the ozone layer Substances Harming the Atmospheric Ozone Layer (SAO) by 50 percent by 2005 and to eliminate all such substances by 2010.

The general population of the Dominican Republic is actively engaged in the protection of the natural resources and the environment. It plays an important role in this field, as do a large number of institutions and organizations, such as the Ecological Society of the Cibao, PRONATURA, the Integrated Fund Pro-Nature, the Dominican Federation of Associated Ecologists and the universities and schools of the country.

It must be emphasized that since the Stockholm Conference (1972), the Dominican Republic has been engaged in a dynamic process of participation in and ratification of treaties, conventions and protocols related to the protection of natural resources and the environment. This is especially true since the Earth Summit (1992). The country subscribes to such important instruments as the Protocol of Montreal, the Agreement on International Trade in Endangered Species (1987), the Convention on Biological Diversity (1992), International Convention to Fight Desertification (1997), the framework Agreement on Climatic Change (1998), the Agreement for the Protection and Development of the Maritime Life of the Great Caribbean (Agreement of Cartagena) and the Protocol of Cooperation to fight the Contamination of Oils.

## CONCLUSION

Having a privileged position from a geographical viewpoint as a crossroads between Europe and America, the Dominican Republic is the natural technical landing point for all air and maritime traffic from the countries of the European Union and the United States of America and for all the New Continent. The Dominican Republic is trying to maximize this position by training the human resources needed. The country possesses one of the best communications systems in Latin America and the Caribbean region and has access to two major markets on both sides of the Atlantic Ocean.

The Dominican Republic is committed as a Caribbean country to fostering relations with Central America and the CARICOM countries. To this end, it has signed a Free Trade Agreement with both regional economic blocs and is engaged in the timetable to become part of the Free Trade Agreement of the Americas (FTAA) in 2005, in addition to fulfilling all its obligations as a member of the World Trade Organization (WTO).

The 8.5 million Dominicans living on the island and the 1.5 million living outside the Dominican Republic have a strong commitment to make their beloved country a nation with a future as the strong Spanish culture democracy in the Caribbean region.

## BIBLIOGRAPHY

Almanaque Mundial 2001. Hacia un nuevo Siglo. Editorial Televisa, S.A. de C.V. México, D.F. (2002)

Banco Central de la República Dominicana. (2001) *Comportamiento de la Economía Dominicana Enero-Septiembre, 2001.* Santo Domingo.

Comisión Económica para América Latina y el Caribe. (2001) *Balance Preliminar de las Economías de América Latina y el Caribe.* Santiago de Chile: Naciones Unidas (CEPAL).

Comisión Económica para América Latina y el Caribe (CEPAL) y Pontificia Universidad Católica Madre y Maestra (PUCMM). (2000) *Desarrollo Económico y Social en la República Dominicana, los últimos 20 años y perspectiva para el siglo XXI.* Tomo I. Santo Domingo: República Dominicana.

Consejo Nacional de Zonas Francas de Exportación. (2002) *Memoria anual de las principales actividades desarrolladas durante el año 2001.* Santo Domingo: República Dominicana.

Grey House Publishing Inc., UK. (2000). *Nations of the World 2000/01: A Political, Economic and Business Hand-book.* Lakeville, CT: Walden Publishing, Ltd.

Guerrero Prats, Lic. Francisco M. (2002) *La Economía Dominicana: Un Compromiso con la Estabilidad.* (Disertación ofrecida ante la Cámara Americana de Comercio por el Gobernador del Banco Central de la República Dominicana.)

Programa de la Naciones Unidas para el Desarrollo (PNUD) 2000.

*Desarrollo Humano en la República Dominicana* (2000) Tomo I. Santo Domingo.

Saladin Selin, R. B. (2002) *Remarks on the Dominican Republic-United States Relations in the Political Economic and Social Context on the 21st Century by the Ambassador of the Dominican Republic to the United States of America.* The University of Georgia.

# INDEX